Inconceivable Conceptions

D1322838

It is now over two decades since the first test-tube baby was born. During this period a myth that all infertile women can now have babies has become accepted. Infertile couples often feel under great pressure to seek a medical solution but the psychological and social effects of the changing experiences of infertility remain confusing.

In *Inconceivable Conceptions*, a distinguished range of contributors, including novelist Hilary Mantel and Germaine Greer, examine the experience of infertility from both female and male perspectives, as well as the psychological aspects of infertility diagnosis and treatment, and the often radical and unexpected effects on changing patterns of kinship.

Drawing from a wide range of theoretical backgrounds and compelling personal reflections, this book aims to unravel some of the implications of advancing reproductive technology.

Jane Haynes is a psychotherapist, working in private practice in Central London, with a particular interest in the psychotherapy of fertility.

Juliet Miller is a Jungian psychoanalyst with a private practice in London. She has a particular interest in the psychology of creativity and the interface with fertility issues.

Contributors: George Christie, Dickinson B. Cowan, Germaine Greer, Ronald Higgins, Monica Konrad, Sammy Lee, Hilary Mantel, Ann Morgan, Michael Pawson, Joan Raphael-Leff, Emma Scrimgeour, Flora Scrimgeour, Sue Stuart-Smith, Diane Finiello Zervas.

Inconceivable Conceptions

Psychological aspects of infertility
and reproductive technology

Edited by
Jane Haynes
and Juliet Miller

Brunner-Routledge
Taylor & Francis Group
HOVE AND NEW YORK

First published 2003
by Brunner-Routledge
27 Church Road, Hove, East Sussex BN3 2FA

Simultaneously published in the USA and Canada
by Brunner-Routledge
29 West 35th Street, New York, NY 10001

Brunner-Routledge is an imprint of the Taylor & Francis Group

Typeset in Times New Roman by
Keystroke, Jacaranda Lodge, Wolverhampton
Printed and bound in Great Britain by
Biddles Ltd, Guildford and King's Lynn

Paperback cover design by Sandra Heath

British Library Cataloguing in Publication Data
A catalogue record for this book is available from the British Library

Library of Congress Cataloging in Publication Data
Haynes, Jane.
  Inconceivable conceptions : psychological aspects of infertility and
reproductive technology / Jane Haynes & Juliet Miller.
      p. cm.
Includes bibliographical references and index.
    ISBN 1–58391–167–7 (hbk. : alk. paper) – ISBN 1–58391–168–5 (pbk. :
alk. paper)
1. Infertility–Psychological aspects. 2. Human reproductive
technology–Psychological aspects. I. Miller, Juliet, 1946– II. Title.
RC899 .H328 2003
616.6'92'0019–dc21

                                2002151995

ISBN 1–58391–167–7 (hbk)
ISBN 1–58391–168–5 (pbk)

Contents

Notes on contributors

George Christie is a psychiatrist, psychoanalyst and group therapist, with an interest in psychogenic infertility. He is a Fellow of the Royal College of Psychiatrists, a Past President of the Australian Association of Group Psychotherapists and a Director on the Board of the International Association of Group Psychotherapy.

Dickinson B. Cowan is Medical Director of the IVF unit at the Portland Hospital, London. He has been in the field of IVF since 1984. He worked with Patrick Steptoe and Robert Edwards in Cambridge in the mid-1980s. Before that he remembers the day that Louise Brown was born, when he was struggling with the basic obstetric health needs of the Third World with its huge mortality – maternal and infant. Then he could not really see the point of IVF when the basic needs of the poor were so pressing.

Germaine Greer is Professor of English and Comparative Studies at Warwick University. Her first book, *The Female Eunuch*, was an international best-seller. Her subsequent books include *The Obstacle Race*, *Sex and Destiny*, *The Madwoman's Underclothes*, *The Change* and *The Whole Woman*. Professor Greer makes regular appearances in print and other media as a journalist and broadcaster.

Jane Haynes is a psychotherapist with interests in the therapeutic use of dialogue and relationship. She is a clinical consultant to the Eastern European Institute of Psychoanalytic Studies in St Petersburg and has a private practice in central London.

Ronald Higgins is an ex-diplomat and has written books on global ecology and, with his paediatrician wife, on multiple births. He was Vice Chair of an NHS Trust for eight years and is Chair of the Champernowne Trust for Psychotherapy and the Arts.

Monica Konrad is a social anthropologist and is currently Visiting Fellow at the School of Advanced Study, University of London. Her research interests are in health and comparative medical and moral systems. Currently she is completing a book entitled *Narrating the New Predictive Genetics: Ethics, Ethnography and Science*.

Sammy Lee is a scientific consultant at the Portland Hospital where he directs the ICSI programme. His pioneering work on GIFT at the Wellington Hospital, London, resulted in his Serono Fertility Award (1991). He has served on the committees of both the British Infertility Counselling Association and Issue, for whom he pioneered the world's first telephone counselling service (funded by the Department of Health).

Hilary Mantel is a novelist. She was brought up in the north of England, and has lived in Africa and in the Middle East. She has published eight novels, some contemporary, some set in the eighteenth century, and is a frequent contributor to the *New York Review of Books*. She is at work on a short story collection and a memoir.

Juliet Miller is a Jungian psychoanalyst and has a private practice in central London. She originally trained as a documentary film maker with interests in women's, environmental and Third World issues. She is interested in the interface between psychology and creativity.

Ann Morgan is a paediatrician and group and individual psychotherapist with a particular interest in the development of the infant, and the infant–parent relationship. She is Past President of the Australian Group Psychotherapy Association and Vice President of the Victorian Branch of the Infant Mental Health Association in Australia.

Michael Pawson is a former consultant gynaecologist at Chelsea and Westminster Hospital and has specialist interest in psychosomatic obstetrics and gynaecology. He is Past Chairman of the British Society of Psychosomatic Obstetrics, Gynaecology and Andrology. He is on the Editorial Board of the *Journal of Obstetrics and Gynaecology*.

Joan Raphael-Leff is a psychoanalyst and has for twenty-five years specialised in reproductive issues. She is Professor of Psychoanalysis at the Centre for Psychoanalytic Studies at the University of Essex. Since 1976 she has had a specialised practice, treating emotional problems related to reproduction. She has written for some fifty publications in the field.

Emma Scrimgeour is a painter and lives in London with her partner and two children.

Flora Scrimgeour is a barrister and lives in London with her partner and two children.

Sue Stuart-Smith is Specialist Registrar in Psychotherapy at the Tavistock Clinic and Royal Free Hospital, London. She is in the process of completing a PhD at Birkbeck College. Her areas of interest include psychosomatics and obstetric and gynaecology liaison work.

Diane Finiello Zervas is a Jungian psychoanalyst with a particular interest in spirituality and has a private practice in central London. She originally trained as an art historian. Having published extensively on Italian Renaissance art, she is also interested in the interface between psychology and art.

Acknowledgements

The editors, whilst holding final responsibility for the text, would like to acknowledge the support and input of the following people:

David Arnold, John Haynes, Rozsika Parker, Sammy Lee, Professor Ian Craft, Jenny Clifford, Harry Whitehead, Lesley Sharp, Kate Boxer, Isabella Foreshall, Mikhail Rechetnikov, Joyce Boyd, Clem Herman, Deidre Lewis, Helen Larder, Helen Williamson.

Acknowledgements are also due to:
Michael Pawson for his unique support and inspiration.
The Library of the Royal College of Obstetrics and Gynaecology.
The Human Fertilisation and Embryology Authority for permission to publish their 'Glossary of terms' and for use of sections from *The Patient's Guide to Infertility and IVF*.
St John's College, Oxford and the Random House Group Limited for permission to use an extract from 'The Ninth Elegy' by Rainer Maria Rilke and translated by J.B. Leishman.
Gary Hume for permission to use his painting 'Two Eggs'.

Introduction

Introduction

Jane Haynes and Juliet Miller

Each advance in assisted reproductive technology (ART) raises the question of whether scientific knowledge alone provides an adequate basis for understanding our fertility and its vicissitudes. The issues which emerge from ourselves as fertile/infertile beings have arguably not become simpler through 'miraculous' and expensive procedures on offer from infertility clinics, but yet more complex. The contributors to this book ask whether experiences of infertility can be advanced by the scientific refinement of techniques which take place in the laboratory, and whether identifying infertility as primarily a medical problem remains the best way forward. They highlight the interface between the medical and the experiential and also the borderland where fertility and infertility cannot readily be differentiated. The diverse approach of the contributors opens up a dialectic between the scientific knowledge of clinical practitioners and the multilayered psychology of a complex human experience that we label infertility.

Unlike other books on the subject of infertility this book has been written from multiple perspectives. Its authors come from the disciplines of medicine, psychotherapy, anthropology, literature and from the public. The editors, both of whom are psychotherapists, were drawn to the psychology of ART when they found that a new category of patients was consulting them. These were men and women who, in addition to dealing with the traumas of infertility, were now faced with the confusion of all the complex issues associated with ART. The multiplicity of these procedures, and the dilemmas and choices associated with them, can exacerbate areas of anxiety about an individual's failure to reproduce. Within the last twenty years there have been such radical advances in reproductive technology that a couple who experience difficulties in conceiving are now confronted by a vast area of choices and associated dilemmas which may preoccupy them for the remainder of their reproductive lives. Before the advent of the birth pill most women were more concerned about an unwanted pregnancy and the terrors of back street abortions than they were with fears about their fertility. With the medicalisation of reproduction some people have more intense experiences of loss and ambivalence about issues concerning their fertility. It is now accepted that 15 per cent of couples who want to have a child will seek specialised advice from a fertility clinic. Statistics also indicate that one in eighty babies is born as a result of ART.

With the arrival of in vitro fertilisation (IVF) in the late 1970s, an underlying assumption about the divine act of creation proved erroneous. The idea that Man was created in the image of God, which implies that there is something perfect about the creation of man or woman, no longer prevails. The explosion of technological knowledge that followed IVF has revealed a different truth. We now know, through laboratory research, that every act of procreation carries a possibility that up to 40 per cent of eggs may be chromosomally abnormal. On the male side 25 per cent of sperm may also be chromosomally abnormal. For every perfect human being born there has always been a concealed price to pay in natural waste and imperfection.

So many difficult issues have been raised by the revolution in ART that the editors decided to approach their subject through as many different professional apertures as possible. This decision will become evident in the course of the book where each section presents the subject from another perspective. We also felt it was vital that the book not only represented professional voices but included first-person accounts of some of the vicissitudes of fertility.

It is indisputable that ART has encouraged a destructive split between mind and body; all the contributors agree about this and want to restore a balance. We are concerned that the body has become an object of professional scrutiny whilst the mind, and its emotions, become neglected and isolated in anxiety. ART is neither a science of fertility, nor a science of infertility – it is about isolating, refining and juggling the mechanics of conception. It is not a method by which to understand the Eleusinian mysteries of fertility, or their absence. The individual diagnostic tools of psychotherapy and medicine have both failed, by themselves, to provide a coherent understanding of the experience of infertility. Whilst the editors do not want to dispute the positive contribution ART has made to the lives of many couples, this book should not be read as a tribute to its successes. We are, above all, interested in attempting a synthesis of psyche and soma and looking at the neglected psychology of fertility. It is our hope that the book will act as a bridge that links professional voices with the reality of some people's experiences.

For those who are unable to have a child there are different categories of infertility:

1   Unexplained infertility – infertility for which no physiological causes can be found, and which has failed to respond to any interventions by ART.
2   Infertility as a result of a diagnosed medical condition which does not respond to ART.
3   Infertility which does not arise from a failure to conceive but a failure to carry a baby to term.

Each of these conditions constellates a different set of psychological issues for the specific individual, or couple, with which they may have to wrestle for a lifetime. It is the subtleties of such differences that we hope to address. For those couples who are unable to conceive, despite medical help, the medical failure can impact on their difficulty in mourning the unsuccessful accomplishment of a family. A diagnosis of infertility can result in a couple becoming deskilled in their procreativity and increasingly reliant on medical experts to bring about conception and live birth. Failure can compound the couple's feelings of impotence, and often affects spontaneous expressions of sexual desire. Procreation and creativity become bound together so that some people may fail to separate the two; unable to mourn their lack of procreativity they struggle to regain some confidence in their other creative powers. The medicalisation of procreativity can create its own obsessional pathology and prevent an exploration of loss and destruction which may be crucial to creative recovery and renewal.

For those successful couples who achieve parenthood through ART these issues may no longer seem relevant. In the course of this book some negative aspects of medical successes are also reflected on. Even in fairy stories there is a price to pay, and the editors are reminded of the Grimm's fairy story *Rumpelstiltskin*. In this story the Miller's daughter is prepared to give Rumpelstiltskin anything in return for his skills in spinning her straw into gold. When she has nothing material left to give, he agrees to complete the task for her on condition that when she falls pregnant she will give him her firstborn child. The Miller's daughter, being naive, acquiesces. The tragic consequences of her uninformed actions are only experienced when, having fallen in love with her baby, Rumpelstiltskin returns to demand his reward. In the course of ART many women, or couples, will go to any lengths to spin straw into gold and achieve their golden fantasy of a baby. They do not always take heed of the long-term consequences, or implications, of their decisions. Some couples will change consultant, or even country, to obtain a baby, regardless of ethical, medical and financial implications. It is only retrospectively that they may be confronted by the Rumpelstiltskin consequences of their actions.

In the same way that the Miller's daughter is willing to transfer responsibility for her dilemma on to Rumpelstiltskin it is not uncommon to find patients who imbue their medical advisers with magical properties. Many doctors are honest enough to admit that amongst the greatest pressures they are heir to is an uncomfortable godlike transference from their patients. Psychotherapists do not have a patent on the psychology of transference, which is ubiquitous in its energies. The editors consider that familiarity with its phenomenology – by which we mean the ways in which historical events in the life span of an individual may transfer responsibility for themselves, or unconsciously project themselves, on to contemporary relationships – may throw some light on the intense feelings which become constellated around medical interventions.

Whenever a doctor facilitates a live birth for a hitherto infertile couple, she/he is at risk of becoming godlike to them. (She/he has spun straw into gold where they have failed and now it is likely that they will transfer, through projection, their own sense of divinity on to the doctor.) One of the medical consultants who was interviewed said that a contributory factor in his divorce was that his wife was unable to tolerate the ways in which his female patients perceived him as perfect! In a similar fashion doctors who fail to provide the correct formula for conception and live births may become demonised by their patients. Whatever the outcome, there can be little doubt that the doctors and staff of all infertility units are subjected to stress as a result of their patients' changing and polarised perceptions of them as people and professionals.

Regardless of whether someone is fertile, or infertile, the area of reproduction is redolent with symbolic meaning. Since recorded time menstrual blood has been associated with contamination and the diabolic, and it is of no surprise to find that generations of women have perceived their menstrual cycle as 'The Curse'. One can be cursed with being over-fertile or under-fertile and the whole area is alive with superstition and ignorance. Although the ancient concept of Mother Nature, as the mysterious source of all life, was officially cast aside by the Age of Enlightenment, the archetypal imagery of Mother Nature as a living womb, originator and sustainer of life continues to be a powerful symbol of the feminine. One of the contributors reminds us that classical mythology provides us with archetypal examples of the reproductive dilemmas of gods and goddesses which amplify the issues and compulsions of reproductive technology.

Many young women who begin to menstruate have not yet separated out their own fertility and sexuality from their mothers' bodies. After becoming sexually active they may still feel that their mother holds their body in thrall. Giving birth to a child can act as a rite of passage into separation, and entry into womanhood. For some women a negative experience of this sense of fusion with their mother can be disastrous, particularly if the young woman goes on to experience reproductive difficulties. It is not uncommon to find, in the course of psychotherapy, that the infertile woman can feel as though she has been cursed by her mother.

One woman, undergoing complicated and painful treatment for frequent miscarriages, who felt that her pain remained invisible to her mother, said that she felt as if she had been cursed when she was a difficult adolescent. She recalled an occasion when she was chatting to her friends about what it would be like when they all became mothers and her mother rebuked her, saying, 'What makes you take it for granted that you deserve to ever have a child?' At the time she experienced her mother as spiteful and it was only later, when she experienced repeated reproductive failure, that she felt that the words were a curse. Another woman said that she felt so afraid of her mother's envy that it wasn't until she was in her forties that she became sufficiently individuated from her to become a mother herself. Her own conception of a child was followed by her female sibling becoming pregnant within a matter of months. Whilst it is well recognised that maternal ambivalence may be a contributory factor to non-biological post-natal depression, many of the contributors to this book also consider that it may be a contributory factor in non-explainable infertility.

The revolution in ART means that professionals cannot feel easy about their applications of technical knowledge without being concerned about ethical and legal aspects of their specialisation. If ART is changing the ways in which we think about fertility, then this also revolutionises our relationships to kinship patterns and genealogy. Society is now faced with a discrepancy between what can be artificially made and what can be created, and the age-old question of the relationship between body and soul demands new debate. Whether we are ready for it or not, we are now forced to take responsibility for our hubris in over-reaching the boundaries of what it once meant to be human. What has hitherto been inconceivable, except in fiction, is now unfolding before our eyes and transforming our relationship to our selves, our genes and our procreativity.

It may now be helpful for the reader to conceptualise the biological processes of natural conception and the currently available treatments for infertility, which are both set out in the following subsections.

The reproductive cycle in natural conception

The female partner must be ovulatory and have at least one functioning fallopian tube. Typically she will ovulate every twenty-eight days or so, and this will take place towards the middle of the cycle when the mature egg will be released from the follicle on either her right or left ovary. The fallopian tube will pick up the egg which will start a slow journey down it. Within twenty-four hours of release, the egg will be positioned ready to receive sperm. The male partner must similarly be fertile (i.e. making sperm in his testes). He too must have functioning tubes (the vas deferens). If the male and female have had sex either a day before or after ovulation the timing will be optimal for the following events that may lead to conception and subsequent pregnancy.

After sex, sperm are normally deposited at the cervix in hundreds of millions. The sperm that arrive at the ampulla, the site of fertilisation, must have undergone an epic journey through the cervical mucus, across the uterus and through the fallopian tube. The few thousand sperm that arrive at the ampulla must therefore be an elite sub-group of sperm (the sperm troopers), the roughest, toughest sperms. The poorer sperm, whether they be abnormally shaped or less motile, are lost mainly in the cervix and in the journey up the female reproductive tract. It is important to consider therefore that even in a fertile man there is likely to be a finite number of fertile (viable) sperm per ejaculate (perhaps just 1000 per 100 million). These sperm must find the egg, and there can only be one winner. The first to penetrate the egg is the winner; thereafter most eggs will become impenetrable to further 'attack'. Fertilisation has occurred and the fertilised egg, now described as an embryo, will begin to grow.

Within forty-eight hours, the embryo will have divided twice to form a four-cell embryo. This is the stage routinely used in IVF for embryo transfer back into the female's womb. At this stage the embryo is still located in the fallopian tube. Five days after fertilisation the embryo is now multi-celled and has become a 'blastocyst' and is almost ready to arrive in the womb where it will try to implant. By day seven, the embryo will have shed its outer coating (the zona pellucida) and implantation should be well under way if it is going to happen. On successful implantation conception has been achieved and an early pregnancy established.

Male and female infertility and current technology

The male and female reproductive systems are intricate, and many things can go wrong within a lifetime. Although the word infertility is commonly used, to be infertile is actually rare and means a total absence of reproductive function. Most people seeking treatment have a varying degree of what is known as sub-fertility. One or more parts of their reproductive systems are impaired in some way, and they may well need some medical help to conceive.

Causes

Infertility or sub-fertility equally affects both men and women. For men it is most commonly due to poor sperm quality or quantity. For women it can be due to a number of factors. The causes of female infertility divide into 42 per cent which is unexplained, 33 per cent which is due to tubal disease, 17 per cent which is due to other medical factors and 8 per cent which is due to endometriosis.

Treatments

Because there are many possible causes of infertility or sub-fertility in both men and women there are also many possible treatments.

1 Ovulation induction (hormone treatment)

At least 20 per cent of women seeking treatment will have an ovulation problem. Hormone therapy can be used to stimulate ovulation if a woman is not producing eggs regularly.

2 AI (artificial insemination) using the partner's sperm and IUI (intra-uterine insemination)

AI may be used to overcome potential problems such as thickening of female mucus, premature ejaculation, impotence or anatomical abnormalities. AI enables the sperm to be inserted directly into the cervix via the vagina. IUI is essentially the same as AI but usually combines ovarian stimulation for the woman and preparation of the semen.

3 Tubal surgery to improve blocked or damaged fallopian tubes

Approximately a third of female infertility problems are due to damaged fallopian tubes. Damage may have been the result of previous infection. Depending on the severity of tubal damage surgery may be appropriate and, if successful, fertility may be permanently restored. For some types of tubal damage IVF may be considered.

4 GIFT (gamete intra fallopian transfer)

This technique can be used in unexplained female infertility and, rarely, with male sub-fertility. The eggs are collected from the woman (see IVF), mixed with sperm and then the eggs and sperm are transferred to the fallopian tube before fertilisation takes place. This means that the sperm do not have to travel the length of the reproductive canal before encountering an egg.

5 IVF (in vitro fertilisation)

In vitro fertilisation means fertilisation outside the body. It is a method which has helped many women have babies since 1978 when it was first used successfully. IVF involves the collection of eggs and sperm which are mixed outside the woman's body in a culture dish. Any eggs which fertilise and become embryos are left to grow for two days and then up to three embryos are transferred into the woman's womb. If the treatment is successful, one or more embryos will implant in the lining of the womb and for each a foetus and a placenta will develop. The woman will then be pregnant as if she had conceived naturally.

IVF is often used in cases of tubal damage, endometriosis, low sperm count, mucus hostility and unexplained infertility. The average success rate for IVF is about 17 per cent per treatment cycle, and slightly less for frozen embryo transfer. Generally the chances of success decrease with the woman's age.

6 ICSI (intra cytoplasmic sperm injection)

This involves IVF, with a single sperm being injected directly into each egg. As with IVF a maximum of three fertilised eggs can be transferred back into the womb. ICSI may be appropriate where the male partner has very few sperm or where the sperm have poor or no motility. It is often necessary, for example, when the sperm sample is relatively small or sperm has to be extracted surgically. In some cases ICSI may be successful where conventional IVF fails to produce viable embryos because of a low fertilisation rate.

7 DI (donor insemination)

IVF can also be used with donated eggs, sperm or embryos. Donation may be an appropriate way forward if, for example, the male partner is unable to produce sperm capable of fertilising an egg, or a woman is unable to produce any eggs of her own or those produced are of a poor quality. Donations might also be used if one of the couple is at risk of passing on a serious inherited disease. IVF treatment may also be offered using donated embryos if both partners are infertile but the woman is able to carry a baby to full term. DI involves the use of sperm from an anonymous donor. This process may also be used by single women or lesbian couples.

Chances of success decrease with age. At present women under 30 achieve a live birth rate of 10 to 12 per cent per treatment cycle, but this begins to decrease after that age. Women aged 35 to 39 have a 9 per cent chance of a live birth and women over 40 have only a 3 to 4 per cent chance of successful pregnancy with each DI cycle.

DONORS

Sperm donors are men aged between 18 and 55 with a relatively high sperm count. All donors must undergo health screening to include hepatitis and sexually transmitted diseases such as HIV.

Egg donors are often women who have completed their families and are undergoing sterilisation, or who are themselves having IVF treatment, or who simply wish to help others. Similar selection and screening criteria apply as for sperm donors.

8 Surgical sperm recovery

Sometimes sperm are produced in the man's testes but are unable to enter the seminal fluid because the vas deferens (the tube which carries sperm outwards from the testes) may be obstructed or absent. If this is the case the sperm may be extracted directly from the testis or the epididymis. Sperm extracted in this way would normally be injected into the egg using ICSI.

(From *The Patient's Guide to Infertility and IVF*, Human Fertilisation and Embryology Authority)

Refer to the Glossary for a full list of ART terms.

Chapter 2

Assisted reproductive technology and the fertility clinic

Dickinson B. Cowan

Dickinson B. Cowan is Medical Director of the Fertility Unit at the Portland Hospital, London.

It is so easy for us to take pride in our selves and our achievements, often without a thought for where we came from. Yes, there are parents and grandparents and the family tree and all of that, but what about the specific process which created us, you and me? The single egg and sperm that led to us? Romantic conception at its best. But this is a mere fairy-tale version of what happened. The reality is that we are all fortunate survivors of conception and birth processes. The notion that either of these might be difficult to accomplish seems inappropriate when we are living through a technological revolution. Egocentric self-perception assumes that those processes, which led to our conception, must be perfect too. Human reproduction, like reproduction observed elsewhere in nature, is excessive and often imperfect. For every normal conception there are many attempts that fail. We know that it takes only one egg, only one sperm, but what of these attempts, how do they fare in the cold world of science, statistics, and fertility treatments?

Is it true that man was created in the image of God? Viewed from the harsh reality of the infertility clinic we can observe that there are so many oddities about the physiology of our natural reproduction, so many features of bad design, that, sadly, our natural creation is unmasked as lacking the perfect, or divine, touch. Research into assisted reproductive technology (ART) has shown that up to 40 per cent of eggs may be chromosomally abnormal in women of normal reproductive age. As women creep past the age of 40 the proportion of chromosomally abnormal eggs increases – perhaps to 85 per cent. The sperm story is similar; about 35 per cent of sperm are chromosomally abnormal but this figure may be higher for some men. If a high proportion of eggs and sperm are chromosomally abnormal and we are perfect, then a conclusion must be that chromosomally abnormal eggs or sperm cannot participate in the reproductive process, but it is quite possible for a chromosomally abnormal egg to be fertilised by a chromosomally normal sperm or vice versa. Having fertilised, the embryo (as it is now called) may begin to divide and it may subsequently implant, sometimes for an instant, sometimes for a few weeks, until miscarriage occurs. This relates to chromosomes, but what about the role of genes – those little foci of important genetic information that hide in the arms and convolutions of the chromosomes? Genes are more difficult to see and to quantitate than chromosomes. But it is possible that a chromosomally normal egg and sperm may contain defective genetic material, which may cause pregnancy failure. Such failure may occur before the first cell division, or limit embryonic life to three or four cell divisions, or failure may occur after implantation by which time the pregnancy has become apparent to the couple.

Somewhere along the line we acquire the notion that getting pregnant is easy and finding out that the opposite can also be true may be the first serious misadventure that a couple encounter. The ease with which couples expect to conceive may have its origins in what teenagers are told by their parents. Parents often imply that getting pregnant is disarmingly easy, and are motivated to tell their children this for reasons of morality and social etiquette. They may also, rightly, warn them of the dangers of sexually transmitted disease. Statistics report that in England and Wales approximately 200,000 terminations of pregnancy are performed annually. The fact that the treated pregnancies are unwanted reinforces the conception that humans are intrinsically very fertile.

In our contemporary culture of eternal youth there is the notion that if you look after your body, eat and drink sensibly and don't smoke or take drugs you will be able to retard the process of ageing and be able to have a baby later. But how much later? It is difficult to appreciate now but in the recent past (in the 1960s and early 1970s) a girl was on the shelf if she wasn't married by the age of 25. At the same time a woman was medically classified as an 'elderly primip' if she had her first baby at the age of 30 years or more. This was not obstetric discrimination against 30-plus-year-olds but a means of classifying a group of women who, at that time, were much older than the norm and regarded as being at greater obstetric risk. The pursuit of achievement goals for women in the workplace and some aspects of feminism have deferred the age of settling down and having a family to a point where this may become difficult or impossible. One reason why fertility clinics and IVF units have proliferated in the last decade is in response to the reproductive demands of older women. Women's magazines and the media promote the impossible. Have fun! Have a career! Have your babies later; later and later. This has not done natural conception any favours but it has generated big business for fertility clinics and the corporate providers of the tools of the trade.

The process of conception has become more transparent thanks to the modern treatment of infertility. What used to be a mystery, concealed in the depths of the body, a reckoning with chance and opportunity, has become a spectacle of personal interest and focus so that a couple having treatment by ART have a view of their soma never seen before, but it may be hard for them, or the professionals to interpret.

In an ART treatment cycle the hardest part of the fertility specialist's remit is to try to explain why the patient's treatment failed. With success, no explanation is needed, no questions – just hopes for a normal untroubled pregnancy ahead with an easy delivery. With treatment failure the situation is reversed and the specialist has to try to explain the inexplicable. Statistics about percentages of chromosomally abnormal eggs and embryos are of no comfort to the distressed couple, nor are the given reasons necessarily true. They are probably guesswork by the doctor who can never know for sure. Why should an egg that has been well fertilised by sperm and which results in an embryo, or an embryo replaced correctly in the uterus, not result in a baby eight months later? Logic says it should, but the logical process does not seem to apply. Perhaps the concept of randomness and luck is better. Contemporaneously, an explanation is expected for everything. Our mental processes demand logical explanation. There is difficulty finding any comfort for failure without an explanation. Blocked tubes, or male factor infertility may provide a peg on which to hang one's coat but the categorisation of infertility does not explain the precise reason why a cycle (or any of its predecessors) failed.

When it comes to understanding why reproduction fails, knowledge is supposed to provide answers, but it often fails us. From a psychological point of view it is more satisfactory to have a good reason for infertility, 'my tubes are blocked' being a commonly stated reason. But so often the actual reason for failure remains obscure. One of the most unsatisfactory situations is so-called unexplained infertility, where the couple's parameters of fertility are normal and, as far as investigation can show, their infertility is unexplained and seen to be lacking in any demonstrable reason. When tubal disease has been ruled out by laparoscopy – sperm problems by semen analysis or a semen preparation – difficulty with ovulation by scans and blood tests – what else is left? Perhaps the egg was retained within the follicle walls following ovulation. Perhaps the egg was washed out from the follicle following ovulation but failed to participate in the fertilisation process. Perhaps the egg was of poor quality. Perhaps fertilisation occurred but the egg could not escape from its shell (the zona pellucida) – a prerequisite for the embryo to be able to implant in the lining of the womb. With in vivo conception fertilisation occurs near the ovary. The developing embryo then spends five days travelling down the fallopian tube to enter the uterine cavity. The embryo can get lost and fail to arrive in the uterine cavity. Perhaps, despite safe arrival, there is a failure of implantation. Understanding of these scenarios is conceptual rather than something that can be factually proved. Any firm reasons for the patient to clutch on to, to account for her failure, sadly are often lacking.

Denial is a common feature of patients going through a treatment cycle, as it is a common and often unrecognised feature of our lives. Denial may enhance self-esteem but it distances truth. There may be some temporary comfort in denial, but in a patient's search for the truth about their infertility denial has no place and can lead to mistrust and unrealistic expectations. A patient, who has taken a huge quantity of injectables for her in vitro fertilisation cycle and then finds that the treatment fails, may not perceive herself, or her partner, as being the problem. The reason for failure is attributable to the intervention rather than the reason for which the intervention was needed. In the clinic one frequently hears that 'Those doctors don't know what they are doing.' 'This IVF Unit is no good.' These are commonly heard comments about a patient's treatment which failed; the clinic failed to deliver what the patient so desperately wanted. Men, too, are often in a state of denial about their semen.

Guilt is a common emotion in patients who are undergoing infertility treatment but it has no positive connotations in this context. It is expressed through feelings such as, 'I am a failure because I can't produce a child myself', and 'I can't give my parents a grandchild.' Or, 'If only I hadn't contracted a sexually transmitted disease and blocked my tubes, what should have been my right has turned into an expensive nightmare.' Other frequently heard expressions of guilt include, 'If only I hadn't had that termination years ago my child would be . . . years old now.' Or 'I don't want anyone to find out that I am doing IVF because I am so ashamed of myself, I feel so guilty, such a failure.' Or 'I hate my periods but at least they seem better when I know that I can't be pregnant.' Even success brings guilt in its wake: 'It's not me who should be congratulated, it's you doctor. You did it all, I couldn't get pregnant on my own, you did it for me. I couldn't deliver my baby without a Caesarean section, you did it for me and now I can't even breastfeed my baby I am such a failure. I feel such a mess, I was just the vessel.' Not only are these distressing emotions but their content contains difficult projections for any professional to endure on a daily basis.

Blame also features between the couple in the infertility scenario: 'Whose fault is it we can't have a baby? Somebody must be to blame, somebody has to be! Is it me, or is it you? If it is me I will feel awful, and if it is you I will feel better and relax a bit, but how will that affect our relationship since I now know that you are the culprit?' Our society loves to establish blame. Who is defective in this couple?

Given that a couple have infertility, what can be done? The advice given is going to be based on some basic considerations that will include the age of the woman (about which nothing can be done), the state of her fallopian tubes, the condition of her ovaries, the quality of the sperm, etc. If the tubes are normal then the range of treatments can be hugely varied – ranging from timing sexual intercourse, to ovulation induction with timed sexual intercourse or intra-uterine insemination. It may be possible to offer GIFT (gamete intra fallopian transfer) or even IVF.

If the tubes are blocked then it is advisable to perform IVF but the success of treatment is related negatively to the age of a woman, particularly when she is over the age of 35. If her partner has good sperm then standard IVF may be attempted, but as the semen parameters decrease the IVF may be attempted by using IVF with a higher than normal insemination concentration of sperm or even IVF using the ICSI process (intracytoplasmic sperm injection). When the couple's embryos are produced, how many should be replaced in the uterus? It is well known that the pregnancy rate for a woman is proportional to the number of embryos replaced, that is, the more embryos replaced the greater the pregnancy rate. Unfortunately in the UK a maximum of three embryos has been imposed by the Human Fertilisation and Embryology Authority. It has recently become a criminal offence to put back more than three. As women who are 40 years old or more often need more than three embryos to become pregnant the UK legislation is ageist and becomes increasingly so as the woman's age increases. If an older woman succeeds in producing more than three embryos then she should have the right to have more than three replaced.

Treatment by ART and embryo replacement is a biological lottery. Embryos are replaced in the uterus, but will pregnancy result? Perhaps a congenitally abnormal embryo has been replaced with a diminished potential for implantation and life. Perhaps the embryos are chromosomally normal but should have been hatched artificially; perhaps the intra-uterine environment is hostile to the implantation of the embryo or there is a deficiency in the adhesive molecules between the embryos and the cells of the lining of the womb. Who knows?

Success rates with ART have plateaued in the last ten years. When three embryos are replaced in the uterine cavity there is a global success pregnancy rate of approximately 35 per cent and this figure has not changed much over the years. The flip side of this statistic is that when three embryos are replaced there is a 65 per cent failure to achieve pregnancy. With the high proportion of chromosomally abnormal eggs, sperm and embryos perhaps the high failure rate is accounted for by embryonic chromosomal abnormality. If it were possible to identify the chromosomally normal embryos and if they could be replaced, then perhaps success rates would increase. It is possible to test embryos before replacement by a technique known as pre-implementation diagnosis but this is a difficult and extremely exacting technique. The technique involves removing one cell from an embryo and subjecting it to analysis. Bearing in mind that an embryo is approximately the size of a pinhead and the cells inside are approximately a tenth smaller still, the size difficulty becomes apparent. And what about testing one cell on its own? What about contamination with other cells that might confuse the situation? How can one examine the chromosomes, or one chromosome of one cell, and look at it, or its gene code, or the components of its gene code? It is possible to do this, but only with extreme difficulty and it is only undertaken in a few specialised centres with specific diagnoses in mind. This technology is in its infancy. These tests, however, are also end-point specific. For instance the testing may reveal whether it is a Down's syndrome embryo specifically and not generally whether the chromosomes of the embryo are normal or not.

The treatment of infertility is exceedingly stressful for all staff working in the infertility clinic: doctors, embryologists, nursing staff, the secretaries and coun- sellors. In a good clinic all staff will know their patients well; their personal problems, emotions, anxieties, previous fertility histories and even details of their psychosocial lives. To offer a valuable service the staff members really have to engage with all the problems of their patients, including the most intimate aspects of their lives. Maintaining a wall of professionalism, which is often advocated, is no longer appropriate where trust, relationship and a realistic perception of the problem, or problems, are so important. It is crucial that the patients experi- ence that the people looking after them do have a real and more emotional dimension than would be expected in other less personal areas of medicine. When a patient experiences a failure of her eggs to fertilise, whether this occurs through in vitro fertilisation and embryo replacement, or insemination, she may experience extreme distress. Clinic staff who ride with the patient's experience may also become distressed, but they have to accept their limitations. However, in the course of lengthy processes most staff get to know their patients extremely well and it is only human that they will develop personal hopes and aspirations for their patients, and inevitably will be affected by the many adverse outcomes of their work.

There is great pressure on the doctor not only to become the expert but also the woman's/couple's friend, rather than someone who is aloof from their pain. Inevitably this means letting down the professional barrier and becoming a human being alongside the patient. Their hopes and fears become yours, as does their misery. The despair felt by some disappointed patients is unbelievable until you are touched by its potency. The hopelessness, the sense of failure, of biological rejection, often turns the infertility clinic into a minefield of emotion and distress.

ART and related treatments are regulated in most countries. In the UK ART is regulated by the HFEA Act, which is complex and requires the interpretation of the Authority which in turn grants licences for clinics and individuals. However, as with most areas of innovation and development, the law lags far behind science. Individuals often feel that the law should determine what can or cannot be done, but it does not work like that. The breathtaking way in which science moves forward is outstripping the legal mechanisms that are supposed to regulate development. Should this fact be regarded as good or bad? ART, as with all other life-related issues (termination of pregnancy, euthanasia, eugenics), is an emotional subject and each person has his or her own ethical views. Whilst regulation has political benefit, and it may even pacify a worried electorate, it also contributes a constricting detrimental impact on future development. For instance, the first IVF pregnancy in the world occurred here in the UK in 1978. This was a result of research by a Cambridge scientist, Robert Edwards, who found a willing gynaecological companion to help him, Patrick Steptoe. It was a British invention. The original pioneers involved in IVF realised there was public disquiet over what they were doing and formed a voluntary licensing authority long before there was legislation. The HFEA Act was passed in 1990, twelve years after the birth of Louise Brown who was the world's first IVF child. The statute was twelve years post-partum! Britain's importance in the field of assisted reproduction has diminished ever since this legislation was introduced. Since 1990 Britain has basked in the political glory of having regulation but has dropped from the cutting edge to becoming a mundane service provider. The innovation and development currently happening in this field are now occurring abroad. In the United Kingdom bureaucracy and politics seem to be preferable to change, development and innovation.

Experiencing infertility

Chapter 3

Clinical waste

Hilary Mantel

Hilary Mantel is a novelist.

A couple of months ago, I was reading a book called *The Therapeutic Purpose of Creative Writing*. In a section called 'Healing Narratives' I came across a sentence that must refer to me; it must, because my name is in it. 'Hilary Mantel had half her insides, including her ovaries and her womb, removed when she was 19.'

The words on the page gave me a physical shock. I felt shaky, as if blood had drained from my head to the (allegedly) missing parts of me. It was the inaccuracy which shook me. It wasn't just the implication that my eight novels are a way of patching up my biography, doing a job on the defects of my life. It was more the matter of poundage, or whatever measure you use to weigh a person's insides; there should be some Old Testament sort of measure, you feel, with a short, blunt, bloody name. I wanted to protest that, though I might be damaged, I wasn't quite as damaged as that. I wouldn't like to say what proportion of my insides is missing but I don't think it's half. As a doctor once remarked to me – or perhaps I dreamt it – 'one has plenty of bowel to spare'; but only two ovaries, and a solitary womb. It's true I was sick when I was nineteen, but I was sick when I was eighteen, when I was fifteen, when I was twelve. No one diagnosed my sickness till I was twenty-seven. Then I was 'cured' surgically, leaving behind the rattling lightweight of which the book speaks – a woman without her due portion of guts.

While I was puzzling over this misinformation, and wondering what I had said or written that had given rise to it, I was conscious of a picture forming – of a hollow person stalking the world, holding open a door in its solar plexus so that everyone could see the empty space within. And it occurred to me that, at whatever age it was created, there is such a gap, always waiting to open, wider and wider still, a black hole into which all the accomplishments of the years might vanish.

The disease which made me infertile and childless – there is a difference, of course – is endometriosis. I will give a lay-person's definition. Endometriosis is a condition in which the kind of cells which line the womb are found elsewhere in the body. These cells have the property of bleeding each month, and do so wherever they are. When the bleeding stops, scar tissue is formed. If there is room for it, the condition may go on for quite some time without causing a problem. If space is tight, pain ensues; sometimes, because of pressure on nerves, the pain is felt elsewhere in the body, which makes the condition hard to diagnose. Mostly, the endometrial cells are found in the pelvic area. Sub-fertility and infertility ensue. Besides pain (at menstruation and through the month), common symptoms are nausea, bowel problems, and infinite and ineradicable fatigue. Women with endometriosis often seem to suffer from the premenstrual syndrome at its most severe, and so they have a mad, jagged air, exacerbated by not being believed when they say how much they hurt and where. The cause of the condition is unknown. Doctors used to think it was moral. They called it 'the career women's disease'. They told women who complained about painful periods that childbirth would sort them out. They told women who complained about pain throughout the month that they were hypochondriacs and nuisances, that they were really complaining about their bad marriages, that they could have a nice Valium if they liked, and take it on a repeat prescription so you're not back here every five minutes with the same old story. 'Have an aspirin!' say your friends. 'Go to bed with a hot-water bottle!'

This, more or less, is what happened to me. It's not an unusual story. When I was growing up, my convent school friends didn't mention period pain. Only later, talking to them, I realise I needed no red camellia; my time of the month was evident from my chalk-white face. (I imagine them standing closer to me at these times, moving in with wordless solidarity, breathing patiently, like ponies in a field.) By the time I was nineteen I was living on the recommended aspirin and in pain most of the time. I turned myself in to the student health service. They thought I was mad. It seemed an accepted thing in those days, around 1970, that female students were only looking for an excuse to manifest psychopathology – a little chink to let their madness steam out. The student health service referred me to a psychiatrist. He diagnosed excess of ambition. 'What did my mother do?' he asked. I said that she was a fashion buyer in a large department store. Thereafter he called her place of work 'the dress shop'. Wasn't it true, he asked, that if I were really honest with myself, I'd like to go and work in the dress shop too? Instead of bothering my pretty head with contract and tort, with express and implied terms, with damages and negligence and Acts of God?

After I'd been out of university for a year or so I gave up my aspirations to a profession and took up writing a novel. To earn money – and as a form of satire, I like to think – I worked in department stores. The novel I was writing was a historical novel, it had nothing to do with my own life, with the 1970s, with the daily life around me. I didn't go too deeply into the question of whether I would have children. Sometimes I thought they were a good idea. Mostly I thought the book was a good idea. It didn't occur to me, and wouldn't until much later on, that after I was fourteen or so children were probably not a choice. When at last the endometriosis was found, its spread and its scavenging nature and the damage that it had done hinted at the length of time that it had flourished. I could only have been fertile, it seems to me, by becoming a source of dread and disgrace, a 'teenage unmarried mother', a stench in the nose of piety.

In 1977 I went with my husband to live in Africa. (I had been married when I was just out of my teens; the part of my life when I was not married feels hazy, as if it were pre-natal.) In Africa I taught in a school and worked on my book, turning a mountain of notes into a story. I found a sympathetic doctor who gave me strong painkillers for my bad periods. He didn't enquire as to the cause of them. In time, the pain grew over the top of the pain relief. But I had a schedule. I had to finish my book before coming home on leave so that I could try to make contact with a possible publisher. I marked out a schedule. I typed and typed. The pain was now daily and grew but still I typed. I thought that if I died I would at least have done the book. Then the date of our leave came and the book was finished. When I set foot on my home soil I collapsed. My face turned grey and the pain filled up every moment. My timing had been perfect.

The removal of 'half my insides' occurred in a London hospital, over the Christmas of 1979. In the end, I had diagnosed myself, from reading a textbook; there is great satisfaction in being a textbook case, and I have never been anything quite so definite since. However, the doctors' choice of reading differed from mine, and this caused some trouble at first; the senior consultant thought I had cancer and was a goner, but the registrar, more cheerful, thought I was pregnant, and ran to get a foetal heart monitor to prove it. I tried to imagine what kind of clawed child I might be carrying; something like the foetus in *Rosemary's Baby*? I made friends with the patient opposite, a member of a South London girl gang, who used to summon the nurses by whistling for them. What I noticed was that people kept winking at me. The spotty young houseman winked at me. The man who did the ultrasound scan winked at me. The senior registrar winked at me, and ruffled my hair. Over the head of other patients the houseman winked at me again. My advice to patients now is this: if they start winking, start running.

The untangling of my convoluted innards, the excision and the rendering redundant, the casting away of body parts which are normally wanted by a woman of twenty-seven: these processes were something of an embarrassment all round. The hospital dealt with me like someone who'd had an ingrowing toenail removed. It was painful, but I'd feel the benefit. My dead womb was clinical waste. No one asked if I'd had uses for it; if I'd had anything planned.

If the chain that links you to 'biological destiny' is severed, you are left winded and bruised on the road, the casualty in an accident. You come up hard against the question: what's the use of me? At the date when I was carried into the operating theatre I was ambivalent about whether I should have children, and I always had been. The issue of childlessness was something I explored gradually, and am exploring still, as I reach the age when (in nature) my chances of conception would be slight. The impact of childlessness, for me, has been subtle and long-delayed. But the issue of infertility confronted me at once, before my stitches had been taken out.

Infertility would be a tragedy for many women but I cannot say it has been a tragedy for me. How not? Well, for one thing, I cannot bring myself to use the word 'tragedy' of what seems at worst a steaming frustration. Like most people, I don't like being told what I can't do. After the surgery, the words in my head were 'Pigs might fly, but you'll never give birth.' I got quite attached to these pigs; they dominated my mental landscape, skimmed through my sky. I kept rehearsing this saying . . . pigs might fly. It was a harsh form of healing but it meant that I could move on to the next thing.

Certainly for me infertility has not been a tragedy at the mental level, but I believe that possibly my body has a different response. I believe that there is a large part of me – at a basic psychic level – which never recognized that the catastrophe had taken place. It was a matter of non-recognition of a pattern: as if the package that is me were actually several autonomous systems speaking different languages, and in most of these languages there was no word for 'can't'. There was no 'pigs', no 'might', no 'fly'. It is not possible to realise fully, at an intellectual level, what infertility means. For sure, the intellect can understand the words, the terms, the idea. The intellect can make guesses about what the loss will do to the spirit. But what afflicts the intellect – the thing that makes it suffer – is the lack of freedom and capacity, the lack of choice, the knowledge that the incapacity is absolute, that nature has made a choice and made it against you. All your life a voice has said 'You'll never' and another voice has said 'Wait, watch, I will.' Now when you are told something is impossible, your spirit rebels. This is Dostoevsky's self-willed narrator, in *Notes From Underground*:

> Upon my word, they will shout at you, it is no use protesting: it is a case of twice two makes four! Nature does not ask your permission, she has nothing to do with your wishes, and whether you like her laws or dislike them, you are bound to accept her as she is, and consequently all her conclusions. A wall, you see, is a wall . . . and so on, and so on.
>
> Merciful heavens! But what do I care for the laws of nature and arithmetic, when, for some reason I dislike those laws and the fact that twice two makes four? Of course I cannot break through the wall by battering my head against it, but I am not going to be reconciled to it simply because it is a stone wall and I have not the strength.

I came from the hospital battered and slashed, hollow and grateful: glad to be alive. My previous clothes, already a small size, now washed about my body. It was as if my flesh were still clamped by the surgeons, and for a year I shrunk, until I was dismayed to see one day that when I turned sideways to a mirror I was like a pencil line waiting to be erased.

No one had told me that the disease might come back. It had flung its net wider than the surgeons had, and it was eating me again. I wrote in my diary that I thought I was dying. I went to see a woman in Harley Street, eminent in her field. She believed in the pain, and prescribed a hormone treatment. At once I began to grow. I grew like Jack's beanstalk – but outwards. 'Look here', I said to the eminent doctor, 'when I came to you I was seven stone three and now I'm nine stone.' 'Well', she said (as the chair creaked under her, and the groaning desk shrank from the weight of her forearm), 'now you know what it feels like for the rest of us.' Six months later, when I weighed twelve stone or so, she took me off the medication.

I still had the pain. I complained about it. 'Well', she said, 'I should think it's your bad marriage, isn't it?'

In the years following I became involved with a self-help group for sufferers of the disease handily abbreviated to 'endo'. The group was founded by a brave woman who could get no help, and its early newsletters were primed with atrocious stories. When the group grew, became a registered charity, it became less interested in the end-game of people like myself. It was full of 'how I got better' stories, which I found alienating, because they usually culminated in the triumph of running in the London Marathon, and frankly I had trouble walking. When we sufferers met, the girls were all 'working towards pregnancy'. They knew all the treatments and what they cost and what their chances were. Their sheer endurance and self-belief impressed me, but I thought that if they didn't get the child in the end they would collapse: body and soul. 'Why don't you adopt?' people would say to them. The answer was and is that adoption agencies pick and choose and they do not choose women with chronic illnesses – and there is no simple, once-and-for-all way of clearing this malady, of which the cause is not yet known.

A young woman who is married, but who is childless, infertile, or both, is in a no-win situation. In my early thirties I was an expatriate wife in the Middle East, in a country where women were not allowed to work outside the house. Motherhood was, then, an overwhelming preoccupation, in which the European and American wives shared. I found that if you don't take an interest in people's babies, they think you're a hard career-minded bitch. Perhaps you are, but you ask yourself – by this stage in your life you are angry – what gives you the right to think anything about me? You repudiate their moral judgements. But if you do take an interest – bill and coo – then what happens? People say 'Soon you'll be having a lovely family of your own.' And you rebel again, inside; you thank God there's more to your life than reproduction. At least, I would say to myself, by writing, I am originating something.

At this stage, which I now think of as the first period of my mourning, I was thankful about what I had been spared; the ungainly head-down posture of the woman waiting for her time, the seepages and milk-leak, the secretions which have no drawing-room name. I shrunk away from femininity and its implications, like a mincing dandy in a frock-coat. I had become, not so much a man, as a sneery little queen. I was not satisfied with this identity, intellectually; but it was fun, up to a point. The snag was that people on the outside didn't, in the least, see what I'd become on the inside. They continued to ask me 'And when are you going to start your family?'

A woman friend, a lawyer, said 'When you come back to England, and you are established as a professional woman, people will not ask you whether you have children.' I was sceptical; but she was right. What I had to face instead was the interest of strangers, their kindly concern. Why? Because I was still fat and becoming fatter. The prescriptions of the large woman in Harley Street had tripped something in my metabolism. When I began the drug treatment I was a size ten: then a bulky sort of twelve: and then (within weeks) an eighteen. Very soon, I was a size twenty-two, and in a department store I could bypass 'Fashion' and go straight to 'Upholstery'. I came to resemble – I who had once been the darling of all men whistling from scaffolding and holes in the road – nothing so much as a large sofa with an extra padding of bolsters and cushions. For a while, with my steroid moon-face, I looked like a real fat woman, but then my face became (relatively) small again, and that caused puzzlement. Only bits of me were fat, so 'When is your baby due?' people ask. If it is a casual contact, a smiling granny on a station platform, you can murmur something unintelligible and move away. You can't do this if your questioner is, for example, a new neighbour, because you are both going to have to live with the consequences of your answer. It's best to be brutal, I find; have it over with. Then again, you can rely to an extent on people's absent-mindedness. There is an elderly, very famous literary man who always escorts me to a chair when he sees me. I used just to thank him – and sit on it. It was a while before I realised he was doing it because he thought I was expecting a baby. What, again? He's known me for about twelve years, during which he has never – according to his lights – seen me when I'm not pregnant. I wonder what he thinks my home life can be like.

Hardly anyone has ever asked if I minded about being childless. People assume you mind. Sometimes, you have to explain yourself. I don't owe an explanation about the state of my soul, but I don't mind so much talking about my body. 'I had this illness', you have to say. 'Never mind', they say back, 'there's an awful lot that can be done these days, I'm sure they'll be able to do something.' A vague, restless look crosses their faces, because they don't like to think too closely about what the *something* might be. Occasionally I venture to say, 'No, there is nothing that can be done', because it annoys me that people imagine that doctors are omnipotent. Then a blank look of fright replaces the vague benevolence. More than once or twice, people have said to me, 'Never mind. Perhaps it's for the best.' I find the comment sinister. And also true.

I didn't cry until sometime in the 1990s. I was sitting up in bed, working on a review, my papers and pens and the dissection of a proof copy strewn about me, and the little black tracks of my handwriting on white paper like early blood. My husband brought the news that his youngest sister (herself last of five) had given birth to her fourth child: a boy, after three girls. We knew that it would be the last child of his family; an era was over. I was pleased of course, in the conventional way, but I could not fool myself that my tears were an expression of pleasure and surprise. They were unexpected to me, and contained every sin: envy, pride, and a sullen babyish anger at being outdone. I was not born to be outdone and within my fleshy upholstery (it became evident) lurked Tamburlaine the Great, equipped with scimitar, who was born to lay waste. Great dictators usually want a dynasty, and it's peeving to learn you can't have one.

And oh, how I cried! For all of a minute or two. I never asked for sympathy, in this particular matter, and I feared that I had passed beyond the point where I could ask for sympathy in any matter at all. I did not grow up assuming I should have a child of my own. I hardly assumed my own survival, and was barely four when I first thought of the merits of suicide. The dead and embalmed babe that was me is, we must assume, strapped to the back of Tamburlaine's chariot; a young child in a carapace of linen, lashed together to preserve its shape.

Since 1979, the date of my evisceration, I have lived carefully and responsibly, as if I had children to answer to. I have lived in houses larger than I needed; in case, perhaps, children should arrive. I have kept the cupboards stocked with food and bought the household basics by the dozen. There is a sense in which I am not good at not being a mother. The crying of a baby is not a sound I can block out; it is as if the child puts a hook into the flesh above my navel, and reels me in. The touch of small children can make my breasts ache. My head said I couldn't have children and didn't want them, or probably not, *so why go on about it*? A large part of me has not got the message. Infertility is a concept for the scientific conference, it is a theme, it is a topic. Childlessness is something else entirely.

Sometime about the year 2000 the second part of mourning began for me. My friends were beginning to have grandchildren. The woman lawyer who had advised me to such astringent effect was now a judge, and a grandmama four times over. Again, I was taken unawares. I could not have predicted the evolution of my sense of loss. Finally I began to realise that it was absolute, and act on the realisation. We moved out of our house and into an apartment. We said, isn't it great not to have a garden? We said, we'll please ourselves now. As if we had been waiting nervously, till now, for some late baby to come and commit a breach of the peace.

I can think about fertility in a detached way. I can have opinions about it. The millionth IVF baby – or so the papers say – was born in 2001. The laboratory can make most 'infertile' men into fathers. Women born without ovaries can deliver a child. The potential for abuse – sex-selection on social grounds, 'spare-part' babies – must be balanced against the perception that what scientists are fulfilling is a natural desire – perhaps a human right? In these days we casually and frequently employ the language of rights, and are told that there is a 'right to family life'. More, we have got used to the idea that our bodies are obedient machines. A card in the slot brings cash out. Won't a penis in the slot bring a baby? We take a pill and avoid pregnancy. So shouldn't another pill bring pregnancy about? Doctors can remodel the face and resculpt the body; can't they fulfil our need to reproduce? And make model babies?

One thing: what scientists can do, they will do, unless limited by a firm social consensus expressed in effective regulation. There is virtually no public debate about the new technologies; there is no forum for it. And here is a case, if ever there was one, for scientists to exercise their imagination about the consequences of their work. There is no reason why they should be spared the effort.

Autumn 2001. When I am out buying groceries – in sensible quantities – I see a little boy in his first week at school. His skin is as soft and white as petals, his newly-cut hair pale and sleek on his tiny head; his woollen blazer stands out stiffly from his sides. His new sandals – the weather is still warm – have soles the size of plates, so new that he can hardly flex his feet inside them; when he goes across the zebra crossing he has to stomp with his legs apart. His mother, affluent and well-spoken, forges ahead, pushing her supermarket trolley, talking and talking; he follows her, a lamb. In any rational society, he would still be at home; she would be glad to be at home with him. I wonder if he was afraid of going to school, and if his mother took a photograph of him dressed up like that for the first time. I wonder if she made it into a celebration for him: whether she made him feel how good and special he looked. I think, I would have made it into a celebration; made him armoured against fate.

But then, you are always thinking what you would have done. That's your condition. Your whole life exists in the realm of potential. The people in my novels are always losing their children in the most desperate, desolating, indeed diabolical ways; I feel rather more, though, for the lost children themselves. 'No children?' a woman once said to me. 'Never mind, you've done your books.'

Chapter 4

One man's story

Ronald Higgins

Ronald Higgins is an ex-diplomat and has written books on multiple births.

In my first forty or so years, I can't remember ever having needed or even wanted children. Nevertheless I always imagined that sooner or later fate or fortune would spring them upon me, just as rain must fall. And I did think such rain at the right time might well be good – with the right partner it could perhaps be satisfying and refreshing, if only as a new challenge.

As a much-travelling diplomat and then newspaperman, life had always seemed so hectic and stimulating that I had never thought much about domestic matters. Nor did this change with my first marriage – to an ambitious journalist. Moreover, I knew nothing at all about children.

I had of course been one, and in part remained and remain one. But I did not really meet a child until I was about 44. By then I was divorced and living alone, writing in a country cottage in Herefordshire. There I got to know a neighbour's small bright girl, Vicky, age 6 who often came by to chat and help weed the vegetables. She seemed heart-warmingly glad to learn from the morose recluse I had rapidly been becoming. (I was writing a pessimistic book on the global prospects.)

Children, I then arbitrarily concluded, were not necessarily the distracting, indeed demanding, deafening and spasmodically destructive creatures I had always rather feared. I had not started wanting my own brood but parenthood had started to become quite interesting.

After about four more years of living alone I gratefully met and fortunately married a wonderful woman whose central passion in life had always been children. Being a paediatrician was therefore not enough. Elizabeth was clear from the outset about wanting our children and I quite simply wanted her to be happy.

Not that either of us had the slightest doubt that we would succeed. She was 36 and I nearly 50 but we were healthy and granted a little patience would surely experience the sheer wonder of making another being together. Indeed we would have liked two or three.

Soon after our first anniversary the home-test kit showed the vital blue ring. We were overjoyed. It was what Elizabeth had always wanted, always expected, always longed for. To me it was like some sort of extra blessing on the happiest marriage I could imagine, and it was at once exciting and awesome.

We were so delighted and proud that we told everybody. Ten weeks later, returning from the theatre, she found some faint brown staining. She looked ghastly and we fell weeping into each other's arms. Soon it was confirmed that we had had a 'blighted ovum'. Gradually we recovered from the blow. We had managed once. We would manage again.

We did not manage. We were patient. We still did not manage. Elizabeth's pain and frustration was now multiplied by her two (much loved) sisters having five children between them in no time at all. We took advice from practitioners of every kind of medicine. By turn we tried almost everything – acupuncture, Bach flower essences, homeopathy, prayer, personal growth weekends, meditation, t'ai chi, lowered bedheads, swinging lodestones, total abstinence from caffeine and aluminium saucepans, measured abstinence from sex. We even tried, idiotically, to relax by doing 'nothing'. Meanwhile Elizabeth's orthodox medical colleagues came in on the case, carrying out appropriate examinations and tests on both of us. They showed up no obstacle. We were apparently among the 20 per cent infertile who have no diagnosable impediment to conception. Unfortunately this meant we had nothing that could respond to treatment.

Furthermore time was running out. (Already at 40 and 52 respectively we had been told we were too old to adopt.) Our only serious remaining hope now was the circumnavigation of the problem – getting round it via the 'test-tube'. IVF (in vitro fertilisation) did not cure infertility but it could produce babies.

It had only been four years since Louise Brown, the first 'test-tube' baby, had been born and very fortunately Elizabeth's own hospital, where she ran a twins clinic, was one of the few offering an NHS programme of IVF. As she was over 40 they could allow us only one attempt. We were pathetically grateful: for even the remotest chance of success we would go through almost anything. We had now become tense, deeply tired, sometimes overwrought. Elizabeth's religious faith was in crisis, and less articulately my own. The saga had already been a long one.

I shall not describe the now familiar stages of IVF except to mention that at one point I had to drive 150 miles through the night to produce the sperm to fertilise the eggs that Elizabeth had produced that might make us happy.

She had produced four of them. If they were all successfully fertilised, we would have to decide how many to implant. As a specialist in multiple births Elizabeth knew full well the vulnerabilities of quadruplets but also that on a single trial with IVF four embryos would give a somewhat higher chance of producing a live baby. Rightly or wrongly I left this decision to her and just held my breath. As it turned out, only one egg was fertilised and, in retrospect, Elizabeth is horrified to think she might have chosen to have all four transferred. (The law now only allows a maximum transfer of three embryos.)

Our single fertilised egg was transferred to Elizabeth's womb and after a night in hospital we returned to Herefordshire to wait. We were told to behave normally. One can forget what that is, especially if treading the cliff edge. After four days there was spotting. That was the end of our quest for a baby.

That at least was what Elizabeth decided. Just like that. I was amazed. She was able, amidst the shaking grief, to close the door on her brightest, longest dream. Retaining hope she believed could now only be destructive. Life and work and we ourselves must go on. There was indeed objectively no further source of hope except a faint chance of natural pregnancy. It never occurred.

In describing more of my own inevitably changeable feelings about this long and ultimately fruitless process, I must of course avoid generalisation about 'the male response'. There will be no invariable pattern.

For Elizabeth the desire for children was not just emotional and rational but profoundly visceral. My viscera were quiescent. My own basic desire was that her needs be satisfied: the desire for children came indirectly. The child was still for me largely an abstract idea, one that had in the past, after all, been suffused with apprehensions if not aversions.

For me the long chronicles of test and experiment, trial and failure, hopes raised and dashed, had produced multiple disappointments but nothing like the depth of feeling Elizabeth suffered. Where I had only to be patient she had to be committed. Where I needed adaptability she needed resilience. It was enough if I was determined: she had to be endlessly brave.

Our life had to be ruled by the prospects of pregnancy. It dominated our conversation, our planning and of course our sexual behaviour. The frustrations for both of us seemed infinite. Nothing in private or professional life could be reliably planned. There were delays, disruptions, diary conflicts, draining distances, unexpected costs. The strains on Elizabeth were all the greater as she was having to deal with bereaved parents in her paediatric work. This while struggling with her own threatened bereavement in the quest of the elusive child.

Her stresses inevitably meant I had to curb the expression of my own: I felt I had to do all I could to avoid adding to her burdens. It meant sometimes concealing irritations, frustrations and resentments and certainly the shameful if only occasional twinges of relief when it looked as if I might not after all need to cope with sleepless paternity.

To some of the many pains of infertility we were partly or wholly immune. Since no organic impairment was to be found in either of us, we need not feel intrinsically inadequate as animals, or as sexual partners or as spouses. Neither of us needed to feel partly, let alone irretrievably, guilty towards the other. Elizabeth was no less of a woman, I no less of a man. Neither the female angst nor the testosterone torment of popular psychology afflicted us. We were not strictly infertile, just mysteriously unlucky.

And yet, and yet. These are all rational responses, and dark feelings are not so easily dispersed. Were we each separately fertile but not – a matter of acidity and alkalinity – possessed of compatible gametes? Was either of us being punished? Were we in some way cursed? Were we at the least disfavoured by a previously loving God? At a much less rarefied level, we had to cope with the sometimes indelicate probings, uninformed suspicions and over-generous sympathies of some relatives and some friends. No, I was not firing blanks. Yes, we did know how to do it. Sometimes it seemed we were becoming typecast whether as valiant fighters or pathetic losers. Sometimes it felt as if people were ducking when they saw us coming and, in fairness, obsessions hardly brighten the social scene.

For practical purposes we were now infertile. When the door finally closed we took a holiday, then threw ourselves into work. As the wounds healed over we found ourselves commissioned to write a Penguin book on the subject (Bryan and Higgins 1995), and being invited together to talk about 'Coping with Childlessness'. We have done this from Hammersmith to Sydney and Auckland.

As various parents we know run into various forms of trouble, we are prone to say that childlessness is becoming somewhat easier.

Incidentally neither of us felt we needed psychotherapy either during or after this episode although we might well have sought counselling had we not been receiving a lot of support and understanding from friends and colleagues in that world.

But of course the pain never wholly goes and, although our marriage remains strong and happy, the grief sometimes catches us by surprise. Love them as we truly do, our nieces are not a substitute for the daughter we nearly had twenty years ago. To her we had to say goodbye without ever being able to say hello.

And corny as it may sound, I should have loved to teach a boy cricket. I would show him what, because of the war, my own dear father, now 98, never had the chance to show me.

The other evening I was watching an old movie, *The Sea of Grass*, when Spencer Tracey said, 'Every man should have a son.' Suddenly, from out of the blue, I wept.

Bibliography

Bryan, E. and Higgins, R. (1995) *Infertility: New Choices, New Dilemmas*, London: Penguin.

Psychological aspects

Chapter 5

Eros and ART

Joan Raphael-Leff

Joan Raphael-Leff, a psychoanalyst, has for twenty-five years specialised in reproductive issues.

Psychoanalysis has informed our understanding that sex is not merely a meeting of bodily parts or their insertion into the other but *flesh doing the bidding of fantasy*. Between two bodies locked in erotic attraction, a delicate tissue of interwoven imagery is fabricated, so strong it can withstand the cruellest of tests; so fragile, the magic of desire can be dispelled as irrevocably as belief in the tooth fairy.

Having discovered infantile sources for adult passions – 'Originally we knew only sexual objects' (Freud 1912: 105) – Freud also indicated both the specificity of each individual's 'preconditions' for falling in love and the generic origin of desire: 'Sucking at the mother's breast is the starting-point of the whole of sexual life, the unmatched prototype of every later sexual satisfaction.' Noting that this initiation underpins later elaborations : '. . . I can give you no idea of the important bearing of this first object upon the choice of every later object, of the profoundest effects it has in its transformations and substitutions in even the remotest regions of our sexual life' (Freud 1916–17: 314).

In adulthood, sexual partners are often unconsciously selected not only for their resemblance to those significant early carers but for their 'transformational' capacity to re-elicit and transmute primary emotional states (Bollas 1979). We surrender ourselves to evocation and succour.

On many levels, magnetic attraction and/or being in love constitutes a form of *re*-cognition, investing the 'familiar' stranger with heightened desires transferred from internal familial figures. Not only is the mesmeric 'stranger' recognised as familial and ascribed attributes and functions of the original imagoes but these unconscious projections probe and occupy the other, intending to activate the desired familial response. When alchemy does spark off a corresponding 'live nerve', it may excite equally intensified, although not necessarily dovetailing, core states of mind in the other.

On some register (whether acknowledged or denied awareness, reciprocal or asymmetrical) in their lovemaking many lovers briefly occupy a nostalgic reconstruction, a 'sanctuary' of suspended restrictions, woven of intertwining tendrils from their respective internal worlds. At times, either or both partners may temporarily experience an illusory undoing of human severance. Poised on the threshold between familiarity and strangeness, Eros effects a momentary collapse of inner and outer by locating self in the other and alterity in the self. A mutual-infiltration leading in health to 'hospitality' (to use Derrida's felicitous term) and a sense of being 'at home in the other' (Derrida 2000) as one was within the pregnant maternal body. But where trauma or deprivation have prevailed, and fantasies of primordinate restitution abound, entry into another's body may unconsciously signify salvation, rebirth and, *in extremis*, an orgasmic state of indistinguishable merger or regressive return to imaginary infantile bliss or intra-uterine fusion. Sex becomes re-entry into the place from which one was ejected (Ferenczi 1938) or a fleeting glimpse of unconditional placental nurturing (Raphael-Leff 1993). Similarly, a meeting of grasping vagina and thrusting penis depositing bodily fluid inside her may evoke pre-symbolic parallels with the milk-filled nipple and sucking mouth of breastfeeding (Deutsch 1944), an inextricable mix of hunger, desire and yearning. The childhood fantasy of robbing the mother's body of its contents due to jealousy and envy of her capacity to bear a baby (Klein 1937) may feature in penetration unconsciously associated with an aggressive attack and/or anxieties about the intactness of the reproductive organs. In cases of perversion it is the intensity, duration, and sadistic and addictive enactment of such fantasies that renders them pathological.

My emphasis here is that, within the normal range, sexual excitation taproots an archaic reservoir in each individual, stirring up residues of time-worn desires for creative discovery of the unknown – interiority and the darkness within, sensual exploration of the (M)other's loving body, revival of erotogenic themes of generative (or destructive) coupling.

For a cohabiting couple, these fantasies and desires may or may not coincide. Each partner brings a multi-layered sedimentation of his or her internalised familial dramas which get played out in interactive dynamics, and undergo subtle trans-figurations during the life-cycle of the couple's sexual transactions. Structurally then, we could envisage an intimate relationship as composed of a reciprocally changing 'cat's-cradle' of intertwining reflections of past and present fantasies and desires, conscious and unconscious emotional residues of the internal worlds of both partners and their respective introjects, enactment in concrete, bodily and verbal and interactional dynamics within the pair.

Eros and desire

The contrasts Freud included within *Eros* 'between the instincts of self-preservation and the preservation of the species, as well as the contrast between ego-love and object-love' (Freud 1940: 380) are highlighted by the self-determined use of effective contraception. Erotic intimacy provides a playground where self and other, ego and object limitations and dividedness can be temporarily suspended. But a playground not without its self-preservative dangers. During the course of their sexual transactions with each other, a couple may surrender to passionate reciprocity, dismantling psychic and physical boundaries between them. Transcendence of time and gender limit-lines generate ecstatic expansiveness but carry a risk of relinquished control. Hurtling through orgasmic boundaries may also release floodgates *within*, dissolving intrapsychic barriers. Transient blurring of difference and separation can initiate joyful mutuality in partners who trust each other and have an inner sense of solid integration enabling each individual to resume his or her own ego boundaries. However, for vulnerable people the risk of too intense or prolonged fusion or sameness may cause anxiety, threatening personal integrity with fragmentation, dissolution and even extinction. Likewise, during transitional periods when sexual distinction is heightened or tinged with failure as in cases of infertility, the sense of separateness and difference may feel insurmountable, and profound loneliness ensues.

In addition to the elusive experiences which find expression within erotic relationships, such as voluptuous fusion, disavowal of time and severance, attaining the unattainable, access to the lost, disavowed and/or prohibited and re-enactment of archaic scenarios, is gratification of a narcissistic wish for bisexual completeness. Through identification, heterosexual encounters may tap wished-for possession of both sets of genitalia and their magical powers of intercourse. (Eroticisation of differences that distinguish male and female sexuality can also be invested cross-sexually and bridged with similarities, uniting masculine and feminine aspects inherent in each partner, whatever their gender.) This echoes Jung's 'animus/ anima', and Freud's notion of bi-gendered internalised bodily and empathic connections with significant others both male and female. 'I am accustoming myself', wrote Freud to his friend Fliess in 1899, alluding to this human capacity for psychic bisexuality, 'to regarding every sexual act as a process in which four individuals are involved' (Freud 1899).[1] For the child, working through the primal scene offers a 'triangular psychic space' (Britton 1989). Tolerance for the parental relationship entails the 'possibility of being a participant in a relation-ship and observed by a third person as well as being an observer of a relationship between two people' (Britton 1989: 86). Thus, unlike the engrossed self–other dyadic perspective this opens a third mental position from which to view the parental pair.

By rotating the triangle of these three participants, identifying with aspects of each parent and with both sexes, the child mentally creates an oscillating 'pastiche' of hetero- and homosexual genital and pre-genital sensualities (Aron 1995). However, in cultures where gender attributes are polarised, such psychic bi-sexuality poses a threat. The fear of being 'infected' by the woman's 'feminine weakness' is a variation on the theme Freud described as a generalised sexual dread of women (Freud 1918: 198). Thus the capacity to surrender may be marred in men in whom femininity engenders anxiety. As Mariam Alizade notes, in her native Latin America, fear of becoming feminine through a display of tenderness, coupled with fear of participation in a woman's 'erogenous overflow', may result in a man's control of his partner's sexuality or even use of violence to assure his masculinity (Alizade 1999: 90). Likewise in females, detachment, passivity or frigidity may express fear of forceful aspects of their bi-sexual sensuality.

In addition to the erotic, there is also dawning awareness of the procreative function of parental sexual union. The child's growing awareness of sexual and generational differences instigates reassessment of several facts of life:

- of *sex* (I am only female or male, not the other sex, neither or both);
- of *genesis* (I am the product of others, not self-made), of *generation* (adults have babies; children cannot) and of *generativity* (females carry/suckle babies, males impregnate).

'Generative identity' (Raphael-Leff 1997: 200) is consolidated between 18 and 36 months when the child who previously imagined s/he could be *everything* faces these restrictions – and accepts being only *one sex* (rather than both and unlimited); *pre*-potent (rather than omnipotent) and only *half* of future procreative coupling (interdependent rather than autonomous). Painful loss of omnipotence and relinquished belief in bi-sexual 'over-inclusiveness' (Fast 1990) result in acute feelings of jealousy towards adults and penis/womb envy of the other sex. Achievement of 'generative identity' involves accepting restrictions and finally resolving to revisit the scene as procreative adults, entering and extending the familial genealogy by pledging the self as future progenitor.

In adulthood, under the auspices of Eros, two bodies locked as one in sexual activity may temporarily suspend these limitations of gender, genesis, generation and generativity. However, when the reality of infertility intervenes to thwart the early promise of producing descendants, generative resolutions are dramatically destabilised as the adult is thrown back into a state of infantalising im-potence and generational confusion (Raphael-Leff 1986, 1992, 1994).

The wish to reproduce

In adulthood, of all chosen relationships, the one between procreative lovers is arguably the most complex. For those who grew up in nuclear families, the reproductive act draws part of its emotional current from a childhood source, replete with the mystery of secret activities behind the parents' bedroom door. Reproduction is what children originally understood sex to be about – the archaic mother and father bringing their parts together to create a baby – themself, or a sibling replacement. Once partners decide to have a baby, anxiously or triumphantly intent on breaking through that barrier, no longer excluded from procreative activity, they now *become* the copulating couple of origination.

While Freud deemed the woman's desire for a baby as substituting for the coveted penis, Klein saw the desired penis as a means to an end of having a baby. However, clinical experience reveals that unconscious motivation for childbearing is multifaceted far beyond the baby wish:

- cheating death of its finality
- emulating progenitors

- providing proof of undamaged fertility
- cultivating the lineage of generational replacement
- reparative urges to repay old debts of generosity
- pressure to meet (or refute) internalised parental ascriptions
- becoming fully 'adult'
- renegotiating incomplete developmental tasks
- articulating further maturational growth
- rewriting history by actively guiding the passively encountered
- vicariously recapturing lost aspects of the (baby) self
- conjuring up the partner's unknown childhood
- physically releasing pro-generative capacities
- fleshing out the longstanding unconscious fantasy baby
- and, in some cases, resolving incomplete childhood mourning.

Reproductive sex is approached with some trepidation and retains the imprint of archaic parental influences of (ascribed or imbibed) unconscious attitudes towards sexuality, corporeality and bodily substances.

When two people make love with the conscious aim of creating a baby, numinous ideas of the originary prototype arise: possession of, or competition with, the potent power of the paternal penis and swelling bulge of the archaic fertile mother's belly are but two unbidden images which come floating into the foreground. However, if, unconsciously, sexual intercourse often carries imaginary hermaphroditic completeness (comprised both of childhood wishes to be both sexes, and the fantasy of a combined parental figure or idealised primal scene couple), conception promises its realisation. A melding of the partners' genetic material, in *actuality*, creating a real hybrid of male/female unification.

Trying to conceive

Generational transition is a stressful one, fraught with tensions about rotating the original triangle. This ongoing period of sex without contraception leading up to pregnancy thus may seem extraordinarily exciting as the couple await the magical moment of conception: 'I feel incredibly alive' says Melissa during the initial months of 'trying'. 'I'm not used to being on this level, a mixture of joy and excitement filtering into everything, and generating so much energy it's quite overwhelming!' Some may experience this transition as a stressful one, flooded with anxiety of overcoming parental prohibitions about emulating but displacing the same or other-sexed progenitor. Melissa has referred herself to me for psychotherapy, wishing to explore her complicated relationship with her own mother before becoming a mother herself. For yet others, generative defiance may prevail, disavowing the gravity of the transition.

For many fertile heterosexual couples, the ongoing period of coitus without contraception leading up to pregnancy feels perilous as they await the catalytic moment of conception. Imagery of impregnation centres on hidden facets of reproductive (as opposed to sexual) genitalia with the smooth transmission of semen to the appropriate place inside, and modes of internal combination and compatible functioning of unseen parts. However egalitarian a heterosexual couple has been, once sex is geared to producing a baby, they shift into a register of sexed factuality which may or may not include cross-sex identifications and envy of the other. He is the male – virile, impregnating, siring his offspring via his woman. Conception by his ejaculate meeting her ovum. She is quintessentially female, doing what only members of her sex can do. Her womb will be the one to nurture their baby, her body will carry it, give birth and lactate. Or will it? 'Wherever I look there are pregnant women' says Verity after a few months. 'Am I being singled out and punished, forbidden to have a baby? Or is it that I'm not good enough to grow one?'

Anxieties focus on the enigmatic interior and feminine mysteries of formation of the foetus, its retention, nourishment and cultivation; its transformation from speck to baby, and later the female magic in transforming bodily fluids into milk.

As a primordial process, childbearing reactivates primary identifications as the woman identifies with the woman who carried her, revitalising fantasies of undifferentiated intra-uterine bodily space between foetus and mother.

'I'm not pregnant. Again' says Melissa as weeks, then months, of excited anticipation and non-fulfilment begin accumulating. 'I don't know if I'm making too much of it. People imply I should accept that it will take time, but I want to know the very *second* I become pregnant so I can begin to nurture the baby straight away. I feel so ready – inside me there's a nest just waiting to be filled', she says, gently cupping her hands to show me. 'I carefully plan where we are on ovulation days and make sure we eat well and listen to nice music. I'm so much more aware of subtle changes in my body; when my breasts get tender I find myself wanting to *talk* to the cells that may have begun dividing inside me. I think of it with such delight and want to make it welcome from the very start, knowing I was an unexpected "mistake" for my parents. Would I know if I was pregnant right now? Could I detect subtle changes in my body forty-eight hours after conception of a baby smaller than a full stop? I say "Hello" to the dot just in case it's there.'

As cycles pass unfructified, superstitious thinking and behaviours proliferate, instigating an increasingly desperate quest for optimal circumstances to produce the much awaited combination of egg and sperm. When this pre-conceptive period is long, intercourse 'to order' as ovulation occurs, and the monthly menstrual crash from elation to deflation of a couple's hopes, denude sex of spontaneity, taking a heavy emotional toll. 'We live each month under the tyranny of her cycle', says a despondent man.

Unconscious doubts, oedipal conflicts and archaic anxieties are re-triggered while one or both partners become increasingly preoccupied with impregnation. Trust in natural conception is undermined by the vagaries of a seemingly recalcitrant body and the constant focus on the body during the weeks of wondering and weathering dashed hopes. Magical thinking and superstitious behaviours begin to proliferate, as an increasingly desperate quest is instigated to produce the ideal circumstances to ensure the perfect combination of egg and sperm. Rich uncon-scious fantasies abound during the period of trying to conceive. It may seem as though the yearned-for baby was hovering in the wings waiting to be called into reality. It is often felt that under special conditions of closeness and love the illusive baby may be conceived.

'I so envy women who just get pregnant and don't have to agonise or root for the baby' says Melissa sadly some months later. 'Every day I search – I *will* there to be a sign. I count up the months when the baby would be due. I fix on special dates on the calendar and when my period comes at first I tell myself "It's only a little bleed", then when I can no longer ignore it I comfort myself that never mind, this is the wrong month but February for sure is the right one. I will most definitely be pregnant by Valentine's Day or at the very latest Easter – that's all about eggs and fertility . . .'

Under the repeated impact of lovemaking geared to reproduction even a hitherto egalitarian couple often become sexually polarised. The partners may begin to live out their unconscious image of an inactive ovum passively awaiting impregnation by the fittest piercing sperm in the sexual fantasy of their male–female bodies coming together, as she patiently awaits his urge to penetrate her in the hope of uniting in fruitful procreativity. Alternatively, she might feel as helplessly and angrily dependent on her partner to fertilise her, as she believes her ripe ovum is upon his sluggish or reluctant sperm. A man who once delegated the trajectory of his ejaculate to seek its womb-home may now feel trapped or suctioned into the dangerous womb. Unconsciously, a male partner may fear female engulfment of his masculinity or have a more specific sense of her grabbing, snapping vulva grabbing his penis or her sucking vagina sapping his vitality during repeated lovemaking.[2] He may feel sapped by his procreative endeavours. In some cultures semen is regarded as non-regenerative, or as precious as life-blood. Hindus, for instance, believe a hundred drops of blood go into making a single drop of semen.

Inevitably, the protracted disillusioning experience of attempting to conceive and failing month after month, alters body- and self-image, permeating the life of the individual on every level, affecting the relationship, sexuality, spirituality, even work.

'I feel so raw. Like an egg without a shell' says a highly placed professional woman after ten months of trying to conceive. 'I used to like my periods – a sign of my body working. Now they're a sign it's *not*. My partner and I used to be so close when we made love. Now it feels mechanical; a means to an end. I have been crying for a week – feeling trapped – yearning for a baby. I sit chairing important meetings but it feels as if I have a thin veneer of grown-upness over a chasm of craving to be looked after. I just couldn't bear yet another month of high hopes and disappointment. I pray and plead to some invisible God – "release me from this interminable phase so I can go on to the next" – but feel I'm caught up in a process that's indifferent to my fate.'

'I watch my friends with their babies and feel there's this whole world being denied to me', she says a few months later. 'But whatever I do – I still can't *make* it happen. . . . It's as if I'm standing on a cold empty platform waiting for a train to arrive; there's no indication when, but people keep saying: "it's bound to be along" – but I'm losing faith in it ever coming. My mind is blank and wordless and I've run out of strategies that make waiting bearable. I try to fill the gap by being ferociously over-busy at work. And at home – I take my temperature; I use a prediction kit. We practise abstinence before I ovulate. But every time we make love I feel myself tensing up, will I, won't I? Is this the moment? I feel I should be more relaxed, less wound up and preoccupied. But somehow having a child has become the most important achievement. Funny, up till recently I wasn't at all bothered but now I can't even stand seeing other people's babies. I prefer to stay at home . . .'

Diagnosis of infertility

With postponement of childbearing and environmental pathogens, problems appear to be on the increase. It is estimated that at least one in five couples in Britain has difficulty conceiving. Today, infertility is defined as failure to conceive after a year of normal intercourse without contraception. The actual diagnosis may follow investigations, once the increasingly despairing couple decides to seek help, or in some cases it may be the outcome of a medical emergency, such as an ectopic pregnancy. To many it constitutes a severe blow to self-esteem, particularly in a culture of contraception that cultivates an illusion of reproductive control. All those assumptions, tacitly held from infancy, that each of us, like our parents, has the natural capacity to make babies, are suddenly called into question. That aspect of gender I have called 'generative identity' can no longer be taken for granted. Lineage stops, as the infertile person sees themselves as the end, rather than the middle, of a genetic chain. The intensity with which each couple or individual reacts to the specific diagnosis is determined by the historical investment in their own generative identity.

Medical distinctions are drawn between sterility resulting from irreversible damage or defect, infertility due to correctable causes, and sub-fertility attributed to a single cause or several factors in one or both partners, or their particular combination (such as cervical mucus incompatibility), producing problems at any stage before or after the successful meeting of sperm and ovum. Clearly these definitions become invested with personal fantasy.

To some couples, the diagnosis constitutes a blow to their most cherished hopes, threatening the very epistemological centre of their world. Where only one partner is afflicted, he or she may feel extremely guilty towards the fertile mate, self-sacrificingly suggesting they separate to enable the other to find a new spouse, or even contemplating suicide. The other partner may be reassuring and able to ride the crisis, or, feeling profoundly cheated of their own birthright, may propose drastic solutions. Some couples draw closer in their sorrow. In others self-recriminations and/or accusations proliferate as previous sexual transgressions or postponement of childbearing are blamed for the current tragedy. Where there is asymmetry in the desire for a child, or when one partner feels hard done by and let down by the other's failure, the partnership may end or deteriorate. In such situations counselling, or therapy are crucial.

In all cases, tensions rise within the relationship as rage, grief, despair, dissatisfaction and derision fester below the surface or erupt in desperate attempts to regain equilibrium. In a world now divided starkly into haves and have-nots, fertile friends may be resented and their own parents unconsciously blamed. The infertile couple may isolate themselves, feeling that those who have had children cannot possibly understand what it is like to be faced with genetic extinction. Assailed by primitive forces of shame, deprivation and envy, the infertile person feels singled out, excluded, stigmatised or even ostracised in being unable to fulfil the most fundamental requisite of the human race. Endangered couples often retreat into reticence or even self-chosen social isolation to protect themselves from the threat of well-meaning inquisitive friends. Some may fear their own antisocial impulses as emotional pressure and turmoil accumulate.

In time, some couples gradually come to accept childlessness or accustom themselves to the idea of fostering or facing the many hurdles of adoption. Others, determined to have a child of their own making, may embark on intensive investigations and expensive fertility treatments if they can afford them, including surgical procedures, or chemical and physical interventions, hopefully leading to medically assisted conception.

Eros and ART

With fertility treatment the nature of intercourse changes. A third, the medical expert or team, now invades the intimacy of a couple's lovemaking. Reports must be made, post-coital tests, sperm counts and temperature charts intrude into the private space between them and various invasive procedures highlight their inadequacies. Sexual disturbances are not uncommon and studies report up to two-thirds of men experiencing transient impotence lasting one to three months, following the discovery of male infertility. Throughout treatment, emotional conflicts and fantasies continue to operate, including idealisation of the Godlike medical specialists who, like the childhood parents, can produce babies, and resentment at their own infantilisation and dependence on the control and interference of these powerful authoritative strangers. Where treatments include gamete donation, the unknown donor is a further stranger in their midst, invoking mythical or paranoid ideas about the source of the biological contribution. The necessary sperm or egg donor/surrogate may be disavowed or, alternatively, elaborate fantasies may be constructed around their omnipotent qualities.

In psychotherapeutic work we note ways in which, infused with archaic significance, reproductive technology and its bizarre happenings play into inner-world intricacies, replicating infantile theories, reinforcing narcissistic splits or offering legitimated escape routes which differ for each individual within the reproductive framework. For instance, for a survivor of incest, gynaecological examinations or fertility treatment often arouse genital anxieties with highly emotional resonances. However, gamete donation itself may, at first, represent not a second-best curative option but a triumphant way of bypassing genetic or seminal continuity with the abuser.

'Fertility treatment means I'm no longer just helplessly waiting for conception, like a dependent child waiting to be rescued', says a particularly insightful patient, who, with menopause approaching, over the past three years has repeatedly failed to conceive. Following a series of asexual relationships, her healthy marriage was somewhat disrupted in the wake of a recovered repressed incident of sexual violation by her father at an early age: 'With the donated embryo it feels I can finally establish my distinct core – a separate family of my own, released from bondage to my past.'

Needless to say, there can be no bypassing the complex web of multi-layered unconscious connections: 'I worry about the social consequences for the baby' she says thoughtfully while debating the idea. 'If the donation becomes known the child will be marked out as special and different. If it is kept a secret, am I recreating the explosive secretive conditions of my own childhood? And I wonder, can I accept an embryo burrowing deep into the privacy of my body without feeling exploited and forced to expel it? Can I nourish it or am I so contaminated inside that I'll poison it? . . . And if the egg comes from another woman will my jealousy make me hate it? My sister always was my mother's darling . . .' In time, as she better understands psycho-historical conditions in her father's life which led to her abuse and even contemplates forgiving him, she is able to mourn the 'blood baby' she and her husband cannot make together.

The 'slow motion' process and constant need to re-question the desire for a baby enable us to draw distinctions between hitherto conflated aspects of gender, sexuality, fertility, fantasy, desire and reproductive urges. For some people, it becomes apparent that the desperate wish to conceive represents not a wish for a baby but the desire to be pregnant, or even just a need for evidence of fertility. On occasion I have been consulted by a puzzled medical expert: 'Can you explain this!? I've [sic] spent three years getting a woman pregnant and then when finally she conceived, do you know what she did? She went and had an abortion!'

Needless to say, compulsion to ratify fertility and/or prove intra-uterine retentiveness is not limited to those with fertility problems but also operates in some couples where conception occurs spontaneously. As in cases of unassisted promiscuous impregnation or repeated abortions, the distinction between the need for proof of fecundity and a wish to have a child becomes transparent: 'If only I could be pregnant, even just for a day, just long enough to prove I am not rotten inside', says a sub-fertile woman on my couch who was abused as a child. 'I'm OK', gloats a virile man whose partner is having fertility treatment. 'The eggs *did* fertilise in the dish [in vitro]. It's not my fault that *she* can't make them stick.'

Thus, if new reproductive techniques offer hope where barrenness has resided, their positive aspects are also fraught with conflict. It seems that science fiction technological interventions, taking place not 'out there' but actually lived out in the innermost space of a woman's body and the inner sanctum of a couple's home, resuscitate archaic unconscious puzzlement about where babies come from and wild theories of how they are made. Increasingly, experts take on the aura of seemingly omnipotent fertile but withholding parents. Rational cognition, geared to ordinary events of birth, copulation and death, lags sorely behind the uncanny reality of these bizarre treatments. And their emotionally and financially draining consequences come on top of the generative confusion of prolonged failure to conceive naturally. In addition, at the very point of struggling to produce their joint baby, treatment techniques may conspire to separate a couple even further. 'It seems so obscene that our beloved baby will originate in a Petri dish from a combination of my wanking off in the clinic toilet and her egg "harvested" up by a pipette.'

Unless they blindly follow the roller-coaster of reproductive treatments, many couples grapple with these questions as they debate whether or not to continue pursuing the next phase of treatment. Some discover that their need to parent involves utilising capacities which may be diverted or sublimated into a social activity. Others focus on creating a genetically related baby; yet others feel content in lavishing their love on an individual baby or child.

With treatment, sexuality and procreation become further separated and the sexual act is drained of its excitement and suspense as hope and responsibility for fertilisation are allocated in another place. Stripped of its potential procreative function, intercourse may feel futile and empty of desire. 'Our whole sex life has shut down', says a woman who has been undergoing prolonged infertility treatment. 'When he wants to make love I feel murderously angry. What for? It can't lead anywhere. We can't make a baby ourselves. I can't bear him to touch me – it's just a reminder that we're useless. As each period approaches I plummet down again. Such a long expensive haul getting nowhere. We've blown another chance. I dreamed I'd left the front door unlocked and squatters were invading our flat. I was trying to shout but had no voice and woke my partner by shouting "No!" I know I'm furious with him for putting me through the humiliation of IVF because of his low-motility sperm. We're both such utter failures. I suppose I'm worse than him. My womb's not good enough and I think I destroy the fertilised embryos as soon as the doctors put them back into me. Life is so pointless. I hate myself. I hear this voice inside berating me with such loathing – "you're stupid; incompetent; barren". It builds up inside me like electric power waiting for discharge and I turn on my partner screaming: "why can't you even do what any animal can?" We can't take control of our lives – we lie there in bed, just he and I together – awake, not touching each other, trapped, separate, wretched, sick with frustration; and sex, the very thing that once brought us comfort, is the very last thing we can contemplate.'

The technological primal scene

Creation myths exist in all geographical locations, cultural contexts and across differing realities of parental age, appearance, skin colour, temperament and mother-tongue. The reproductive primal scene occupies a central place in both personal and collective accounts of origin. Human narratives reflect individual fantasy elaboration and mythological cosmology which arise both to express and to counteract fundamental strictures, often rebelling against the limitations imposed by generative identity. The 'big bang' theory of origins, where two bodies, male and female, come together to conceive a third, carried within and then expelled out of the mother's body, is merely one version among these imaginative stories.

However, within the last few decades, eternal and seemingly immutable facts of life have changed dramatically *in reality*, blurring fact and fiction, as science races ahead changing the story of origins faster than the unconscious can keep up. Not only is sex now possible without pregnancy but pregnancy has become possible without sex! Contraception redesignated intercourse as hedonistic, primarily for pleasure – sex for 'recreation' rather than procreation. Indeed, conception frequently occurs in the absence of the procreative couple themselves, as commonplace laboratory conceptions by in vitro fertilisation testify. Sex-change surgery belies fixity of gender, cloning negates two-sex reproduction, while post-menopausal pregnancy and implanted foetal stem-cells rupture generational boundaries. Egg transfer means a woman may be pregnant with a genetically unrelated foetus or have a baby by proxy, through 'rent-a-womb' surrogacy or a relative's generous incubation. Indeed, generations may be breached as grand-mothers gestate their own grandchildren. Reproductive technology moves us into new domains of kinship; with embryo freezing, twins can be born years apart, and gamete donation introduces new parent/child/sibling connections, including known or unknown surrogates and sperm/egg donors.

Self-insemination introduces the possibility of a woman on her own achieving fertilisation without a potent male in her external (or internal) life. Female partners may choose conception by egg swapping or nucleus removal – thereby bringing procreativity out of the exclusive possession of heterosexuality, or indeed, twosomeness. As reproductive technologies play out the stuff of science fiction, gametes may even be borrowed from the dead; necro-impregnation is now possible – utilising eggs from adult cadavers or cultivating them from dead girls or aborted foetuses. Apart from banked frozen sperm, a widow's recent successful bid to the European Court of Human Rights for insemination with semen mechanically removed from her comatose husband before his death recaptures an ancient myth of posthumous impregnation of Isis by dead Osiris.

Efficient contraception, safe abortion, reversible sterilisation, the 'morning-after pill', selective foeticide and egg-freezing potentialities create an illusion of self-regulating control while offering women real choices as to whether, when, how and with whom to have a baby. In this illusory realm of omnipotent reproductive control not only are generative representations affected, and psychosexual disturbances unleashed, but our wildest fantasies may be actualised, flaunting reality restrictions and taboos.

Clearly, the emotional impact of prolonged failure to conceive and fertility treatments which may continue for many years permeates every aspect of life –

intrapsychic, interpersonal, psychosexual and occupational. Given this ongoing reappraisal, psychotherapy or counselling are not luxuries but a vital necessity in providing a safe place and time-out to put into words the emotional impact of infertility and treatment on each partner's sense of generative identity and creative capacities. In a fraught love relationship therapy offers space to explore, at a time of high technological hype, the vicissitudes of the unusual journey of transition from being sexual partners to becoming, or not becoming a parental couple.

Notes

1   While this formulation has been intercepted as two prescribed sets of heterosexual couplings (Butler 1990) it can also be conceptualised as a *multiplicity of choices* originating in the oedipal child's identification with any aspect of each parent in the fantasied intercourse. Freud's reference to four 'individuals' rather than part-objects, suggests the child's elaboration of the *primal scene parents* as separate subjective individuals by contrast to a more primitive pre-oedipal combined parent figure (Klein 1946). This conceptual development assumes *meaningful* sexual interaction thereby differentiating and integrating previously inchoate, violent or everlastingly joined aspects of the parents (Ogden 1989). However, the latter possibly continues to operate as an alternating phantasy system in the mind, to include the 'dark side of sexuality' (Aron 1995: 214).
2   The fear of being 'infected' by the woman's 'feminine weakness' is a variation on the theme, one Freud described as a generalised sexual dread of women (Freud 1918: 198).

Bibliography

Alizade, A.M. (1999) *Feminine Sensuality*, London: Karnac.
Aron, L. (1995) 'The internalized primal scene', *Psychoanalytic Dialogues*, 5: 195–238.
Bollas, C. (1979) 'The transformational object', *International Journal of Psychoanalysis*, 60: 97–107.
Britton, R. (1989) 'The missing link: parental sexuality in the Oedipus complex', in J. Steiner (ed.) *The Oedipus Complex Today*, London: Karnac, pp. 83–101.
Butler, J. (1990) *Gender Trouble*, New York: Routledge.
Derrida, J. (2000) *Of Hospitality, Anne Dufourmantelle invites Jacques Derrida to Respond* (trans. R. Bowlby), Stanford: Stanford University Press.
Deutsch, H. (1944) *The Psychology of Women*, New York: Grune & Stratton.
Fast, I. (1990) 'Aspects of early gender development: towards a reformulation', *Psychoanalytic Psychology*, 7 (suppl): 105–118.
Ferenczi, S. (1938) *Thalassa – a Theory of Genitality*, London: Karnac, 1989.
Freud, S. (1899) *The Complete Letters of Sigmund Freud to Wilhelm Fliess, 1887–1904* (ed. and trans. J.M. Masson), Cambridge, MA: Harvard University Press.
—— (1912) *The Dynamics of Transference*, Standard Edition, vol. 12, London: Hogarth Press and Institute of Psychoanalysis.
—— (1916–17) *Introductory Lectures on Psychoanalysis*, Standard Edition, vol. 15, London: Hogarth Press and Institute of Psychoanalysis.
—— (1918) *The Taboo of Virginity* (*Contributions to the Psychology of Love, III*), Standard Edition, vol. 11, London: Hogarth Press and Institute of Psychoanalysis.

—— (1940) *An Outline of Psychoanalysis*, Standard Edition, vol. 23, London: Hogarth Press and Institute of Psychoanalysis.

Klein, M. (1937) 'Love, guilt and reparation', ch. 19 in *Love, Guilt and Reparation*, London: Hogarth Press and Institute of Psychoanalysis.

—— (1946) 'Notes on some schizoid mechanisms', in *The Writings of Melanie Klein*, vol. 3, London: Hogarth Press, 1975.

Ogden, T.H. (1989) *The Primitive Edge of Experience*, Northvale, NJ: Aronson.

Raphael-Leff, J. (1986) 'Infertility: diagnosis or life sentence?' *British Journal of Sexual Medicine*, 13: 28–30

—— (1990) 'If Oedipus was an Egyptian . . .', *International Review of Psycho-Analysis*, 17: 309–335.

—— (1992) 'The Baby-Makers: an in-depth single-case study of conscious and unconscious psychological reactions to infertility and baby-making technology', *British Journal of Psychotherapy*, 8, 3: 278–294.

—— (1993) *Pregnancy – The Inside Story*, London: Sheldon Press; Aronson, 1996; Karnac, 2000.

—— (1994) 'Transition to parenthood – infertility', in *Infertility & Adoption*, Seminar Series, London: Post-Adoption Centre.

—— (1997) 'The casket and the Key: thoughts on gender and generativity', in J. Raphael-Leff and R. Jozef Perelberg (eds), *Female Experience: Three Generations of British Women Psychoanalysts on Work with Women*, London and New York: Routledge, pp. 237–257.

—— (2000) '"Behind the shut door" – a psychoanalytical approach to premature menopause', ch. 5 in D. Singer and M. Hunter (eds) *Premature Menopause – a Multidisciplinary Approach*, London: Whurr, pp. 79–97.

Chapter 6

Mourning the never born and the loss of the Angel

Juliet Miller

Juliet Miller is a Jungian psychoanalyst.

To see the *Annunciation*, a fresco by Fra Angelico in San Marco in Florence, you approach the painting from below. It is on the wall at the top of a steep flight of steps that lead up to the monks' cells. Along the bottom of the fresco is an inscription: 'Virginis intacte cum veneris ante figuram pretereundo cave ne sileature ave.' 'When you come before the image of the Ever-Virgin, take heed that you do not neglect to say an Ave.' This injunction was made to all who entered the north dormitory, which was the place where the lay brothers and important male visitors slept. The Virgin and the Immaculate Conception are to be acknowledged, she and the Angel must not be ignored. This fresco moves me, not because of its obvious devotional aspect, but because the Virgin seems touchingly self-protective as she listens to the Angel's message. Mary has her hands crossed over her stomach in an acknowledgement of the Angel Gabriel's presence, and this gesture is mirrored by Gabriel. Despite the depiction of a miraculous event, the delicacy and lack of artifice of Angelico's painting suggest an ordinariness and humanness about Mary as she accepts her part as intermediary and vessel. As well as joy there is a sadness and a sense of ambivalence. God will be made Man through Mary and as a result as a man he will die. Birth will also bring forth death. The Angel brings a message of both.

The relationship of the birth process to transience and death as well as joy is an existential problem, which we struggle with continuously as part of the experience of being alive. A beginning cannot be meaningful without an end. Birth and death are inextricably linked together and inform each other. This tension and paradox is also true of the creative act. Our ambivalence and conflict about bringing into being was well understood by Rilke who explored in his poetry the complexity of our creative drives. He understood these not as miraculous events through which we attempt to become Godlike, but as our small attempts to make statements about our transient aliveness. In *The Duino Elegies* he struggles with why, as humans, we both need and resist creativity:

Praise this world to the Angel, not the untellable: you
can't impress him with the splendour you've felt; in the
cosmos

where he more feelingly feels you're only a novice. So
Show him
some simple thing, refashioned by age after age,
till it lives in our hands and eyes as a part of ourselves.

(Rilke 1964: 64)

The Angel is to be praised through expression of our ordinary capacities to create. To be fully human it is necessary to acknowledge our connections to a spiritual life without believing that we are also angelic. The depiction of Mary in the Fra Angelico fresco also speaks of how we can be touched by the miraculous and yet at the same time have to accept that we remain human. The Angel has to be acknowledged but not embodied in our creative acts.

To be touched by spirits is one of the ways we experience our humanity. What happens, however, if we feel cut off from this connection? If, through trauma, body and psyche are experienced as unrelated and as a result conception is identified as miraculous. To be infertile is to experience such a disturbance.

In this chapter I shall be exploring how infertility is experienced by women. Although there may be many similar as well as different issues for men, their experiences are addressed elsewhere in the book.

For some women the inability to conceive a child can challenge their belief in a spiritual and a creative capacity and can also keep the infertile woman trapped in a timeless world where mourning is not possible and as a result nothing can change. The capacity to create and the capacity to mourn are both closely related to feelings of aliveness, which the infertile can feel has eluded them. I shall be writing from two perspectives: from my personal experience and also as a psychotherapist. In my practice I have worked with women who face issues of infertility and childlessness and also those who struggle with a loss of creativity in other aspects of their lives.

Conception is one of those facts of our humanity which still holds mysteries for us. It inhabits a place between psyche and soma, somewhere between the Angel and the corporeal body. It is an issue both grounded in the physical world and yet rich with symbolic meanings; an area inhabited by gods and angels and yet made concrete by the conception and birth of human babies. Recently my nephew rang me to tell me that his first child, a daughter, had been born. I expressed my excitement and delight to him on the phone and afterwards wept profusely, a moment of wonder and mystery that grips me every time a baby is born of someone who is close to me. What I didn't tell him was that it was also the birthday of my cat. A comment which I felt he would rightly have responded to as a diminution of the birth of his daughter. However the mutual birth day is significant to me as it connects me more deeply to this child than my nephew would know. My large and very beautiful male cat watched me with an unblinking gaze as I spoke on the phone and I was flooded with the uniqueness of that moment, a moment in which to experience the nod of the gods.

We now live in a world where there is little communal experience of the sacred. It can sometimes be shared in collective moments of grief or joy, but mostly the sacred is now only experienced by individuals in private. We no longer, as a matter of course, nod to the Angel as we ascend the stairs of San Marco. Yet this profound and spiritual dimension to our lives may still be present despite it being relegated to the unconscious. 'In a world which has lost the sense of the sacred, this dimension of symbol has an archaeological quality, or that of scattered fragments of a bygone culture whose meaning has been forgotten' (Zoja 1997: 53).

An experience where a death touches us can also bring forth these 'scattered fragments' and hold a uniqueness and sense of the sacred. A few years ago an elderly woman of my acquaintance who was in her nineties died in her own time and in her own way. When I was growing up she lived in the basement of our house which she rented from my parents, and although she moved to another city when my parents sold the house, she kept contact with me and my siblings. She never married and had no children except us. She devoted her life to writing poetry and supported herself by secretarial jobs. As she became ill she spoke briefly of a man she had been in love with in her twenties and speculated how things might have been. However, she was aware of the choice she had made and that this choice to be a writer rather than a wife and mother had sustained her for over ninety years. When she was taken into a hospice for the last days of her life she insisted that she had a job to do, to die, and that whatever it was like it would be a unique time for her and that she had no intention of being interrupted by visitors. I was allowed the privilege of seeing her for a moment whilst she was deeply engrossed in the process of her death. There was no resistance, just an openness to what I imagined was a spiritual experience. It seemed that the childless atheist whose individuality had informed my childhood had been immersed in the experience of dying and died creatively.

The birth of my great-niece and the death of my elderly mentor were experienced as vibrant energetic events by me. Both of them linking me to life and living. Our responses to births and deaths may be one of the few ways we still allow ourselves to acknowledge that we are connected to a spiritual life. A patient recently told me how her partner had been completely surprised by overwhelming feelings when his brother had his first child. It was as if he had been out of touch with this area of himself before that and was now aware of his own procreative desire and maybe also, as a result, his mortality, his fate as a human being.

Patients who seek psychotherapy are often looking for some kind of spiritual meaning to their lives, which they feel they have lost or never found. This desire need not encompass a religious meaning in the sense of the organised religions, although sometimes a religious faith can hold that meaning for them. More often it is a desire to experience the nod of the gods and to reconnect with meanings that do not come from inside or from outside but which in unique and important moments can marry the two and become a connecting energy to life. If all goes well this *marriage* can be symbolised through the relationship with the psychotherapist where the therapy becomes a liminal zone, and movement and change are possible.

In an interesting Jungian study of the dreams of women who are pregnant, cats appear frequently as liminal creatures, representing a feminine consciousness which contains a capacity to wait patiently for the right moment, to access dark areas of the unconscious and to be both warm but also independent and detached (Abt *et al.* 2000). They also have the capacity to inhabit the worlds of day and night, the conscious and unconscious worlds, and have an ability to cross, apparently, seamlessly between the two, just as 'The cat who walked by himself' in the *Just So Stories* (Kipling 1975). Because they represent aliveness and connection, they can also appear in dreams as creatures who are starving, mutilated and desperate, showing us the shadow side of their liminality. For women who are pregnant the multiple changes in both physical and psychological areas as the foetus develops may be experienced as dangerous and can appear as such in dreams:

> At a table with children. Horrible worms crawl out of the ceiling. . . . The worms turn into cats which start to chew the dreamer. Although she likes cats otherwise, she can't prevent her resistance to them. At last the children say: 'Stroke them!' – which the dreamer immediately does. Immediately, the cat in her arms turns into a quiet little boy. 'Now . . . be quiet, too. This battle is over, too.'
>
> (Abt *et al.* 2000: 222)

In this dream the fears appear to be overcome and the conflict resolved through worm to cat to baby.

In the dreams of women who cannot conceive, dead liminal creatures can also appear as symbols of internal destruction. It seems that the battleground of destruction and creation is symbolised in similar ways in both pregnant and infertile women. Frances, a patient I will refer to in more depth later, had unexplained infertility and during the early years of her therapy dreamt often of dead and mutilated cats.

Many patients come into therapy because they feel barren or empty inside and fear that there is nothing there or that what is there is destructive. For patients who are infertile these feelings can be compounded. Some of my female patients have been unable to conceive children. Some have decided not to reproduce. Many have allowed the decision to be made for them by the passing of time. For those who cannot conceive there is a difference between those for whom a medical reason is found and those who have 'unexplained infertility'. Primary unexplained infertility, where no cause can be found for the inability to conceive, has special issues relating to it which I consider bring up, more acutely, this loss of liminality and which can then be experienced as a loss of soul. This painful psychic state can appear to leave them stranded in a place which is neither of the living nor of the dead – in limbo. Conceiving and miscarrying, or suffering from blocked tubes, or ovarian failure, or any of the many medically recognised reasons for infertility, presents the patient with reasons for and realities of loss. There is a failure to conceive and this can be painful to accept and to mourn. But there is a loss which can be thought about and pictured in bodily terms. For those who have unexplained infertility there is no loss but rather a void. No embryos however young, no damage however guilt-ridden can be focused on, there is simply a space into which a child cannot or will not come, and about which it seems that *nothing* can be known. The Angel simply will not visit, and this lack of visitation can have a broad reach, which may extend beyond the woman's capacity for procreation and into all aspects of her creativity.

In his *Visions* seminars Jung refers to this internal struggle for a woman who is unable to get pregnant as 'a special kind of hell. For a woman there is no longer any way out; if she cannot have children, she falls into hellfire because all her creativeness turns back to herself, she begins to eat herself' (Jung 1997: 794).

As many feminist writers have noticed, for the infertile woman, something more than the possibility of a baby has been removed: 'It seems that once you find yourself involuntarily childless, all other identifying marks are washed away. Of course, such transformations are not unusual; they are the hallmark of socially stigmatised conditions' (Pfeffer 1987: 82). There is more at stake here than an inability to make children. As Pfeffer argues, this may well include a sense of social stigmatisation, but I consider that the lack of 'identifying marks' goes further than this. A woman who has no explanation for her infertility can experience herself as not only socially, but spiritually and psychically severely disabled. This may result in an inability to function on many levels and she may be at a loss as to how to heal herself.

Assisted reproductive technology (ART) may appear to provide a concrete answer to healing this state or it may not. Societal pressures and changing expectations of procreative choice have been widely written about and have had a part in dramatically affecting the expansion and proliferation of medical interventions (Pfeffer 1987, Greer 2000). The changing view of society's belief that all women should have a baby if they want one, regardless of age, or fertility, and the concomitant acceptance that infertility is a medical problem with a medical solution, is reflected in the explosion of reproductive technologies whose end goal is to produce babies. As a result many childless couples have been successfully helped to have families.

To live within this medically vibrant age not only opens up new solutions to making babies but it can also become a defence against other forms of creative awareness and understanding. The medical consultant and ART can be seen as the saviours and can be pursued at all costs. The fertile spirit then appears to reside with them and not with the couple. The hundreds of photographs of babies emblazoned on the walls of infertility consultants' offices appear as signs of the fertility of the consultant or his magical powers and offer up hope to the infertile couple of being included in this abundance. For the couple, sex and reproduction are separated from each other and conception fantasies may involve ideas of parthenogenesis rather than a creative male and female sexuality. Sometimes, to regain a sense of control, and a belief in their own powers, infertile couples who are going through infertility treatments will create their own rituals in an attempt to make conceptive meanings for themselves. A patient told me how she had asked the close-knit group in her office to take turns in giving her the numerous daily injections for her IVF treatment. It seemed that this had a meaning for her in terms of a group/family involvement in the subsequent conception and birth of her son. I felt that it was an attempt to re-inject an idea of relationship into the medical procedure.

Most infertile couples who seek treatment are not successful in producing a child. Yet if the drive for a child becomes an obsession, the couple may feel that hope would be lost for ever if they were to stop looking for a medical solution. This may be regardless of the threat posed to meanings and relationship by repeated technological interventions. Any suggestion that there might be other ways of looking at this deathly state to help warm it into life, apart from a birth, can be experienced as an additional unbearable wound – much like a prisoner might experience if told that her release was not the primary issue and not what she should be thinking about. As a result, take-up rates for counselling services in infertility clinics are low and once couples have embarked on the decision to proceed with invasive medical treatments they often do not want to explore their motivation further in case this disturbs their commitment to the decision they have taken. Studies of infertile couples who attend infertility clinics are now beginning to acknowledge that protracted medical interventions can become anti-therapeutic and anti-healing. Acknowledging an infertile state as permanent can help a couple to adjust (Koropatnick *et al.* 1993, Moller and Fallstrom 1991).

> With IVF came a gradual decay of hope. We weren't in control of our destinies. It's a course of action I would recommend people to think very, very, very hard about. Because it's a high-stake game and the odds are that you will lose, and continue to lose.
>
> (Gerrard 2001: 20)

For some infertile women, for whom reproductive technologies have not turned out to be the answer, an acceptance of their failure to conceive may not release them but may keep them imprisoned in a state of permanent failure. In this prison there appears to be no escape, no space for psyche and soma to talk to each other and no possibility of other creations. Those who suffer from unexplained infertility may then experience a ghostly form of loss and death which appears to be especially difficult to work with or through, as there is no subject to mourn, or death to be known about. Ways of dealing with other losses and usual coping mechanisms for grief seem inadequate and irrelevant. This lack rather than loss may have differing psychological effects. There may be difficulty engaging with the mourning process but there may also be an accentuation of an emptiness that is already felt to be there. Or the effect may be to reactivate old losses. As a result the woman may feel she is presented with an existential difficulty around a loss of identity and self.

Frances had come into therapy in her forties because of her pain about her inability to conceive over a long period going back to her mid-twenties. She longed to be released from a frozen state where a baby would not come and yet she could not move forward into her life. No medical reason had been found for her infertility, which left her with a void. 'It would be a miracle if I got pregnant now. I don't know why I can't conceive and yet I have no hope because all I know is this nothingness.' In using the word 'miracle' it was as if Frances could only see a solution to her problem as happening outside herself. How was it possible to engage with a dynamic internal world when, in a physical way, through her body she appeared to be uncreative?

She spoke of how if she had been pregnant once, even if only for a few weeks, this feeling would have been different. She would know that she was fertile even if the pregnancy never came to term and she never gave birth to a child. Becoming pregnant to prove fertility can be experienced as a separate issue from actually giving birth to a child. In Eva Pattis Zoja's interesting study of abortion, she looks at women who abort again and again rather than using contraception successfully and sees these repeated conceptions without births as attempts to initiate a birth of self through the re-experiencing of their fertility (Zoja 1997: 31).

Pregnancy has always been a visible statement and proof of fertility and virility for both men and women. When a woman is unable to make this happen, the lack of a concrete expression of her procreativity can feel like an attack on her capacity to trust in any of her other creative acts. It may confirm a sense of being empty inside and having nothing to draw on. 'I could never have babies. I felt empty – well I was empty, wasn't I?' (Gerrard 2001: 21). Or it may confirm a fear of being full of unseen destructive forces, which are not available to be known about except through their results.

In Erik Erikson's well-known 1960s study of the adolescent identity crisis he touches on a woman's experience of her own interiority in relation to her identity as a woman: '. . . in female experience an "inner space" is at the centre of despair even as it is at the very centre of potential fulfilment' (Erikson 1968: 278). The womb is both a container for a healthy baby or a coffin for a dead one. It is an organ that is preparing itself for a child or emptying itself out because of the lack of one. This dual capacity of the womb can sometimes be expressed intensely in the fantasies or dreams of pregnant women where deformed or dead babies appear. 'Her refrigerator was closed, and she couldn't open it. She was angry because she was hungry. At last she opened it with difficulty. Inside she found a very small, frozen baby. She was desperate' (Abt et al. 2000: 414).

For a woman who has unexplained infertility, this active duality, in her conscious life, appears to be absent. Her womb is neither a container nor a coffin, simply an empty space. This space not only separates the woman from her creativity but also from her destructiveness. It appears that, unlike a woman who can become pregnant, she can only speculate about the forces within but cannot know about them. A connection may be helpfully reactivated if she does become pregnant: 'Pregnancy, like all transitional phases, reawakens earlier unresolved conflicts and anxieties. The archaic clash between her inner imagined life-giving and death dealing forces is now relocated in the arena of birth, a test, culminating in proof of whether she is destructive or creative' (Raphael-Leff 1985: 16).

If being pregnant can reactivate a sense of an early struggle between creative and destructive forces then being in an infertile state may confirm an earlier impotent state where there was either the lack of a struggle or a fear that destruction had won. If acceptance of an inner world alive with creativity and destruction was never strongly established as a child then an infertile patient may feel confirmed in her inability to work through this void and in her own worthlessness as a result. There may have been a lack of an early satisfactory relationship with a parent. The desire for procreativity may be even stronger in those patients who feel the lack of strong internalised good parental objects. Early parental deaths or other unresolved losses may be re-ignited in the infertile state. As a result, the desire to show that previous losses have not destroyed creative capacities can make procreation seem like an essential healing task. The desired baby may then become symbolic of the rebirth the woman wants for herself, and as a result it can be doubly painful if no baby arrives. Yet to experience a rebirth in this way, whether through the birth of a child or not, it seems that there has to have been enough concrete proof that there has been a good enough relationship both to and between the parents and that a creative union could have happened and therefore could now happen in the present relationship.

Some infertile women connect their own lack of mothering to their present inability to become a mother. If the mother was a negative figure and remains an internally negative one, then to become like her by having a child may be strongly resisted in the unconscious. This resistance and ambivalence is of course around for all mothers and potential mothers. The mother's realisation that she may have murderous feelings towards her own child can be very shocking as well as liberating (Parker 1995). The choice that some women make to abort a foetus may sometimes be an attempt to step outside a recognised feminine identity of belonging to the world of mothers where ambivalent feelings have to be denied.

Whether an unconscious ambivalence can be so strong as to deny conception was one of the questions that Frances had to struggle with and which we could only speculate about in the work. There may be many contraceptive scenarios that the unconscious may play out; an area that both Freudian and Jungian analysts have speculated about. The unconscious fantasy of being able to have a one-parent conception may reduce fertility (Mariotti 1997). Or a difficult intrapsychic relationship between the woman and her own mother may add to difficulties in conceiving (Pines 1993). These difficulties may be played out in the relationship with the therapist, which becomes the stage where meaning can be made from the patient's experience of nothingness.

For Frances the reality of her infertility felt so concrete to her that she defended herself against symbolic interpretations. Early on in her therapy, imagining other ways of making 'babies' seemed to be very painful. It was as if anything that she might create could only be seen as a poor substitute for a real baby. For us to make connections in the process of the work required her not only to trust me and her journey but to allow an intimacy between us and expression of feelings which felt extremely dangerous to her. As the work progressed it was the expression of her rage and aggression which brought us closer together.

Frances's sense of her parents was of a powerful intrusive mother and a passive father. The intrusion meant that getting close had to be protected against and so she protected herself against me. The passivity brought up fear of sexual desire both in her father and herself. As a result her unconscious sense of the parental couple was non-creative. She began to re-experience this as replicated in her own inability to be fertile and to understand what had happened in her own psychic spaces, which had meaningful connections to her infertility. It was as if the inability to procreate had been inherited and lived out by her, through her parents but not actually experienced by her own mother. Her parents had managed to conceive her and other siblings but had not passed this generative capacity on.

Rosemary Gordon suggests that the creative act is similar to the procreative act in that it is a bisexual genital activity necessitating a good identification with the father who gives and the mother who receives. She explores how delicate the requirements are for the creative process to happen and that it requires an 'inter-dependence of activity and receptivity, of control and surrender, of consciousness and unconsciousness' (Gordon 1978: 134). A fluidity between male and female elements is required. Out of this develops a sense of trust, which is essential to be able to bring creations into being. These are life tasks that Gordon is writing about and they require an understanding of the warring forces within us as well as a capacity to acknowledge our limitations without experiencing them as limiting. Not to be able to conceive is to experience an extreme limitation which can suppress feelings of both aliveness and death. There is no sign of a birth but nor is there any sign of a death.

A patient who was questioning her own single state and lack of babies reported, with amazement, how a friend of hers, who was in her late forties, and who had not so far been able to conceive, had a near fatal car crash and became pregnant immediately afterwards. She was not sure how these two events were related but felt somehow that they were, that the brush with death had enabled her friend to conceive. She had come close enough to her own death, looked it in the face, and also her own capacity for destruction, to be able to give birth.

Yet for a woman who is experiencing unexplained infertility to get in touch with destructive thoughts, or dreams, or fantasies, can be extraordinarily difficult. Many of my women patients will do anything to avoid expressing these feelings to me. They cannot experience a difference between the thought and the act and they seem to fear their loss of identity and acceptance as women. Struggling with the difference between omnipotent destructive fantasies and the desire to live them as a reality is a crucial part of becoming an individual and refusing a handed-down identity (Austin 1999). We all long to tear down, attack, release our rage and have murderous thoughts, yet for women to acknowledge these thoughts threatens them with a loss of gender identity. They may therefore be expressed unconsciously through repeated abortions or difficulties in conceiving. This is not to say that all women who have unexplained infertility may have unresolved issues around these destructive aspects. We do not know nearly enough yet about all the factors involved in conception. However, with studies now beginning on work with infertile couples prior to IVF, it does seem that the more these couples are able to be aware of their unconscious ambivalence to pregnancy and parenthood, the more successful the IVF treatment is (Christie 1998).

For many years Frances was unable to express her anger or rage about her infertility, only her unresolved grief. She clung tenaciously to the belief that her anger would only make things worse for herself and those close to her and that it would be destructive of any creativity she might have. Because of their continuing strong desire to have a family she and her partner went through the lengthy process of becoming accepted as adoptive parents. When a seven-year-old girl was finally matched with them Frances realised, at the very last minute, after her initial meetings with the child, that she could not adopt her, although she knew this was her last chance to be a parent. She was incontrovertibly faced with her own ambivalence about being a mother. 'I can't do this because I fear that I will be lost, that what I need will be forgotten about. I am terribly, terribly ashamed that when I am faced with becoming a mother it is not the most important thing in my life. Maybe, if I'd had my own child, I would have had no choice, but here, now with this little girl, I can't do it.' The shame and guilt associated with making this choice for herself, rather than for another, seemed to herald a turning point in the work. The crisis which was experienced as a result of making a decision seemed to open up for Frances the possibility of naming and talking about her ambivalence about becoming a mother and enabled her to acknowledge her capacity to say no to a child.

During the lengthy adoptive process, which consumed most of her waking thoughts for many months, she often questioned why she never dreamt of this future child who was to be so important to her. During this period no representations of this child came into the therapeutic work. In an interesting parallel Zoja compares the dreams of two women who are considering abortion. The one who decides to abort never dreams of her child and the one who decides to keep her baby dreams frequently of 'My baby'. Zoja suggests that both the absence and the presence of an image have an effect on the final decision of the two women, that one had unconsciously decided to embody the child and one had not (Zoja 1997: 79). This relationship to image has been highlighted since ultrasound pictures have become an accepted part of the mother's first pictures of the child in her womb. The daughter of a friend who had decided to abort her second child because of external difficulties in her life at the time, was unable to do this after she had seen the foetus on the ultrasound screen.

For Frances, once the decision not to adopt had been made, the little girl appeared frequently in her dreams as if now the ambivalence had been acknowledged she could be made flesh. This was a painful realisation but it also enabled the beginnings of a mourning process to happen, for now there was someone to mourn. Frances's need to go through the lengthy and painful adoption procedures even- tually enabled her to move on. This was achieved through what she experienced as a destructive act on her part. If the possibility of adoption had been given up before the arrival of the child this would not have had the initiatory meaning for her that she needed it to have. For her the rejected adoptive child was her sacrifice, as with a woman who aborts a baby, a painful choice, which she knew she would live with for the rest of her life. This loss empowered her, as she realised that she did have a choice and that she had *chosen* to reject this child. 'I could have been a parent if I had wanted but I decided not to be, that is very different to feeling that the choice has been denied to me. Now I know I shall never be a parent. Something has come to an end.' It is as if to release themselves from the prison of infertility women need to do that which will mean risking their last vestiges of female identity, which in many ways they already feel that they have lost. They have to give up their sense of powerlessness and contact their destructive side.

Marion Woodman, who sees part of the woman's psychological growth as separating from her mother, suggests that violence and destruction may play a crucial part in this: 'If she can hold the tension until she finds herself, then her baby if she has one, will not have to carry what she has fearfully avoided. An abortion can be the threshold that forces a woman to seek her own identity, in which case the baby becomes the sacrifice through which the woman brings herself to birth' (Woodman 1985: 119).

There is a marked difference between those infertile women who long for children and are never able to move into other areas of creativity and those women who are able in some ways to do this. Neither may ever, as the self-help books suggest, come to terms with their childlessness, but they may learn to cope with it (Bryan and Higgins 1995). The losses and grief continue into middle and older age as the lack of children evolves into the lack of grandchildren and the pains return in different ways and in differing forms. However, there may be a crucial difference, depending on whether the woman has been able to mourn or not, as to whether she can find creativity and fulfilment in other areas. As Woodman suggests, 'The biological purpose of life at the unconscious level is to reproduce itself, the conscious purpose is not simply to reproduce or perpetuate but to *know*' (Woodman 1985: 119).

Mourning is to be in a state of knowing. To be able to acknowledge that there has been a loss. For those with unexplained infertility the process of mourning can be constantly put off as each month holds the possibility of conception. For some women it may not be possible to begin to mourn the loss until the arrival of menopause. For Frances the aborted adoption began this process for her.

The mourning process is now known to be a complicated one with many stages, which may be interrupted at any point. Since Freud wrote *Mourning and Melancholia* in 1917 (Freud 1984) more work has been done on the differentiation of the stages of the mourning process. Yet the essential task of mourning is still seen to be the ability to accept the painful reality of the loss of the loved object. John Bowlby proposes that a normal process of mourning would progress through: a phase of numbness, a phase of yearning and searching, a phase of despair, a phase of reorganisation (Bowlby 1980). All these stages require that the person who has died or is lost did originally exist. For the infertile woman the trigger for her to be able to begin to mourn may remain invisible.

To be able to continue with the mourning process it is necessary to be able to bear the destructive thoughts which accompany loving; to acknowledge that there is ambivalence about the loved object. This may reactivate an infantile state where there are both aggressive and reparative wishes towards the parental object. When someone dies there is loss and grief but also hate. For the infertile there has been no baby, there is no body to grieve over. How can you feel hateful when there is no obvious loss but only an overwhelming feeling of frustrated desire? The hate is therefore projected on to partners, doctors or the self. Mourning for someone who will never come into being appears to be un-resolvable. The relationship to an unborn baby is experienced as a void in which no symbolic processes can occur. Frances externalised this problem by 'creating' a child whom she then chose not to adopt as her own. As a result she was able to experience herself as denying towards a potential daughter, which made it possible for her to face some of her own destructive forces. She knew who she had lost.

Losing a child is acutely painful. It is unlike other losses which may happen in adulthood, the loss of a spouse, or parents, or siblings. There is a sense in which it can never be recovered from. For those parents whose child dies, the pain of loss may be warded against by attempting to replace the child rather than facing the unbearable feelings of guilt and pain. Attempting to replace the child before the mourning process has been completed is to confine the experience to the non-symbolic realm. This is similar to the infertile woman's desperate attempts in the IVF clinic to achieve a baby at all costs. But without the symbolic a psychological balance between destruction and creation cannot be rediscovered and the experience of the loss of the Angel is a trauma without hope of rebirth. The symbolic cannot be retrieved if the death cannot be mourned.

The image of the Virgin and the Immaculate Conception contains within it both the mystery and miracle of a partnerless conception, but also the ability to be open to conception of oneself. It symbolises both a connection with the divine and the ordinary human capacity to be creative within and from oneself. For those who are unable to produce babies this ability to bring about a conception of themselves may also elude them. It seems that the mystery has been lost and that, as a result, conceptions remain in the sphere of the miraculous. This loss of soul may be retrieved if the lack of procreativity can be mourned and space can be made for other creative possibilities and the arrival of the Angel.

Bibliography

Abt, R., Bosch, I. and MacKrell, V. (2000) *Dream Child. Creation and New Life in Dreams of Pregnant Women*, Einsiedeln, Switzerland: Daimon Verlag.

Austin, S. (1999) 'Women's aggressive fantasies. A feminist post-Jungian hermeneutic', in *Harvest: Journal for Jungian Studies*, London: C.G. Jung Analytical Psychology Club.

Bowlby, J. (1980) *Loss: Sadness and Depression*, in *Attachment and Loss*, vol. 3, London: Hogarth Press.

Bryan, E. and Higgins, R. (1995) *Infertility. New Choices, New Dilemmas*, London: Penguin.

Christie, G.L. (1998) 'Some socio-cultural and psychological aspects of infertility', *Human Reproduction* 13, 1: 232–241.

Erikson, E.H. (1968) *Identity, Youth and Crisis*, New York: W.W. Norton.

Freud, S. (1984) 'Mourning and Melancholia', in *On Metapsychology. The Theory of Psychoanalysis*, Pelican Freud Library, vol. 11, London: Penguin.

Gerrard, N. (2001) *The Observer Magazine*, 14 January.

Gordon, R. (1978) *Dying and Creating: A Search for Meaning*, London: The Society of Analytical Psychology.

Greer, G. (2000) *The Whole Woman*, London: Anchor.

Jung, C.G. (1960) *The Structure and Dynamics of the Psyche*, Collected Works 8. London: Routledge.

—— (1997) *Visions Notes of the Seminar Given in 1930–34*, vol 2, ed. Clare Douglas, Princeton: Princeton University Press.

Kipling, R. (1975) 'The cat who walked by himself', in *Just So Stories*, London: Pan Books.

Koropatnick, S., Daniluk, J. and Pattinson, H.A. (1993) 'Infertility: a non-event transition', *Fertility and Sterility* 59, 1: 163–171.

Mariotti, P. (1997) 'Creativity and fertility: the one-parent phantasy', in J. Raphael-Leff and R. Jozef Perelberg (eds), *Female Experience. Three Generations of British Women Psychoanalysts on Work with Women*, London: Routledge.

Moller, A. and Fallstrom, K. (1991) 'Psychological consequences of infertility: a longitudinal study', in *Journal of Psychosomatic Obstetrics and Gynaecology* 12: 27–45.

Parker, R. (1995) *Torn in Two. The Experience of Maternal Ambivalence*, London: Virago.

Pattis Zoja, E. (1997) *Abortion. Loss and Renewal in the Search for Identity*, London: Routledge.

Pfeffer, N. (1987) 'Artificial insemination, in-vitro fertilization and the stigma of infertility', in *Reproductive Technologies. Gender, Motherhood and Medicine*, Cambridge: Polity Press.

Pines, D. (1993) *A Woman's Unconscious Use of Her Body*, London: Virago.

Raphael-Leff, J. (1985) 'Fear and fantasies of childbirth', *Journal of Pre and Perinatal Psychology* 1: 14–18.

Rilke, R.M. (1964) 'The Ninth Elegy' from *The Duino Elegies*, in *Rilke: Selected Poems*, London: Penguin.

Woodman, M. (1985) *The Pregnant Virgin. A Process of Psychological Transformation*, Toronto: Inner City Books.

Chapter 7

The battle with mortality and the urge to procreate

Michael Pawson

Michael Pawson is a former consultant gynaecologist with specialist interest in fertility.

What is it that makes a gynaecologist take up such a speciality and reflect on mortality and procreation? I am conscious that my motivation to do medicine and then to specialise in women's health and well-being, initially in pregnancy and childbirth, was the positive and creative nature of producing a healthy baby. Probably a deeper and more complex reason was associated with the fact that I had no communication of any sort with my father from the age of 6. This made me interested in parenting and, having seen, understood and taken part in the care of pregnant women, I became aware of the pain of those who were unable to conceive. I became progressively more interested in the problems of infertility and started a clinic within the NHS in 1970 dedicated to those with fertility problems.

My own childhood experiences led me to ask these patients about their experiences of parenting in their childhood and in particular about their mothers. I was soon surprised to find repeatedly a story of a poor relationship with the mother. Time and again, when asking women about their mothers, I got evasive or frankly unhappy replies. It was a similar story in the general gynaecology clinic, which suggests that it may be a widespread problem. I began to reflect on whether there was not a more powerful psychological undercurrent than I had perceived, and that perhaps my dualistic, traditional medical education had faults.

My generation was taught to keep the patient at arm's length at all costs, that a line was drawn in the sand between patient and doctor that one could not cross. This dualism goes back to Descartes, the 'architect of scientific thinking'. Descartes believed that science needed to explain mechanisms and functions at what he called a 'micro level', at what we might call today a quantum level. He was a reductionist who believed that all function could be reduced to the mechanism of the smallest possible particles. But there was a caveat: all can be explained in this way in all things which are 'devoid of thought and mind'. Descartes addressed this by dividing the world into the three-dimensional physical world, and the thinking world. This led to the widely-held dualistic approach which divided the world into a physical, objective, visible world on the one hand, and a subjective, thinking, feeling world of values and aesthetics on the other. Science and the spiritual were divided. This dualism has been a problem ever since and the mind–body problem remains. It was in this tradition that my generation was taught medicine. When there was something physically wrong that could be demonstrated by blood tests, x-rays, etc., you could treat it. Otherwise the patient had a psychiatric problem such as depression, which was passed on to the psychiatrists. To look at a patient as mind and body was, and remains, a very difficult attitude for a doctor to adopt. This approach, in my view, is wrong. The woman who has lost a baby, or who is ravaged by the grief of her infertility, is more likely to be helped by the doctor who shows emotion, who shares her grief, perhaps even with tears, than by the doctor who maintains the approach of, 'You are a patient, I am a doctor. Emotions cannot be shared.'

If feelings and emotions are important in the patient and in the doctor's response to ill health, could they not also be important in causing ill health? Everyone, whether medically trained or not, would recognise the reason for a young woman to stop menstruating for some months if her husband and child had died in a car crash. No one would question the psychological or emotional element in her responses. There are other emotional traumas, just as severe but buried in the past, or less obvious recent or current psychological factors which might affect the body's function. It was Henry Maudesley who wrote, nearly a hundred years ago, 'The sorrow that hath no vent in tears makes other organs weep.' This is one of the earliest descriptions of psychosomatic disorder.

Failure to produce a child not only confronts us with a sense of that failure in our immediate environment, but also with the realisation that we are neither special nor immortal. Our birth and death are the two most important and significant events in our life. The intimate and close relationship between the two is clear in the word consummation, which for Christ was death, as it was for Hamlet in 'A consummation devoutly to be wished'. Consummation of marriage or a female/ male relationship often carries with it the expectation of engendering new life and birth. Existence itself is a lottery and we have no conscious knowledge of our prenatal and birth experience, nor of our death experience. We now value life so much that death has become unacceptable. Doctors battle to save life and to preserve it as long as possible, and in the same way that they are now beginning to employ technology to create life, so they use technology to prolong life with intensive care, organ transplants and attempts to defeat the ageing process. Cloning may well be the next step. Death is biologically final and irreversible and we increasingly attempt to postpone it for as long as possible. We have no control at all over our birth and only little control over our death. Our very existence is a matter of extraordinary chance. Why did that particular sperm fertilise that particular egg and create a unique individual that is oneself? With the advent of assisted reproductive technology (ART), the question has an even more complex nature. Why did the embryologist choose the embryo that developed into me and dispose of my potential siblings?

A question that is frequently debated in the ethical committees of fertility clinics is whether the person being created by ART would prefer to exist under circumstances that would appear to be very difficult, i.e. with some sort of physical or social handicap, or never to have existed at all. The conclusion reached is that it is very difficult indeed to imagine any life, however painful, however difficult, where a person would have opted not to exist. In order to experience life and to enjoy it we have to be born, and throughout the world birth is welcomed and celebrated. A birth that would be unwelcome in much of the Western world may now be prevented. We judge new life to merit celebration and this judgement is made from our own experience. Life stretches ahead of the newborn with all its vicissitudes and fateful interventions, but we judge that to be good and worthwhile. Furthermore, the newly created life guarantees continuity of the species and of the individual's genetic inheritance.

We build defences against our knowledge and fear of death which are based largely on our belief in a God of some sort. Each person believes that he or she is special. 'It won't happen to me.' The smoker who knows someone who has smoked for forty years and is healthy will convince themselves that they also can be an exception because they are different, they are special. The same applies to the career woman who does want a baby sometime but defers pregnancy until her late thirties so that she can fulfil her career or other ambitions. She will also quote a friend or relative who conceived at 40 – why should she not do the same? None of us should expect to be exceptions or subject to a different set of biological rules; other than genetically, we are all the same.

Darwin's ideas have robbed us of a belief in an afterlife on which our defence against mortality has been based. Now that the credibility of God has been seriously questioned and for many removed, we have lost the person, the being, who could intervene in our suffering. God was our individual, personal saviour. We could pray to God and ask for our prayers to be fulfilled. Furthermore we had someone to blame when things went wrong. If we are found to be infertile, if we are to be childless, whom do we blame now? Gaia, or Nature, is no good because she has no interest in the individual, only in the species and we are too self-interested to accept that. As Adam Phillips has said, 'Modern lives, unconsoled by religious beliefs, could be consumed by the experience of loss' (Phillips 1999: 14). We now have to make sense of the transitory nature of our life and adapt to that finitude. If we fail to come to terms with our mortality, then our lives become dominated by this negativity. One way around this is to create something permanent that will always be remembered. Few of us are a Mozart or a Rembrandt; however, most of us can reproduce. Since Darwin the best way to achieve immortality is to survive and procreate. For most of us this is all we can do, pass our genes on and thereby ensure a degree of immortality. The old must die so that the young may inherit their habitat, thus preserving and benefiting the species.

There is, however, a difference between creating and procreating. To create means to make, to form, or to constitute, unless it is referring specifically to the divine when it means to form out of nothing, to produce where nothing was before. To procreate means only to beget, to generate offspring. Trying to develop their creativity, whilst it may be the best that they can do in the circumstances, is for many women second-best to procreativity. Anxieties about the difference between creating and procreating are often expressed by couples undergoing ART. They are concerned that they are not procreating but artificially creating. They may feel that creating an embryo through technology is too scientific, too mechanistic, and this is a step some couples will not take. Some perceive that the ability to use technology to harness nature may release them from the tyranny of infertility but at the cost of what is 'natural'. 'Men have always had to choose between their subjection to nature or the subjection of nature to the self' (Adorno and Horkheimer 1997). The further our reproductive technology advances the more critical become the choices that confront both those receiving and providing treatment.

Woman's need to procreate

The creative need is satisfied for many through the birth of a child. How fundamental and desperate this need to procreate is, is revealed to the doctor treating the infertile. Many of our patients are unable to live with the reality of their infertility and defer recognising the truth by maintaining their illusions, and the illusion of a child is very powerful.

A group of women attending the author's clinic some years ago were asked to write down a description of the baby that they believed they would have one day. All responded with moving images and with one exception all described a daughter. Why should this be, that the fantasy child is so often female? Winnicott, the psychoanalyst and influential paediatrician, suggests that when a woman becomes pregnant there is a feeling that she has stolen the baby from within her mother's body (Winnicott 1991). The mother's baby to which she most obviously relates is herself – a female. The whole process of reproduction is essentially female. It is the female who plays the most important part; she only needs the male for a few minutes to start the whole procreative process going. She can give birth and nurture her child without any further male input. She may therefore relate more naturally to a female child than to a male.

A childless woman, for whom it was imperative to have a hysterectomy, wrote a letter to the child she was never to have which she generously shared with me, from which I now quote:

> Dear little child I'll never have, I don't really know what to say to you but I so want to make a connection with you. First of all I'm very sorry, guilty that I never gave you life. All those years when I took the pill to stop you happening and I didn't realise what I was doing to both of us. . . . Maybe I conceived and lost you, I'll never know. But you were wanted, you were very wanted and I just know that you would have been a little girl. I know what you would have looked like. Bright-eyed, wide-eyed, innocent . . . happy and with a ready smile, good fun and very loveable. You would have been full of mischief and very stubborn. And if I had you now I would have nurtured all of that . . . I would have given you lots of time but I would have also given you the freedom to grow and to learn and be there to catch you when you fell and it hurt. And best of all we would cuddle 'cos cuddles are the loveliest thing in

the world . . . it's not to be and it can't be and I feel a great sense of longing and loss . . . I want you to know that I did want you only I didn't really understand and I have so much love for you and somehow if you are at peace then I can find peace too. I love you very much.

By creating a fantasy child that she can talk to, write to, the infertile woman has someone to mourn which helps her to come to terms with her grief. To be able to grieve a loss is essential. When a woman has never been pregnant, or lost a child, grieving can be doubly difficult.

A difficulty which confronts the infertility doctor is treading the line between telling the patient the truth and making them face their reality on the one hand, and allowing them the defence of their illusions on the other. How justified is it to allow the illusion that my patient will conceive to continue? Even more difficult is deciding when to call a halt to treatment. Is it better to refuse treatment where conception would be a miracle, or better to, at least, try some plan of treatment on the basis that retrospectively the woman will look back and feel that she tried everything? Sadly, miracles do not happen outside the context of myth and the Bible. The incidence of natural conception after adoption is more of a myth than a quantifiable reality, although there are some remarkable and unexpected conceptions when scientific aid has been exhausted, but these have psychogenic explanations.

Many women who suffer involuntary infertility feel that they are worthless, empty, that their life is no longer useful, they are a 'failed female'. Furthermore, women have another physical and emotional milestone, the menopause, which may be a reminder to the woman that she is a mammal who is degenerating and she may now feel as though it is downhill all the way to death. Men have no such clear yardstick.

Causes of sub-fertility

It is generally accepted that 15 per cent of couples who want a baby will consult a fertility clinic. The explanation of their failure to conceive may include failure to ovulate, a blockage in the fallopian tubes, male infertility, coital problems and others. The doctor is left with as many as a quarter who have no clear explanation for not conceiving, and these couples form a very difficult group. One possibility is that they may have psychogenic reasons for not conceiving. This is a difficult area to investigate. How much may the psyche be a cause of sub-fertility; how much may the sub-fertility affect the psyche? There is, in general, little credence given in fertility clinics to the possibility of psychogenic infertility. Psychological factors are difficult to measure and can seem grey and inconclusive. If the psyche is considered at all it is usually only after all physical investigations have been completed. Pure science demands a hypothesis that can be supported, disproven or otherwise. In the area of the psyche this is difficult.

I would like now to present some brief case histories to illustrate how psychological trauma appears to affect fertility:

Mrs A. presented in my fertility clinic having never conceived. She had tried to conceive for seven or eight years with her husband. The marriage was unable to cope with the failure to conceive and ended. Mrs A. was a Roman Catholic. She found a new partner with whom she had been trying to conceive for a further six or seven years. She had, therefore, a story of at least thirteen years' infertility in total. She was fully investigated and no explanation was found. Considering the possibility of a psychogenic factor she was referred to a psychoanalyst, who could find no obvious problem in the hour that he had to assess her. He did, however, give her his contact number should she feel the need for it. A few weeks later she rang him in great distress and returned to see him. She related very tearfully how she had been living with her parents and at the age of 18 conceived an unwanted pregnancy. Her boyfriend arranged what was then an illegal abortion, and during the night, with her parents asleep in the next room, she aborted. She took the aborted foetus, broke it up and flushed it down the toilet. She continued living with her parents and then two years later she came home to find her mother dying in the same toilet, being administered the last rites.

She was consumed by guilt and over the next few years tried to get some sort of absolution from the church, but on each occasion was frustrated by fate. A priest she approached was 'not on duty'. On a further occasion she was waiting at the end of mass to approach the priest when a nun came up to her and asked her to sign a petition against the pill. This story unfolded in a cathartic consultation at the end of which she said, 'Now you know why I have not got pregnant', and asked to be put on the pill to prevent pregnancy. I referred her to a Catholic priest whom she saw regularly. After about three months she returned describing the side effects of the pill which were unacceptable and asked to be taken off it. She conceived spontaneously within a few months, and had a healthy baby and a second one two years later.

Mrs B. discovered that she had been adopted when she became engaged and needed sight of her birth certificate. It was a profound shock. She conceived easily but the baby was stillborn following a medical error during labour. She presented at the fertility clinic two years later having failed to conceive again and no explanation was found. When reviewing her after all the investigations I brought up the question of her birth mother and family and asked whether she might be interested in trying to find them. Could her problem lie not only in the lost baby but also perhaps in the lost mother? She traced her mother and half-siblings and had a joyful meeting with them. She became pregnant and we subsequently calculated that she conceived on the night that she met her family. She had another child thereafter.

Mrs C.'s first child was stillborn due to haemorrhage. She and her husband felt unable to face a funeral and asked the hospital to make all the arrangements. She subsequently was referred with secondary infertility. Nothing wrong was found on investigation. We traced where her baby had been buried and suggested that she visit the grave. She resisted the suggestion until persuaded to 'try anything' by her continuing failure to get pregnant again. She and her husband went to the grave together on their wedding anniversary and she conceived shortly afterwards.

Such stories are not uncommon in a fertility clinic, particularly if one is aware of the possibility of psychogenic sub-fertility. Where the psychic pain has been so severe as to stop menstruation, and therefore ovulation, the explanation for sub-fertility is obvious. But when a woman's cycle is normal, how can psychogenic infertility be explained? The answer is often difficult and complicated and requires a sensitive and comprehensive history-taking where the doctor listens with an attuned ear. Most doctors are untrained in these skills.

A patient referred for IVF (in vitro fertilisation) had an accompanying letter from her previous specialist stating that she had a daughter of 19, had been trying to conceive again for three years and that the investigations were all normal. What the letter did not state was that she had had her child when she was only 16, that the father took the child back to his own country of origin after only six months and that the patient had only seen her child once in the past nineteen years. The letter did not state that the patient was one of twelve siblings and was constantly abused by her alcoholic father, put into care and ultimately adopted. Neither did it state that she was the only one of the siblings to be thus treated.

Typically the woman with psychogenic infertility will not recognise her psychic suffering as a cause, and will deny any relationship between past or current emotional pain and her failure to conceive. She may be seeking to please a partner and existing child or her family by trying to conceive when her psyche recognises the threat of pain, of death, of stillbirth and responds by preventing conception. Many people respond to psychic pain by action rather than by reflecting on their situation. They immerse themselves in work leaving no time for lovemaking and creating a baby. There are women who have great difficulty in communicating not only with themselves but also with others. The doctor caring for such patients needs to explore other means of communication, perhaps through dreams and the comments of husband or partner.

Effects of infertility on the couple

Most couples seek advice about a year after they began to try to conceive. Some cope with the investigations with equanimity and in a positive spirit expecting an explanation and treatment. The menstrual period is dreaded and increasingly the couple can become depressed. If a cause is found and there is a clear treatment plan, this is felt to be positive and sustains morale. If, however, no explanation is found, it can be difficult for both the couple and the doctor. The couple are angry that science, capable of performing near miracles, is unable to come up with the answer to what seems a simple question. They are vulnerable at this stage because they are desperate and will try anything. It is equally frustrating for the doctor. It is not easy to say to a patient that you do not know what is wrong, and difficult to say that therefore you are not sure what to do. There is no situation more dangerous than one where the doctor is uncertain about what to do, and is confronted by a patient so desperate she will do anything.

The woman's psychic pain is emphasised every month that she continues to menstruate and by the thoughtless questions of those around her. There are many stresses imposed even by simple treatment regimes when, for example, couples are instructed when to have intercourse rather than to make love spontaneously. Many infertile couples feel isolated, and that their problem is a taboo subject that they cannot discuss freely with friends, family or even their partner. They no longer feel in control of their lives. The final insult and indignity comes when they enter a programme of assisted reproduction and the couple perceive that even their lovemaking is no longer good enough and that technology will take that over too.

The relationship with the male partner is put under pressure, sex becomes a duty and not a pleasure. It is not uncommon to see couples where the demand for intercourse at the time of ovulation makes the male impotent, when he is normally potent for the remainder of the cycle. When a woman has had a previous pregnancy terminated there is often a deep feeling of guilt – 'I feel God is getting his own back on me, doctor.' If the couple continue failing to conceive, despite all that has been offered, the relationship may break down. There may be a strong cultural factor when this happens, particularly in Afro-Caribbean, Orthodox Jewish and some Asian cultures, where if a woman fails to produce a child she is a sterile and negative object and is discarded.

In general, society rejects or marginalises those that it perceives as failures. Doctors also find their failures hard to handle. The 'success' of a fertility clinic is measured by pregnancy rates and published as a league table. Clinicians do not give enough emphasis to any assessment of those who do not conceive, how they are cared for and how they cope. They are the failures that the doctor wants to forget and they are discarded in the medical waste-paper basket. It was C.S. Lewis who, when asked his opinion of a young poet, asked first to see the contents of the poet's waste-paper basket. Medicine gauges success in terms of survival and positive measurements, which are important, but its failures are important too and they are neglected. Until the introduction of the hospice movement doctors were not encouraged to be interested or involved in their failures. In the current ethos of the National Health Service within the UK, the market, statistics, waiting times, league tables and blame are the new language. The failures such as handicap and chronic disease, both mental and physical, tend to be discharged from medical care to the inadequately supported umbrella of social services. The fertility clinic failures do not even have this support and are left to work out their own salvation as best they can. If you are trying to 'sell' your fertility services in a competitive market you are not going to talk of failures.

Ambivalence and generativity

We know that there is a natural regulation of fecundity and that births are reduced in times of war and famine. Fecundity is higher in rural areas than in urban areas and may even be affected by the type of dwelling in which one lives. Population is further checked by abortion and infanticide. The discrepancy between the numbers of recorded female and male infants in some countries indicates that infanticide is much more common than we would like to acknowledge.

There are situations where the body switches off its ability to conceive. For example, menstruation and ovulation are frequently stopped in anorexia. A woman who is underweight is more likely to have an underweight baby if she does conceive. Such babies are more likely to have problems during and after birth. So the body, quite rightly, takes its own steps to prevent conception and this is achieved through higher centres in the brain. These centres in the brain are those which recognise and respond to stress, grief and psychic pain. The suppression of ovulation is at a subconscious level.

Our motivation to procreate is complicated and full of ambivalence, and that ambivalence is at three different levels. Superficially we want a child in order to conform, to be like other people or because it is expected of us. There are pressures on a woman to conceive from family and society. But there are good reasons not to have a child also. A child will make demands on our freedom to do what we want, will cost us money and time. A child will be the cause of many anxieties and for modern, Western women may interfere with a career. Ambivalence at this level will be recognised and accepted.

There is ambivalence at a deeper level. An unresolved grief, such as a stillbirth or previous termination, may be preventing conception. This is more difficult to recognise and accept. At a deeper level still there may be failure to achieve what Erik Erikson called 'generativity'. This seems to me to lie at the core of our motivation to reproduce and its relation to mortality, and I want to enlarge on it briefly. Erikson described, in his epigenetic theory, eight stages of development. The seventh stage is that of adulthood where generativity competes with stagnation. The heart of generativity lies in establishing and guiding the next generation. One can do this through one's own creativity, through art or even through influencing the lives of those with whom you come into contact every day. Alternatively it can be achieved through procreativity, that is, through one's offspring. The adult needs to be needed, to be of value to someone else. We need self-verification and can achieve that only by the products of our own creation or procreation. The introspective, self-absorbed individual is likely to stagnate and become emotionally impoverished.

Erikson postulates that the prime virtue of the mature and complete adult is that of caring; as he puts it, the 'Widening concern for what has been generated by love, necessity or accident' (Erikson 1984: 222–247). This quality is essential for man's psychosocial evolution, but is balanced by a degree of 'rejectivity' in that one cannot be generative and caring about everyone. Even monastic communities, which reject biological procreation, still work to achieve a greater understanding of care through the agency of God. Failure to achieve a state of generativity may offer a psychogenic explanation of why some women fail to conceive. They are not ready emotionally for a baby.

Erikson's eighth and final developmental stage is that of old age when 'ego integrity' is opposed to despair. If the previous ages of one's life have been negotiated successfully, then at the end of one's life one may have achieved wholeness. Then one is ready for death, for the closing of the one and only life. The life, for which one did not ask, which had to be and which allowed no substitutions. Such a person will come to death with courage and acceptance. Failure to accept the end, an inability to accept it, leads to despair; the final realisation is that one's time is not infinite and that one cannot start again.

I have deliberately dwelt on Erikson's ideas because it seems to me that they do draw together the theme of procreation and death. At each stage of life one can only flourish if one is evolving into a whole person. In adulthood one has to be careful of oneself, others and a future generation. Failing to accomplish this may leave one's psychic self unable to allow procreation. There are of course countless couples who are not 'whole' in Erikson's terms but have children successfully, but it could be that the idea of generativity is important in the couples who do not conceive and for whom there is no clear, scientific explanation. Not only do we have to create psychic space for a baby, but we also have to continue to become a whole person to accept death with dignity. For 'good' procreation and 'good' death we need similar qualities.

The feelings of those working in infertility clinics

I have tried to explore briefly what motivated me to get involved in this special area of infertility. I cannot speak for others. For the scientist it is certainly an exciting area for research and at the forefront of the new world of genetic medicine. It is a very emotional area for the doctor and those working in the clinic, as well as the patient and her partner. There is nothing more rewarding than sharing a woman's joy when she has conceived after treatment.

Whilst I have earlier argued for a sharing and non-dualistic approach, the doctor and fertility team need to be aware of the power and effect of 'transference'. Patients refer to 'your baby', and some doctors do become paternalistic and sit in offices surrounded by photographs of *their* babies. There is a danger of the doctor becoming addicted to his power and feeling arrogant about what he is able to do. We do well to temper our cleverness with wisdom and remember that all scientific knowledge is there to be discovered by someone. If Newton had not discovered gravity then someone else would have done. If I had not treated Mrs X with IVF and helped her achieve a pregnancy, many hundreds of others could have done so, but it takes much more than knowledge and skill to treat a couple sensitively with assisted reproduction. But in Descartes' other world no one could have written *Hamlet* except Shakespeare. Most doctors, however, are in awe of the potential for creation in which they are involved; but there are and should be doubts and questions that we all ask of ourselves, and new difficulties that have to be confronted and navigated therapeutically.

There is the problem of money. Very few health authorities fund IVF treatment within the NHS, and where funding is available it is rationed. With an average pregnancy rate of about 30 per cent, across all patients and across the better clinics, and a 'take home' baby rate of about 20 per cent, how justified is one in treating someone whose financial resources are slim and whose chances of success remote? Is it better to refuse treatment, or let the couple make an informed decision which is unlikely to be rational? Is it possible to make a so-called informed decision in this emotionally highly-charged situation?

Other problems constantly of concern to those working in assisted reproduction include: the age to stop treatment, what to do about the risk of congenital abnormality, whether to treat where one or both partners are HIV-positive and many others. We ask ourselves if we really know what we are doing 'playing with nature' and 'acting God'. What do we know about the outcome for babies of assisted reproduction? The evidence from Golombok and others is that they do as well in all respects as children conceived naturally (Golombok *et al.* 2001). But there are still many unanswered questions.

We have long been aware of the surviving twin syndrome and the guilt and emotional problems of a twin where the other twin was stillborn or died early. Similarly there is the well-recognised holocaust survivor syndrome and now also acknowledged is the syndrome for the children of holocaust survivors. What might the growing child or adult conceived through IVF feel when he or she realises the number of potential siblings that were discarded? What will the survivor or survivors feel about a pregnancy where selective reduction was performed?

ART is now posing more and more questions that doctors and others working in this area have to ask themselves. Each advance leads to more ethical questions and more doubts and soul-searching about what is right in general and what is appropriate for an individual. Decisions about what treatment is right and acceptable in reproductive technology have to be made by a wider representative group than just that of medicine.

Conclusion

Western medicine has been plagued by the dualistic Cartesian inheritance of dividing the mind from the body. The increasing specialisation in modern medicine has brought benefits to patients. The doctor who does nothing but assisted repro-duction all the time is likely to be more skilled than the one who only does it part of the time. However, the super-specialist can become tunnel-visioned and frequently the psychological may be overlooked.

If a woman is allowed to tell her whole story in relation to her infertility when she consults a doctor, psychogenic causes will possibly emerge. They are not necessarily the only cause for not conceiving but they are certainly contributory. Different people will respond to emotional trauma in different ways. Their response will depend on their physical and psychological health at the time and also on how they perceive their situation. Some women, threatened by the demands of those around them and maybe by fear of their mortality, will become more and more distressed during investigation and treatment. They are desperate and very vulnerable. If there is no physical explanation the doctor may collude with the patient because neither wants to face the possible cause within the psyche. The doctor then authenticates the physical nature of the problem by giving a physical treatment.

I have tried to show that in our society, for many, being successful means being rich, beautiful and essentially having children. We have existential problems which are posed by our awareness of our mortality, by our loneliness and by our lack of purpose. Having a child dilutes our isolation, provides a purpose in life and for some may alleviate the problem of their mortality by ensuring a partial immortality through their genes. The failure to have a child breaks down our defence mechanisms, we are no longer special, we have to confront our isolation, there is no saviour and death is the end.

There are ways to help. Infertility may not always be regarded as a disease although it is certainly a dis-ease. Those advising and caring for the infertile need to recognise that there are as many dis-eases as there are patients. To paraphrase the author Robertson Davies, every doctor seeing a patient has to recognise that everyone is unique, that nobody has ever suffered like her before because nobody has ever been her before (Robertson Davies 1983: 316).

The treatment of infertility has become focused on a successful positive outcome – pregnancy. Annual league tables only measure success in terms of pregnancies and babies born. What happens to those who do not conceive? The Hippocratic teaching is that the art of medicine lies in the complete removal of the distress of the sick and this means psychic distress as well as physical. The rider is added by Hippocrates, 'knowing that everything is not possible to medicine'. Medicine does therefore have a responsibility to those who it is not possible to help conceive. That responsibility is to help them come to terms with their isolation and ultimately their mortality. The psyche plays an integral part in the motivation to procreate, in the reasons for failing to procreate and in the investigation and treatment of infertility. While fertility specialists are unable and unwilling to value the psychological background, psychogenic infertility will remain unrecognised and untreated. Remedying this is best achieved by letting patients tell their own story and relate their own feelings. The best diagnostic tool in medicine remains the spoken word, the best therapeutic tool the listening ear.

Bibliography

Adorno, I. and Horkheimer, M. (1997) *Dialectic of Enlightenment*, London: Verso.

Davies, R. (1983) *The Deptford Trilogy*, London: Penguin.

Erikson, E.H. (1984) *Childhood and Society*, London: Triad/Paladin.

Golombok, S., MacCallum, F. and Goodman, E. (2001) *Child Development* 72(2): 599–608.

Phillips, A. (1999) *Darwin's Worms*, London: Faber and Faber.

Winnicott, D.W. (1991) *The Child, The Family and The Outside World*, London: Penguin.

Chapter 8

Myths and reality in male infertility

Sammy Lee

Sammy Lee is a scientific consultant at the Portland Hospital.

Male infertility accounts for up to 60 per cent of all cycles of ART (assisted reproductive technology) in the Western world today, yet little is said in public about it, which reflects the isolation and desolation experienced by those with a diagnosis of male infertility. Male infertility challenges how men think about themselves – shattering their own beliefs in male supremacy. Even in today's world, being male is still all about male dominance, which means that men have a free rein over which roles they adopt, so long as they are manly ones: hunter, breadwinner, head of the family, and so on. Female roles are forbidden and inferior. Men do not cry, they are not allowed to love, or display love as women do; they rarely display their emotions in private and especially not in public. Men are men, which means that they are responsible, macho, virile and do not need help. They are rational and objective, but they are also afraid of their emotions. Through their emotional distance, men seek to have power and control, which is a key part of their value system whereby work, independence and dominance become all-important.

A diagnosis of male infertility is shocking, not only because of its social stigma, but also because those who seek a second and third opinion find themselves becoming confused, isolated and frustrated. Until very recently, little attention was paid to the man in most infertility clinics (which even now are often held in gynaecology clinics in maternity buildings). As a consequence, men willing to acknowledge male infertility and to 'come out of the closet' are few and far between. The fact that most infertility specialists are men trained in gynaecology has also served to maintain myths about male infertility.

I am a clinical scientist and have been working in IVF (in vitro fertilisation) since 1985. Even as a 'lab rat' directing busy IVF laboratories, I have found the exposure to couples undergoing treatment extreme. In ART there is nowhere to hide. Patients will seek you out when they need advice and information, which all too often can only come from the laboratory itself. By 1991, having directed laboratories which had completed over 10,000 cycles of ART, I was shell-shocked, perhaps even punch-drunk. Even in the best of clinics at that time, more cycles failed than succeeded. The failures began to haunt me. I therefore trained as a counsellor and have been counselling IVF couples since 1991. The counselling skills have helped me greatly. They have lent me a robustness which has extended my career as a clinical scientist as well as endowing me with special insight into the pain that the infertile feel. The skills also allow me to carry out 'counselling without counselling' (more about this later) as I apply 'band-aid and Savlon' to the walking wounded that limp daily in and out of the clinic.

Sometimes I find the two roles in conflict with each other. This is so when dealing with couples who have reached a watershed and are struggling with life-changing decisions. It is never easy to accept a future which will be childless. How do I help a couple decide? I weigh up the need to 'move on' and develop other aspects of their lives against the scientific side of myself, which relishes the challenge. Perhaps they will succeed if they try one more time . . . or perhaps they will not. Unrealistic expectations are around every corner. My struggle is equally poignant when dealing with new patients who are so desperate. I want to protect them from themselves. In recent years, I have become the harbinger of doom. They sometimes tell me they do not wish to hear my information, which may have the ring of a death sentence, but some do thank me for helping them take off their rose-tinted spectacles. Nevertheless, few heed my advice and almost all end up with their eggs and sperm in my laboratory and I spend months and years entrusted with their hopes. In spite of the travails, I am thankful that the journey has enriched my human experience and thank God for the successes. Through the opportunity of working with men struggling to enter the ranks of fatherhood, I have learnt much about myself and my fellow companions. This chapter is dedicated to all of them, especially the ones who continue to suffer.

Male myths

Men avoid talking about their infertility. Where workmates or friends know about 'it', cruel jokes follow: 'I hear you are firing blanks.' Graffiti suddenly appear on toilet walls offering help with 'servicing' the wife. It is only 'boys' talk', but it may sometimes be a bitter pill to swallow. Like women, men also suffer from loss of self-confidence, a feeling of incompetence, a feeling of failure, isolation, guilt, anger, shame, bitterness and frustration, when they are struggling with male infertility (Lee 1996, Mason 1993). Other feelings expressed by men after they have been given 'a sentence' of male infertility consist of feeling an outcast and different from everyone else. Man's right to be supreme is challenged by male infertility, so that not only is the diagnosis a shock, but manhood is also called into question. Many feel that their virility (man's last iconic/symbolic role) is in doubt, since it is common amongst men to brag about their children and to acknowledge that those who have children have accomplished a rite of passage and 'proved themselves' (Lee 1996). Some men report: 'We couldn't have a family because of something I couldn't do and that hurts', 'You can't do your bit . . . I have to put on a brave face with my male friends . . .'. Many men obviously feel that they have let their partner down. Because men with children see parenthood as being an important aspect of manhood, childlessness, especially infertility, is seen by them as an indication of male weakness, which is why most men (and women), including gynaecologists, find it difficult to talk about male infertility (Lee 1996). In some cases the loss of self-confidence and feelings of failure are so strong that a man's work performance will suffer. Some men (probably those stuck in denial) will immerse themselves in their work, working longer and longer hours and trying to avoid their partners, friends and families, but most commonly of all, men feel impotent, sometimes in a sexual way, but more often in a general sense, because they feel so powerless. This type of general impotence leads to massive frustration and anguish because they had taken this aspect of their future life for granted.

Male infertility in the Western world

Marie-Claire Mason has written of the desire to be a father. Some men wanted to improve on their own experience; some wanted to prove themselves to the rest of the world; some just wanted to have children. The idea of not being able to seemed to play a strong role in the resultant desire, which is then paradoxically heightened. The striving and the failure seem to feed on their growing yearning for a child. One man described how his yearnings involved fantasies about what he would do with his child. His pain was made worse when he saw other fathers realising his fantasies. There were also aspects of property and ownership for some men. One man resented the fact that he would be unable to pass on the benefit of his life experiences to any children. This idea of passing things on and, in a way, becoming immortal through having offspring is a deep-seated kinship belief. Many men reported feeling resentment that those lucky enough to have children seemed to take them for granted and did not cherish them as they imagined they would. Some felt even more strongly, not just about their experience but also about their inability to pass on their family characteristics, their genetic genealogy (Mason 1993). Here there may be issues of competitiveness with siblings who have succeeded in procreation. The need to be a biological parent is locked deeply into the male psyche. It is possible that this need is archetypal and that children represent an archetypal image.

It could be argued that the desire to become a father when it presents in an obsessional form might be a demonstration of a disturbed psyche, indicating that a person who was previously a well-adjusted adult becomes imbalanced as his unconscious exerts a powerful influence on his conscious attitudes. The pursuit of this generative need to its ultimate end leads many men to the doors of the fertility clinic, which seems to offer the 'promise' of restoring the psyche to a healthy balance (by the production of the desired symbol of fatherhood and thus communicating a visible demonstration of virility). Therefore the increasing dependence on assisted reproduction, by both men and women in the West, assumes a new meaning and significance. The technology in ART seems to be feeding on and fulfilling new desires (Strathern 1992) since, before the advent of technology, people would accept their plight and get on with their lives, or look for different solutions, such as adoption or fostering. These issues are inevitably linked to the changing attitudes of women, as they pursue independent careers, making a choice to have their children later. Ovum donation (not surrogacy) has opened up new avenues, where women past normal reproductive age may now become pregnant and deliver babies. In this case it is the father who has the genetic 'rights' and not the mother; technology changes legislation and begins to change the way we look at kinship in the West. We may begin to imagine why ART has become so powerful in the minds of those who must have children. It is conceivable that the desires that drive this rush towards ART inevitably expose men to risk, since men are most uncomfortable in a medical environment. The ill man rarely seeks medical help; to do so is to admit 'weakness'. That men, desiring to be fathers, are willing to risk exposure and be seen to be weak tells us how powerful the unconscious desire to enter the ranks of fatherhood is.

Emasculation and rebirth: paradox in the fertility clinic

Most men seem to find their visits to the clinic an unpleasant experience. Since fertility, equalling virility, is a fundamental part of the male psyche, it is understandable that facing up to the clinic, which may represent both their own shadow and society's negative view of infertility, may not be a task they view with relish. Couples are scared of showing anger or hurt because they fear the doctors may retaliate and withdraw treatment. This puts a great deal of pressure on them, because they have to perform and be well-behaved. Furthermore, although many doctors acknowledge that infertility comprises both male and female components, in practice, within the clinics, men are still ignored and marginalised.

For men, burdened by the shackles of male myths about their manhood, the idea of being the partner with the 'problem' often results in a strong sense of guilt and blame. For men, particularly those in Europe and the USA, the fact that men don't cry and that they somehow 'manage' all types of life disasters by 'toughing it out' means that infertility becomes a bitter pill (Hite 1991, Lee 1996). Men face immense pressures as they strive to maintain a public face, desperately clinging to their persona (social mask), whilst inwardly their self-fabrics have been shredded. Some men never come to terms with their infertility. Technology makes it even harder because their desires are fired by the hope that someone will find a solution, which is just around the next corner. In the main, most men achieve a type of balance, whereby they learn to live with the pain, which inevitably makes them more susceptible to severe stress and life crisis. Men are not comfortable in themselves about seeking help (Greenstein 1993, Lee 1996, Mason 1993), so infertility is a cross they have to bear in solitude. In the clinic, men are already reduced to the role of 'man the sperminator', whose primary role is to be the sperm 'donor', apart from which he remains the helpless onlooker. To add insult to injury, they are not allowed to prove their manhood by producing the sample in the normal way, but must do so by masturbation. Men do not use the word 'wanker' to describe an inadequate male without reason. Thus to be reduced to being the onlooker, the 'sperminator' and 'wanker' to boot, places men in a humiliating position. To have to do all this in addition to being told that you have poor sperm is too much. In some cases, where even this limited role is taken away – for example, in cases of azoospermia – it is altogether too much.

Why masturbation?

ART requires a male sample to be produced by masturbation. The male must perform to order. Hitherto, until this point in treatment, he has been neglected, playing the role of the partner waiting in the wings. Now he becomes all-important and is expected to perform. He must produce a sample of semen, usually in the clinic, and more often than not, he must produce it on his own, knowing that everyone is waiting expectantly. The sample itself takes on a type of symbolism, sometimes men are unable to produce it in such difficult circumstances. Perhaps, when the occasion arises, the man is saying something about ART! Such events, when they occur, are hardly surprising; not only are there high stakes riding on the production of the semen sample, but there are also religious aspects as well. To both the Catholic church and Orthodox Judaism, masturbation is an abomination. This may also add a further burden of guilt for many couples. Throughout Africa, and amongst Arab countries and other countries in the non-Western world, there may also be taboos against masturbation, which makes this method of semen production even more stressful than it might normally be. This act further exacerbates the removal of sex from ART, perhaps reinforcing the idea of reproduction without sex. The requirement of masturbation as a means of production of the semen sample for use in the treatment ensures patient compliance. It ensures that the laboratory gains access to the sample within an hour of its production, which helps in assessing and preparing the sample for use. It also ensures that couples are not in a position to swap the sample with a known donor. In my experience there are a number of couples who might try the latter given the chance. Part of the reason for masturbation is for the clinic to maintain control over the patient.

Why do professionals stop couples from producing by coitus? The official answer is that recovering semen from the vagina might be a messy affair. Samples obtained by interruptus are usually poor. Both these methods are unreliable because semen is made up from the secretion of several glands, the most important emission being that from the epididymis, which is

continued

where the sperm are stored just prior to ejaculation. Unfortunately, the emission from the epididymis is the first one, so that by the time the other glands – the prostate, seminal vesicles and the bulbo-urethral glands – have also emitted, the first portion may already be widely dispersed (the first portion is only about 0.5 ml, whereas the rest may be 2 to 8 ml). Thus, even with interruptus, we usually only get the fluid from the accessory glands rather than the epididymis, which has been left behind in the vagina. Samples produced by sex, for treatment purposes, are likely to be of poor quality, unless we collect into a seminal device – a device which must be non-toxic and non-spermicidal. Such devices exist and most men are able to produce through coitus into these devices. Why do we not routinely use these devices? It remains unclear. Some embryologists are reluctant about handling the devices (most are female, which might explain this), and there may be issues of cost (£5 to £10 per device), but ultimately, it could be about patient control and compliance. A researcher, Zavos (1985, Zavos and Goodpasture 1989, Zavos et al. 1994), has studied the use of these devices extensively in the USA. He has carried out a number of studies which show that semen samples produced with the devices are improved over samples produced by the same men through masturbation. Some of the studies are possibly flawed, but the implication is that masturbation semen samples may be sub-optimal, begging the question, if we assume masturbation produces poor samples, how meaningful is IVF's failure to fertilise? Is it possible that such cases might be reversed if we were to obtain a further sample from coitus using a seminal device to catch the whole sample? It is a moot and ironic point. More research needs to be done. Almost certainly there are benefits to be obtained from the use of such devices, with the only risk being that some couples might swap samples on us!

The cult of children

Jung believed that myth and the collective unconscious of the human mind are inextricably linked. Myths concerned with fertility abound in all cultures. Marriage in our society is mainly about providing replacements for ourselves. Western men are in some ways reborn through their children, who then take on a new significance. Now we have a linear model of time, history becomes more important and life becomes meaningful in terms of generativity. Man's religious expectations also change; the idea of salvation becomes more important, since in the linear model you only get one chance. In the cyclical model you are constantly reborn with infinite chances. Jung was in tune with the idea of salvation and rebirth and he looked on them both as a pathway to wholeness. If we regard having a child as being part and parcel of 'salvation' and rebirth, then becoming a father may be compared to an important station on the way to becoming whole and through a family of creation becoming an adult. Continuing with this theme, it seems pertinent to wonder if becoming a parent has become the modern equivalent of a pilgrimage.

As our symbols, rituals and beliefs have all been eroded, are we now left with the cult of children as the last meaningful symbol in life? The act of becoming a parent is probably a primal urge buried in the human collective unconscious. The obstruction of this need is further exacerbated in our modern age for archetypal macho men when they have a diagnosis of male infertility, for whom the act of becoming a father may be vital for maintaining the balance of their psyche. In their absence children can become an all-consuming desire.

If we have a cult of children, then fertility assumes a new importance. The idea of duty is an important concept amongst most men. This ideology has served Western man well for millennia, but now it is no longer appropriate and is currently partly responsible for men's increasing disarray (Greenstein 1993). Women are beginning to assert themselves and express their needs more openly, which is threatening to men, even though it has brought about a reproductive revolution that has exploited women, according to the feminists (Lee 1996). This legacy has produced a phenomenal explosion in the provision of infertility treatments (albeit almost entirely in the private sector). In IVF terms alone, this has meant an increase in IVF from 6,000 in 1985 to 37,000 in 2000, effectively a reproductive revolution. The number of IVF clinics has also increased from fifteen in 1985 to over eighty in 2000. Undoubtedly, the explosion in availability of IVF is a remarkable phenomenon. The more remarkable because, for the first time ever, the emergence of this fertility cult actually promotes reproduction without sex.

A number of issues arise here. Why are we reinforcing reproduction without sex in clinics? What value have samples which are produced by masturbation? If we bemoan reproduction without sex, would it not be better to allow couples to produce semen samples through coitus? What is going on here? The reproduction revolution is all about technology. Technology that has heightened people's reproductive desires and hence expectations, as well as changing future possibilities regarding our Western kinship system, since we are assisting not only in the making of persons, but also in the making of parents (Strathern 1992). The price is loss of control as technology assumes the reins of control and we give in to almost any aspect of human desire regarding reproduction. Although most infertility clinics are exploiting a new class of consumer, because reproduction technology extends choices and possibilities for people previously left in limbo (Lee 1996, Strathern 1992), fertility treatment, especially if it works, assumes the guise of a free gift. The free gift is a symbol of modern Western society and as such creates an infinite appetite for what is on offer (Lee 1996, Strathern 1992), such as treatment, one of modern times' ultimate manifestations of consumerism (the baby supermarket).

Those providing treatment, embryologists and especially gynaecologists, have become the new high priests and priestesses of temples (infertility clinics) infused with supposed fertility power which is believed, by those seeking children by these means, to reside in modern IVF clinics. Many of these couples therefore come to these modern temples of fertility to achieve redemption from their sins (guilt and punishment) by paying for their treatment (which equates to sacrifice and atonement).

Therapy and the clinic

The Human Fertilisation and Embryology Act of 1990 prescribed therapeutic intervention (which they called counselling) for patients in licensed clinics. In spite of this, men remain staunchly reluctant and avoid counselling, even though many are in pain and crippled to such an extent that their marital relationship is placed under great strain. Few men seek help. Most will suffer in silence since men rarely discuss their feelings and 'when the going gets tough, the tough get going'. Men are expected to be self-reliant, they cannot be seen to need help from anyone else. Consequently, it is rare to arrive in a counselling setting that has been initiated by men. When men attend sessions, it is usually as a result of a mandatory referral (no further treatment until . . .) arising from a label of a difficult or angry patient. Because of the loss of self-esteem, men may feel vulnerable and in need of love and support, which is often lacking because infertility is a taboo subject. An unwanted conspiracy of silence therefore comes about. In a way, male infertility becomes the secret which is the rock on which men are themselves shattered. Since men cope with male infertility by developing an introverted approach to it, part of their own method for survival involves studiously avoiding counselling.

Fatherhood may be viewed as a developmental stage in a man's journey through life. There is a parallel between the reality of life's journey – birth, childhood, adolescence, adulthood, parenthood, middle age, old age and finally death – and the journey the psyche goes through. If becoming a father is a crucial stage, then we can see why fatherhood is such an important part of a person's continuing development; fatherhood allows a person to understand their own childhood better and if necessary relive and put to rights any defects in their own upbringing. Fatherhood also gives a person a sense of the passing of generations; it is one of the rites of passage that are so important in realising the meaning of our existence.

Most men do not find bereavement as important an issue as it is for women, although it is likely that this is due to denial and introversion (Lee 1996). Mason found that only five out of the twenty-two men that she interviewed had significant things to say about loss and bereavement of the prospective child (Mason 1993). Certainly, when dealing with bereavement in this setting, we need to understand the uniqueness of suffering and try to find ways in which each individual may ritualise the 'passing' of their 'dream child(ren)'. Mahlstedt suggests that patients are faced with all the losses that characteristically cause clinical depression (Mahlstedt 1985). By consciously grieving their losses, patients may be able to move on and thereby benefit more from their treatment or, in rare cases of resolution, get on with their childless lives. Because of the overwhelming tendency of men to deny their plight, there is an irrevocable commitment to isolation. This self-isolation makes men particularly difficult to deal with, both from a medical aspect and a counselling aspect. The isolation results in tremendous feelings of loneliness and is further exacerbated by friends and family beginning to avoid them as they feel guilty when they realise how distressed infertile persons and couples can be. Isolation is compounded by a conspiracy of silence. This veil of secrecy also exists because many men are too embarrassed to bring the subject of infertility up amongst their peers, because of its associations with sex and masculinity. The more technology moves on, the harder it is for these patients to accept their diagnosis and to resolve their feelings about their infertility. The pursuit of treatment is, for some patients, an act of denial, but for others it is part of a process by which men, whose psyche has been wounded, struggle to reintegrate their unconscious through the self-regulating aspects of the psyche. By reconnecting to the symbolism of fertility and children, the male archetype may be restored through the treatment (in the modern temple of the fertility cult, by fertility specialists – the new high priests and priestesses), and the psyche healed and restored to balance. One patient who was first diagnosed with azoospermia in 1988 disappeared without trace. He resurfaced in 2000 and had taken the trouble to seek me out. During the twelve intervening years technology had moved on. Now he might be treated by ICSI (sperm micro injection). He said, 'Now I know I am treatable, I feel like a man again, you don't know what this means to me!'

Sperm

The mature sperm containing a haploid (n=23 chromosomes) number of chromosomes (n=22 + a male chromosome-Y or a female chromosome-X) is a few microns long only, but, considering its relatively small size, it must travel an epic distance of up to 40 cm in the female genital tract to fertilise the oocyte. Sperm have a complex structure which consists mainly of the nucleus (a genetic package consisting mainly of chromosomes). The nuclear portion of the sperm is 'capped' by the acrosome (an enzyme-containing portion of the sperm head which is vital for the penetration of the outer membrane of the oocyte – the zona pellucida), a mid-piece (the energy source) and a tail (which provides motility and propulsion). During the process of production, sperm pass through the seminiferous tubules to the rete testis, on to the vasa efferentia, the head of the epididymis and thence twelve days later to the tail of the epididymis. Transport of the

continued

mature sperm is via muscular activity within the epididymis and vas. During this time, the sperm acquire motility and undergo the final biochemical changes that confer them with the ability to fertilise the ovum following ejaculation. Seminal fluid coagulates at ejaculation (it is made up from the secretions of a number of glands, such as the bulbo-urethral, seminal vesicles and the prostate, all of which add up to the half a millilitre or so of epididymal fluid), but under normal circumstances then liquefies within twenty minutes, its basic pH protecting the sperm in the acidic vagina. Sometimes, when certain enzymes are missing, the coagulation persists and can bring about infertility by restricting the sperm from gaining access to the cervix. Within minutes after ejaculation, sperm may be found in the cervix and are released constantly over a period of up to seventy-two hours, during which time the sperm will move with great speed and direction to the ampulla where fertilisation of the ovum (mature ovulated oocyte) will occur. To achieve this, the sperm must undergo capacitation (attaining fertilising capability; oestrogen dependent) and activation (readiness to undergo acrosome reaction; a change in movement pattern also occurs; the inner membrane underneath the acrosome cap becomes primed for fusion with the inner membrane of the ovum-oolemma; calcium dependent).

Armed with the insight that men are utilising the clinics as a means of dealing with the pain of male infertility, it is important to realise that, even so, men still suffer at the hands of those who run these 'temples'. Men need to be active and in control, but in the clinic where the medical specialist, usually a gynaecologist, is all-powerful, the man is reduced to the role of 'flapping' around helplessly, trying to exert some control. The clinic makes all the decisions, which renders him ineffectual. The men try to sort out treatment and to get information, but they are rendered impotent at every turn. Thus infertility demonstrates one thing above all else: that the drive to have children owes little to reason. No wonder men become disoriented.

Men are often unaware of their own emotional needs, and, even when they are, seem incapable of demanding that they be addressed (Lee 1996). As issues and problems arise in the clinic environment, most men remain reluctant to consider any support, let alone counselling. Furthermore those who have been counselled do not seem to cherish the process. They are clearly worried about coercion to have counselling or to go to support group meetings, probably because any of these actions implies even more loss of control.

Modern men with male infertility look to the clinic for their 'salvation', yet, in the clinic, we fail their spiritual needs, inflicting uncertainty and taking away their self-esteem and right to be in control. One of the great challenges therefore is how to support these men and their partners through the process. They need to be empowered. In my work as a clinical scientist, my daily work is concerned with the mechanics of the science of injecting sperm into eggs to create embryos. I routinely spend time with patients doing my best to ensure that they are properly 'consented' with regard to the complex treatment(s) they are receiving. I also see a great deal of pain, misery and fear (of the unknown) but, in spite of this, they will not seek help. I have a diploma in counselling and am happy to offer them counselling 'pro bono', but less than 10 per cent avail themselves of the service. Over the years, I have developed the strategy of 'counselling without counselling'. The coffee machine in the clinic is in the waiting room. We have two consulting rooms next to the waiting area and one is usually free at any one time. I drink a lot of coffee. This makes me freely available. My routine is to greet everyone waiting. I am always amenable to the 'By the way . . . can you tell me about . . .'. My antennae are always out. In this way I try to deal with floating anxieties, which the men will not make appointments for, but if it can be dealt with on the fly it seems to be the way men like to work. I am forever taking patients 'on the fly' into one of the rooms, and generally we do not emerge until an hour to an hour and a half later. Up to three hours of my working day are spent this way.

Conclusion

Collective beliefs in the myths of what it is to be a man have contributed greatly to the way in which men respond to a diagnosis of male infertility. Ignorance alone, however, is insufficient to explain all the problems that exist in the field. How a man feels when he realises that becoming a parent, and a father, might not be so easy as he originally thought, clearly relates to his unique outlook as a man. Because we all have role models that we follow, and because the male psyche produces supposedly self-reliant and self-contained individuals, most men suffer terribly when told that they have male infertility. It is as if the unconscious feminine aspect of them is torn asunder, whilst they struggle to maintain their social mask. As roles and rituals have been eroded, one of our last symbols of life are children. Children are a symbol of hope. So strong a symbol that children now dominate news media. We not only have a reborn fertility cult in the West, but also a cult of children, which has been a vital cog in the re-emergence of fertility itself as a modern cult.

Men in the infertility setting are private persons, with a few extrovert exceptions. A common summation of all these feelings, especially within the medical setting, is a growing feeling of uselessness. There seems so little that can be done for male infertility. Most treatment options centre on their partner. Undergoing cycle after cycle of ART can be soul-destroying. The stresses and strains of treatment can devastate relationships. Being able to acknowledge one's fears and to face up to them may help some couples to make decisions which allow them to control their own destinies.

A public acknowledgement of the existence of male infertility and the ignorance surrounding it may lead to more openness about it and therefore less public stigma about male infertility. Perhaps more access to counselling will also help to alleviate the stigma, anxieties and isolation. How we begin to help those men, who feel the blow so badly, is one part of the story. Where individuals are resistant to asking for, or receiving, help, the impotent render those who would help impotent. Part of the answer also lies in becoming adept at the art of counselling without counselling. The world is changing quickly. Female empowerment, technology and the millennium impact on the collective unconscious and come together in compelling men to adjust to the reproduction revolution. This revolution involves reproduction without sex, which is ironic, since the decade before IVF arrived was the beginning of the era of sex without reproduction (sexual revolution and the pill). The winds of change, first brought about by Steptoe and Edwards, have heightened public expectations about fertility. The cult of children and of fertility, having brought about the new religion centred on fertility clinics as the 'church', has rapidly become established in the psyche of Western man. Though men and women suffer in the process of treatment, the paradox is that they are attending to their needs on another level, that of moving into and through the important rite of passage and entering the age of parenthood. This is an archetypal image, so strong that, to fulfil it, many will undergo extreme pain to achieve their grail, which may be akin to the various processes undertaken in the mysterious *vas* of the sixteenth-century alchemists. Consider as well the sperm's journey in the testes, vas and female reproductive tract (the vas is a crucial element in the transportation of sperm), which are also steps on the psychological path to enlightenment and psychic integration.

Reproduction technology touches on the collective unconscious in such a powerful way that, in the space of fifteen years, reactions to the technology have gone from public outrage to complete acceptance. IVF is now an everyday phenomenon. People have IVF in the same way as they go to the dentist. Its impact upon the public psyche is such that even couples who are probably fertile submit themselves to IVF for convenience. For men with male infertility, their fertility is often synonymous with their virility and they will submit to anything which will restore it. The fertility clinic is the modern temple where the cult of fertility and of children is practised. Infertile men project their desires on to the 'temple' and its 'high priests'. For some men the medical world of reproductive technology still needs to become better integrated into consciousness as it is their only route to 'salvation' which, when successful, allows them to enter the ranks of men by becoming fathers.

Bibliography

Greenstein, B. (1993) *The Fragile Male*, London: Boxtree.

Hite, S. (1991) *The Hite Report on Love, Passion and Emotional Violence*, London: MacDonald Optima.

Lee, S. (1996) *Counselling in Male Infertility*, London: Blackwell.

Mahlstedt, P.P. (1985) 'The psychological component of infertility', *Fertility Sterility* 43: 335–346.

Mason, M.C. (1993) *Male Infertility – Men Talking*, London: Routledge.

Menning, B.E. (1980) 'The emotional needs of infertile couples', *Fertility Sterility* 34: 313–319.

Strathern, M. (1992) *Reproducing the Future*, Manchester: Manchester University Press.

Zavos, P.M. (1985) 'Seminal parameters of ejaculates collected from oligospermic and normospermic patients via masturbation and at intercourse with the use of a Silastic seminal fluid collection device', *Fertility Sterility* 44: 517–520.

Zavos, P.M. and Goodpasture, J.C. (1989) 'Clinical improvements of specific seminal deficiencies via intercourse with a seminal collection device versus masturbation', *Fertility Sterility* 51: 190–193.

Zavos, P.M, Kofinas, G.D, Sofikitis, N.V., Zarmakoupis, P.N. and Miyagawa, I. (1994) 'Differences in seminal parameters in specimens collected via intercourse and incomplete intercourse (coitus interruptus)', *Fertility Sterility* 61: 1174–1176.

Chapter 9

Love, hate and the generative couple

George Christie and Ann Morgan

George Christie is a psychiatrist, psychoanalyst and group psychotherapist.
Ann Morgan is a paediatrician and group and individual psychotherapist.

Introduction

Over twenty years ago the authors first came together at the Royal Children's Hospital, Melbourne, as co-therapists for a group of mothers of disturbed children. As our professional relationship developed we began to conduct analytic groups with psychotherapy patients in private practice. Over time we have become increasingly interested in how a sound co-therapy relationship can strengthen group containment, facilitate trust, and provide a safe space for the emergence and creative transformation of destructive forces within the group. An example of this is the way in which a well-established analytic group can survive a frightening outbreak of aggression involving several members, and then, just before the end of the session, have someone produce a moment of spontaneous, genuine humour that brings everybody alive in a burst of simultaneous and freeing laughter.

Psychoanalysts, philosophers and poets appear to be in agreement that our potential for achieving creative transformations depends upon our being able to retain some intuitive awareness of the powerful destructiveness within, together with a capacity to organise this into an acceptable avenue of expression, as in a moment of generative humour. It is of interest that such a capacity is increasingly being described, intrapsychically, in terms of maternal holding; a holding of the largely unknown destructiveness, and perhaps also a joint parental capacity to start organising it in some way. The Jungian analyst Rosemary Gordon describes the creative person as being able to bring into life, intrapsychically, a genital bisexual activity, requiring an identification both with the father who gives, and with the mother who receives, and bears, the child (Gordon 2000). These ideas link with how the containment provided by a sound parental couple, providing space and opportunity for the emergence of play, can be of importance in facilitating the emergence of a child's creative potential.

We believe these ideas are relevant not only for the creative but also for the procreative potential within all of us. The therapeutic couple have their part to play in the treatment of clients with unexplained or relatively unexplained infertility. Our experience suggests that any individual work we do with infertile clients can be helpfully augmented by an infertile couples group experience, led by the experienced co-therapy couple.

Unexplained or relatively unexplained infertility

The unconscious processes involved in unexplained infertility can be quite subtle. Perhaps we need to keep in mind the words of two German gynaecologists, Petersen and Teichmann, that 'a baby will come when it wants to come', and try to deepen our understanding of what they mean by this, before we contemplate taking action. They were interested in exploring aspects of conception, and also of its inhibition, that go deeper than that provided by our current incomplete knowledge of neurophysiological and hormonal processes, or by our popular notions of external stress (Petersen and Teichmann 1984). We know very little about these deeper levels of awareness. We need a pooling of information, not only from physicians and physiological researchers, but also from infertility counsellors, psychoanalysts, sociologists and anthropologists.

There is an interesting example of psychogenic inhibition of conception in the literature. It is a striking and macabre report of a deep inhibition of spermato-genesis. De Watteville refers to a German book by Stieve, who examined the testicles of men convicted and executed shortly after committing rape. Even in cases where the rape had allegedly led to pregnancy, the autopsy material, without exception, showed inhibition of spermatogenesis, and complete absence of spermatozoa. If a woman is sentenced to death, Stieve says that her uterus begins to bleed within hours, no matter where she is in her menstrual cycle. The rapidity of these processes, evoked by fear of death, suggested a neurogenic, rather than a hormonal, mechanism (de Watteville 1957). The starkness of these images seems to provide an allegory for the primary forces of life and death. There can be no doubt about the power of the human psyche here.

Petersen and Teichmann write of another level, that is, one incorporating such phenomena as the feelings of certainty, perceptual aliveness and sudden sense of a three-person situation that can characterise the onset of conception for a couple who are ready to allow a baby to come and to nurture it (Petersen and Teichmann 1984). Currently infant mental health workers in Australia are exploring the most subtle aspects of the interaction between mother, father and baby, not only post-natally, but also in anticipation, that is, prior to birth, even prior to conception (Paul and Thomson-Salo 1997).

An important area is that of the role of human ambivalence in the psychogenesis of lowered fertility levels. Those who are sceptical of any part played by the mind in infertility often make the understandable point that if a frightened, angry, rape victim can be impregnated by such an assault, how can ambivalence about pregnancy possibly be a factor in the lowering of human fertility levels? Ambivalent feelings about producing children are, of course, universal, and are currently heightened for Western women by their increasing freedom to seek higher education and careers, and their increasing success in these areas.

However, our clinical experience suggests that one factor that can contribute to a lower fertility level is where the negative, rejecting component of ambivalent feelings is warded off from conscious awareness, and its return prevented by a defensive idealisation of the prospect of pregnancy, and an idealized image of the baby. It is of interest that the Strauss opera *The Woman without a Shadow* is about an ideal woman who, lacking awareness of the negative side of her feelings, is subsequently sterile.

The psychotherapist Rozsika Parker even suggests that ambivalence provides a woman with a sense of individual identity: 'I would say that it is ambivalence that makes passions circulate, as well as firming boundaries, forcing reflection, provoking both separation and unification, and thus providing a spur to individuation for mother and child' (Parker 1995: 21). This is in line with Winnicott's view that the reliability of mother–infant relating is dependent upon the mother's genuine feelings of love and hate, and not upon her psychological defences (Winnicott 1975).

Any good, sound relationship, whether with parent, sibling, partner or child, can perhaps be regarded as a generatively ambivalent one, as compared with a destructively ambivalent one, or an idealised one. A generatively ambivalent relating is one where the periodic emergence of genuinely expressed derivatives of hate in certain situations provides no lasting threat to the mutual love and respect, and where the conflict is eventually resolved, often helped by access to a shared sense of humour.

Pre-conceptive ambivalence and readiness for parenthood

The psychoanalyst Luis Feder includes the infanticidal wish in his concept of 'pre-conceptive ambivalence', an ambivalence towards pregnancy present in all of us, that is, the wish to have a baby, accompanied, at varying levels of consciousness, by a wish to prevent the baby coming, or to destroy it. This is an ambivalence experienced not only before conception, but also during pregnancy, and after the baby is born. Feder emphasises a universal degree of repression in relation to this ambivalence, seeing the universality of the infanticidal component as matched by the universality of its denial (Feder 1980).

According to Feder, pre-conceptive ambivalence, contributing to the inner conflicts we all have as parents, continues to exert its influence during the ensuing development of the child. He recognises its importance as a factor in the genesis of the Oedipus complex. He goes further than this, however, in seeing the failure of the couple to work through this ambivalence as being a major factor in the emergence of hatred and violence in society (arising within all the primarily unwanted children).

However, a stage of personal maturation can be reached where the wish to allow a baby to come becomes predominant. Several writers have set forth ideas about what needs to be achieved here. Erik Erikson wrote of the psychosocial stage of generativity, where, in a woman, a readiness to deliver and mother a child has begun to prevail over all other feelings. He believed that this stage emerges predictably in each one of us when and if we reach a certain level of maturity. At this level we have developed not only the capacity to take responsibility for our own lives through separating, individuating and acquiring a sound sense of self, but also an emerging ability to lose ourselves in a meeting of bodies and minds with another person, that is, a capacity for a deep intimacy with the other (Erikson 1963).

However, many women (and men) whose sense of identity is consolidating during the establishment of successful careers might not feel ready to seek to have children until the second half of their thirties or even later. This can lead to more chances of physiological problems during pregnancy and childbirth than is the case with younger women.

In referring to 'the psychological birth of the mother' as 'a specific form of maturation', Rodin writes of the necessary emergence of a woman's 'tri-generational object structure'. These are her internalised concepts of her own mother, of herself as a child of that mother, and of the foetus as her child. A woman is then ready to become the mother, her own mother or 'urmutter' retreating to a supportive position in the background (Rodin 1993).

According to the psychoanalyst Dinora Pines, a woman with unexplained infertility has often failed to achieve the dual maturational tasks of establishing a sufficient degree of identification with her mother's maternal function and a sufficient degree of separating and individuating away from that mother (Pines 1990). This may mean that she and her husband or partner have not been able to help each other complete their moves in the direction of taking responsibility for themselves away from their families of origin.

Such a woman often possesses deep ambivalent feelings towards both her own mother and a fantasised infant. She may be unable to own, consciously, her underlying hostility, either towards the mother, or the fantasised infant. A genuine love for her mother may be buried beneath an intensified compliance with what she believes are her mother's wishes (e.g. feeling she has to ring her mother every day), a compliance that represents a defence against awareness of the depth of her hostile feelings.

Here the woman's genuine capacity to care for any future infant is sometimes hidden away beneath an idealised and frenetic need to become pregnant. Such a conscious need represents a denial of her infanticidal wishes. However, in a paradoxical way, her latent capacity for care, for sensing what is best for her child, may still be operating through the inhibition of her reproductive processes, an inhibition that derives from an unconscious awareness of not being ready to allow a baby to come, and to nurture it.

In our psychotherapy with infertile couples, one therapist sees the woman individually at first, and the couple together from time to time. The male partner may be referred to the other therapist for some individual work. Our experience suggests that it is helpful if this can be augmented at a later date by the couples entering a supportive-expressive type of group, led by the therapists as an established co-therapy couple. Sometimes the individual approach is enough, as illustrated in the following two cases.

Case I (Dr Christie)

At the time of her referral, Ms A., a 37-year-old woman, had been living with her partner for ten years, and trying to conceive for three years. Ms A. had been distressed by her failure to conceive, and was initially convinced that she had an organic problem. Seeking help for her infertility, she wanted absolute answers, and quick and definitive treatment. At one stage, gynaecological investigation had revealed a degree of cervical mucus acidity, with poor sperm penetration, for which alkaline douches had been prescribed.

When her gynaecologist suggested she come to see me, Ms A. resisted the idea at first. She eventually made an appointment, appearing guarded in the initial sessions. A warm, emotional and articulate woman, she told me of extreme frustration felt in relation to her partner, whom she saw as a silent, introverted man. She also told me of difficulties she had in relation to her family of origin. She had found it difficult, as an adolescent, to separate from her possessive, anxious parents. She had always had a troubled relationship with her mother, and even now was still finding it difficult to differ openly with her. She knew her mother was unhappy, on religious grounds, about the de facto relationship, and Ms A. felt very uncomfortable about this.

Ms A. said she was wary of psychiatrists, and felt resistant to the idea of psychotherapeutic probing. As I continued to listen in an unhurried way, her resistance began to lessen. We settled into weekly sessions, and there were signs of a developing trust. She told me she was feeling increasingly that she would never be able to have a baby. She wanted her gynaecologist to make appropriate tests that would confirm this, so that she could devote her time to a successful career. As our therapeutic contact developed, her frenetic need for answers seemed to recede, and she was increasingly able to own a conscious wish not to have a child, together with a feeling of sadness about this. In other words she was now able to stay with awareness of both sides of her ambivalent feelings (a new and positive development).

After enjoying a short holiday, Ms A. returned to her weekly sessions with me, and almost immediately conceived. The unexpected development aroused intensely mixed feelings in her. She became preoccupied with the question of whether or not she would seek an abortion, initially seeming to favour doing so. Morning sickness was continual, developing into severe nausea for most of each day. She could not bring herself to tell anybody what had happened, and was terrified her parents would find out, feeling sure that her mother would disapprove. Her partner, in his quiet way, seemed delighted with the news.

As we continued to reflect upon the issues in our weekly sessions, there was a steady decline in her wish to abort, and her nausea gradually lessened. She showed a quietly enthusiastic response to successive ultrasound photographs showing a growing foetus. At around five to six months, she was able to find the courage to face her mother and give her the news. The mother reacted calmly to this, and began to do things for her.

Things now began to change markedly for Ms A. Her nausea disappeared. She began to discuss future plans more maturely in our weekly sessions, and seemed to be less dependent upon my support. The birth of a delightful little baby girl was greeted with great pleasure by both the patient and her partner. The baby sucked well and was soon sleeping long hours at night. The sound mother–infant relating, and father–mother–infant relating, was striking to observe, in the light of Ms A.'s initial inclination to seek an abortion. The couple eventually married, and since then a second daughter has arrived.

I consider that this case illustrates several important features in the individual management of an infertile patient:

1 Premature interpretation of her pre-conceptive ambivalence could well have been a persecutory experience for this woman. It was of paramount importance to establish a successful therapeutic engagement, with provision of a genuine containment, so that awareness of her own ambivalence could emerge in its own way, and its own time.
2 Ms A. was able to become increasingly aware of a wish not to have a child, and at the same time experience a sadness about this, because of her parallel wish to have a child. It is interesting to speculate that the creative implication of this emerging awareness of contraries served to facilitate Ms A.'s biological conception.
3 Aided by the psychotherapeutic containment, Ms A. could face her mother during the pregnancy, achieve a further degree of separation-individuation from her, with a positive response from the mother and an increasing emergence of Ms A.'s own maternal functioning.

A study by Brazelton and Als appears to have some relevance here. These two workers followed a group of primiparous women through their antenatal and postnatal experiences. Some of these women became so emotionally upset, at times, during the antenatal period, when interviews, in a psychoanalytic setting, uncovered anxiety of almost pathological proportions, that the interviewers became concerned as to how they would relate to their babies. Yet when these women were seen in action later as mothers, the anxiety and the related unconscious material had clearly become a force for reorganisation and readjustment to the important new role. These women became successful mothers. They were women who could live with derivatives of their own ambivalent feelings, and any related anxiety, because they were not excessively defended against awareness of such feeling (Brazelton and Als 1979).

So if a woman isn't ready to face the maturational crisis of pregnancy, and the uncovering of deeply ambivalent feelings, her pro-creative urges may become blocked, at least temporarily. An analogy for any such defensive lowering of fertility might be found in the way an adolescent can adopt a recognisably defensive position (e.g. a temporary asceticism) until the individual personality strengthens enough to be capable of managing hormonally intensified sexual and destructive impulses.

A number of early American papers are also relevant here. Rubenstein, Ford *et al.*, Rothman *et al.* and MacLeod all reported upon the frequent finding in infertile women of repressed hostile feelings towards their own mothers. This repressed hostility was also leading these women to fear, subconsciously, that if they became mothers they would hate their own children, and be hated by them in return. In analytic treatment, as the women became aware of how much underlying hostility they felt towards their mothers, they started to make contact with the genuinely loving side of their ambivalent feelings, and started to relate authentically with the mothers, rather than over-protectively, usually with a positive response from the mothers. Many of these women conceived during or shortly after a period of analytic treatment that enabled them to achieve further increments of separation-individuation from their mothers (Rubenstein 1951, Ford *et al.* 1953, Rothman *et al.* 1962 and MacLeod 1964).

Many of our infertile patients have shown an over-protective and/or idealising attitude towards their own mothers, as a way of defending against an underlying hostility (as described in the earlier American papers). But we have also seen a mildly paranoid type of resentment towards the mother, operating as a defence against a strong underlying needfulness, and fear of merging. These two attitudes illustrate how either side of a deep ambivalence can be disavowed, and a defence set up against it in the psyche.

On the other hand, a powerful reaction to early maternal deprivation may be blocked from any form of expression, and this may not only inhibit the procreative process later, but also predispose to future life-threatening somatic illness, as in the following case.

Case 2 (Dr Christie)

Mrs B., aged 39, was referred to the author, with a longstanding unexplained infertility, which had persisted despite several unsuccessful cycles of artificial insemination with her husband's semen over many years. She had a good job and what appeared to be a sound marriage. Both she and her husband were aware of mixed feelings about whether or not they wanted children.

Mrs B. had been her father's favourite, and she had wept at length when he died. She had been able to support her mother at this time, adding that she had always had a rather tempestuous relationship with the mother, mitigated by the mutual respect they had for each other. However, Mrs B. had been able to separate and individuate satisfactorily from her mother and take over responsibility for her own life, supported by the sound relationship with her husband. In addition both husband and wife had been able to hold on to an awareness of ambivalent feelings about the prospect of parenthood. How then could a psychological factor be operating in Mrs B.'s fertility problem?

The interesting fact emerged that a year or so previously, when her mother had died, Mrs B. had been unable to cry. A short time later she was found to be suffering from raised blood pressure, diagnosed as essential hypertension. Before initiating any medical investigation her sensitive and supportive woman doctor had asked, 'Has anything significant happened in your life recently?' Mrs B. began to speak of the loss of her mother, burst into tears, and wept at length for the first time. She could not find words for the feelings she was experiencing. However her raised blood pressure level then began to recede.

Mrs B. went on to inform me that she had been conceived 'accidentally' when her mother was 43. After Mrs B's. birth, the mother proceeded to develop a severe puerperal depression which required admission to a psychiatric hospital. The baby was taken from the mother, placed with friends for a short time, and then transferred to an aunt for a few months. She was eventually reunited with her mother, and a reasonable relationship grew into being, with its admittedly 'tempestuous' element.

Thus a separation had occurred at a time in early infancy when psyche and soma are not clearly separated out from each other and when disturbing feelings tend to be split off into bodily expression. Joyce McDougall describes how many of her psychosomatic patients have an incomplete sense of bodily differentiation from the mother in the area of their psychosomatic pathology, together with, as yet, no developed words in which to express their emotional pain (McDougall 1978).

In subsequent sessions it became possible to take up with Mrs B. the possibility that the sudden separation occasioned by her mother's death had revived, in the depth of her inner being, something of an originally powerful response to the first separation in early infancy, a response for which there would have been no words, or images or playfully creative avenues of expression, only a turmoil of primitively ambivalent feelings, revived and expressed through her body later in the form of the raised blood pressure. When she had been able to weep at length in the empathic, holding presence of her woman doctor, had she perhaps at last been able to find an avenue for expressing something of her reaction to the original loss, as well as the more recent one, enabling her raised blood pressure to return to a normal level?

Mrs B. was intrigued by these possibilities, but also found it hard to think about them. As we worked with all this in subsequent sessions, Mrs B. gradually began to emphasise the reasons why she did not want to have a baby at her stage of life, as well as feeling increasing sadness about this, because of a persisting wish to have one. Now increasingly able to hold such ambivalent feelings in consciousness, Mrs B. proceeded to conceive for the first time in her life, at age 40. Nausea in the first trimester was very troublesome for her, but this eventually cleared, and she started to enjoy ultrasound pictures of the foetus. Apprehensive about the prospect of labour, she nevertheless resisted any suggestion of Caesarian section. She eventually had a normal labour, was deeply gratified to achieve her wish to hold a baby boy in her arms, and her breast milk flowed freely. She felt no need to continue seeing me.

On weaning the baby nine months later Mrs B. suddenly felt so depressed that she rang me to seek some literature on post-partum depression. Before I could return her call she started to think about all we had been discussing earlier, began to weep at length, and soon felt quite well again. This further sequence suggests that an increment of mother–infant separation, implicit in the weaning process, had once again revived a trace of the original separation experience deep within Mrs B.'s psyche.

A deep inner turmoil of ambivalent feelings, held at an early preverbal level, had not only blocked Mrs B.'s procreativity, but also predisposed her to future life-threatening illness. An interesting aspect of the outcome is how two people, her sensitive GP and me, were involved in the course of events that helped Mrs B. conceive. Was this an example of the generative effect of a therapeutic couple, even though here we were working separately?

The role of the co-therapy couple

The question just raised is one that does warrant further reflection. What we have not followed up at this stage is whether couples with persistent unexplained infertility would be better seen by a co-therapy couple from the start (with each partner seen individually by each therapist, and the partners seen together from time to time by the therapist couple). However, in our experience, where sound individual work has not led to a successful outcome, inclusion in a couples group seems to have had a powerful augmenting effect. It is fortunate that our couples have been able to move into such a group, led by an experienced co-therapy couple including their individual therapist. We feel this has provided an increased holding and containment for our patients, in a continuity of treatment, as well as increased opportunities for them to work through unresolved difficulties in relation to their own parents.

In reflecting upon the role we have played in the treatment of infertile couples, we would first like to make some points about co-therapy work generally. There is a growing realisation that the parental couple have more to offer than the sum of their individual roles as mother and father, and we believe that the same applies to a co-therapy couple.

Schindler, Durkin, Scheidlinger, and others have developed the theme of the group-as-a-whole as mother. Therapists join with the other members in forming a merging wholeness that can be containing for individual members as they experience the initial marked regressive effects of entering a group, including the emergence of primitive forms of aggression. This wholeness can give the individual group member time and space to survive the experience and to go on to find an increasing sense of self and an increasing access to the creative potential within (Schindler 1966, Durkin 1964, Scheidlinger 1974). We are suggesting that a sound, already established co-therapy couple can add something here. Strengthening the quality of containment makes it safer for the gradual expression of primitive hate and persecutory fears. The group's survival here provides a safer setting for the early pathology to actualise at a more articulate oedipal level, because the co-therapy couple can understand and survive it. In analytic groups, just as in families, there are powerful forces within the group directed both at attacking the couple, and testing the couple's capacity to survive these forces. According to Dick, Lessler and Whiteside, a co-therapy couple need to experience progressively unfolding developmental stages in their relationship, preferably under supervision, until they reach a point where they can survive all crises, come what may (Dick et al. 1980). Not only is a sound couple better equipped to understand and survive these powerful forces, but, in our opinion, the forces might not always actualise so clearly in an individual therapy setting.

As stated earlier, we first started working together as a couple with a group of mothers of disturbed children at the Royal Children's Hospital, Melbourne, in the late 1970s. Ann had been working previously as partner to Dr Bill Blomfield, and was familiar with his application to group work of Margaret Mahler's contributions concerning separation-individuation processes. George was used to working with analytic groups of adults, using the ideas of Foulkes, Bion and Ezriel.

We were very polite to each other, as we came in from time to time with comments from our respective theoretical positions. The mothers were quiet and rather dispirited. One day one mother started talking about how annoying it is when two of your children want to watch different television programmes at the same time. Immediately other mothers began to agree with her. When it gradually dawned on us that this might be a reaction to us, and we said something to this effect, the whole group came alive. As one mother put it, 'We sit in the waiting-room before the session wondering what you are going to differ about today.' We have now worked together conducting once-a-week psychoanalytic therapy groups for almost twenty years.

A co-therapy couple can be put under great strain at times, coping with the feelings that can be unconsciously stirred up in the group interactions. On one occasion we felt exhausted after a group session which had involved considerable tension and where we had both been trying to cope with many confusing developments and trying to understand their meaning. We were not only taking in primitive feelings somehow projected into us unconsciously by other group members, but were also having disturbing conflicts stirred up in our own psycho-pathologies. The group members left, and we sat together silently for some time. George found himself wondering how to tell Ann what had entered his mind during a prolonged group silence. Eventually he found the courage to say, 'Ann, during one of those difficult periods in the session, I was preoccupied with a thought that you might suddenly drop dead!' 'Oh, I wouldn't worry, George', she replied, 'I was giving the eulogy at your funeral!' Our shared laughter gave considerable relief, of course, making it easier for us to think about and discuss the preceding session.

We would now like to give some other examples of growing evidence for the importance of the holding and containing function of a sound co-therapy relating. Over an extended period at the Royal Children's Hospital in Melbourne, both long-term and short-term groups were used in the treatment of certain disturbed mothers whose disturbed children were already in individual treatment. In choosing suitable neurotic and borderline mothers, the co-therapists had in mind those situations where the presenting problem in the child appeared to be related to unresolved deep ambivalent conflicts in the mother.

Christie and Correia have described how a successful group experience enabled some mothers to free their hostility, hitherto covertly directed (via projection of bad internal parent images) on to the way they had experienced hospital depart-ments and staff members. Group containment of this hostility seemed to help some mothers make contact with the hidden pain of their guilt over destructive wishes harboured towards their own children. Experiencing this pain, in the supportive empathic atmosphere of the group, helped them contact the other side of their ambivalence, the genuinely warm, caring and empathic impulses within. Gradually they became better able to find more creative solutions for their intrapsychic conflicts. As they became freer and more whole in themselves, they also became freer to allow the children to proceed with their own development (Christie and Correia 1987).[1]

Group therapy with infertile couples

It is only four years ago that we became interested in the possibility of introducing a group experience for couples already established in individual psychotherapeutic exploration of their unexplained or relatively unexplained infertility. We proceeded to form such a group. After a few sessions one wife informed us that further gynaecological investigation had revealed complete blockage of her fallopian tubes. She acknowledged the help she had received from earlier individual and couple sessions, enabling her to achieve further separation from her own mother and gain a better understanding of the difficulties arising from being the good, compliant eldest child in her family. However, she and her husband decided that they would discontinue group sessions and proceed to try IVF (in vitro fertilisation). They went ahead with this, she conceived at the first attempt, and went on to deliver a baby boy. Another couple left because the husband was transferred overseas. We then settled down with three couples, meeting fortnightly.

One woman had been told that she formed antibodies to her husband's sperm. IVF had been attempted unsuccessfully with seven egg collection cycles. Sometimes no eggs were found, three times fertilisation failed, and any embryos that did form appeared immature. A noticeable early feature in the life of the group was the relief experienced by this woman in finding that it was acceptable in the presence of the other group members to own and express the negative aspects of her ambivalent feelings about having a child at 41, and how having a child would interrupt her developing career. Feeling a lot freer as a result, she eventually decided to have one more IVF attempt during the life of the group, and conceived twins.

One of the other two women was able to express intense feelings of envy about this. A manic defence style of relating had earlier characterised her behaviour in the group, but this now began to lessen as she talked with difficulty about her envy, and then was able to confess to the group how she had terminated a pregnancy early in her marriage. Tearful moments followed, and one session ended up with the three women hugging each other.

Two of the husbands were able to admit that, although they had been supportive of the wishes of their wives to conceive, they really didn't want children. As they began to express these negative feelings, they proceeded to some exploration of relationships within their own background families. The genuine expression of difficult feelings was leading to increasing freedom and spontaneity in relating within the group, and a strong attachment was clearly developing between the three couples. The group came to an end by mutual agreement, following the departure of the first woman and her husband, late in her pregnancy. She eventually went into labour, and delivered a boy and a girl.

The other two couples agreed they would like to join a new group planned for early in the next year. But late in the year one of the women rang to say that she and her husband had decided she would have one more IVF attempt. She had done so, and she also had conceived twins. Then early in the following year we received a phone call from the other woman to say that she and her husband had changed their minds about IVF, had sought this out, and that she, too, had conceived with the first attempt.

So here four couples were able to achieve immediate success with their first IVF attempts taken up *after* inclusion in our group (two of the couples having failed earlier IVF procedures). They have all been adamant in feeling that their individual and group experiences played a significant, and even crucial, role in bringing about the eventually successful conceptions, after their many years of struggle and frustration. The couples sought our permission to have contact with each other outside the group, and we agreed to this. They followed this up with a request that they bring their babies in with them to sit in a circle with us for one final meeting, and we agreed to this too.

We began a new group with four couples the following year. Three of the wives conceived naturally during the continuing life of this group. One baby was born, but the other two pregnancies miscarried. The fourth wife decided against parenthood, and resumed taking the pill. We plan to start a new group early in the year 2003.

We have been interested to realise that our work with the two infertile couple groups has differed in certain ways from what we have experienced over years in working with our analytic psychotherapy groups. We were both struck with the sense of overall containment, cohesion and trust that seemed to develop quickly, particularly in our first infertile couples group. This led us to have relatively little to say as therapists. We preferred to carry out a containing or holding function, and just listen carefully. The infertile couples appeared to identify quickly with each other and welcome the opportunity to express the troublesome feelings they experienced in the outside world, such as extreme feelings of envy, frustration and a sense of isolation, feelings difficult to ventilate freely in their family, social or even fertility clinic settings.

Most of the work was done by the group members, and this increased in parallel with their sense of group containment, that is, their decreasing sense of isolation from others. We intervened mainly during the rare silences, commenting when we sensed something was remaining unsaid in the group. Although we encouraged the exploration of feelings, we did not find ourselves working with the feelings they developed towards us, and feelings we developed towards them, in the way we have done in our analytic groups. This doesn't mean we won't find reasons to work with such transference and counter-transference manifestations in subsequent infertile couple groups, but it has been lacking in our early experience.

We are left with the belief that the holding, containment and quiet listening provided by us as an experienced co-therapy couple have been of crucial importance in our work with these couples. Perhaps something is happening in these groups that parallels what happens in the mother–infant groups, where the mother is discovering the child within herself, the infant is beginning to tune in to the mother, and the mother is gaining access to her own mothering capacity. We also wonder whether there is something about the infertile couple group experience that facilitates 'the birth of the mother' (and the father). As mentioned, Rodin describes, for the woman, the emergence of a trigenerational object structure comprised of internalised concepts of her own mother, of herself as a child of that mother and of the foetus as her own child (Rodin 1993). Our remembered experience of the final session, the two co-therapists sitting quietly to one side, the three couples together, and their babies crawling over the floor, seems in some way to resonate with this concept.

Is it also possible that the co-therapist containment, provided for both the mother–infant couples and the infertile couples, facilitates a regression and playful interaction in ways that open access to a deeper level of experiencing, with its generative possibilities? There is still so much work to be done in these areas, so much for us still to learn, so much room for future research.

The need for a better integration of the technological and psychosocial approaches to infertility

In the field of human infertility there are many areas of high-quality research into reproductive system and immune system pathology. However we still have much to learn about the neonatal and postnatal development of the human brain, including the gradual evolution of the human immune system, and the role of prenatal and postnatal influences there. On the other hand we are similarly still in the earliest stages of uncovering basic intrapsychic, familial and socio-cultural truths relevant to our overall understanding of the variable levels of fertility in our communities.

Mind and body are not separate entities. They constitute a wholeness. It is not easy for many of us to keep that perspective. Surely there is an urgent need for those individuals and groups working in the fields of infertility technology and those exploring psychological and socio-cultural factors to come together more and really listen to each other. The worst situation, and one that is not uncommon, is a polarisation into opposite camps, with little understanding on both sides of what the other side is doing and discovering. This can lead, for example, to the brilliant discoveries in the artificial fertilisation of human ova occupying too central a focus, unmodified by the insights, constraints and new possibilities that can follow from a broader, more holistic perspective.

The little we do know about psychogenic factors in infertility is largely confined to women. For reasons remaining unexplained, there appears to be a world-wide avoidance of enquiry into such factors in males. We also need to find out much more about the interpersonal relating of the infertile couple. It is of interest, for example, that as the level of fertility in one partner improves with treatment, it may simultaneously begin to wane in the other partner.

We need, also, to be sensitive to how transference feelings towards significant members of the treating staff can develop in these patients. A woman can endow her gynaecologist with attributes determined by unconscious wishes directed towards the image of an idealised father (or mother). The frightening intimacy of an AID (artificial insemination by donor) or IVF procedure, carried out in such a context, can sometimes result in anovulatory cycles. How helpful if such unresolved feelings towards significant parental figures can emerge and be worked with in individual and couple therapy, conducted in parallel with the technological procedures. As Joyce McDougall suggests, in relation to psychosomatic disorder generally, 'further insight into the processes at work may alter our way of listening to our patients' (McDougall 1978: 337–376).

Unexplained infertility represents an exciting field for future exploration, if we can stay with 'not knowing', and allow time for an adequate listening to what our patients can teach us. Just as an increasing awareness of contrary feelings can facilitate a creative impulse in us all, so can an increased awareness of a whole range of feelings about the prospect of conception help us, as individuals and couples, to gain more access to our own creative potential as future parents, in both mind and body.

Note

1   We would also like to mention here the intriguing and innovative work with mother–infant groups being conducted in Melbourne by co-therapists Campbell Paul and Francis Thomson-Salo. Of special importance here seems to be a quality of containment or holding that is provided not only by the two co-therapists but also by the mother–infant group-as-a-whole – a containment of the mess, at times, and a containment or holding, not only of the real child and mother, but of the child within the mother as well, which helps the mothers 'to find the answers within themselves', and to gain access to their own genuine creative potential as parents. It is a relief not to be hearing of attempts to educate, train or condition the mothers. There is also the way the two co-therapists relate to the infants in 'the language of action and play', modelling this for the infants, and thereby facilitating an opening up of creative avenues within the mother–infant dyad – e.g. facilitating the emergence of humour in their interactions. A developing concern in the infants for their mothers often follows, which appears to be a facilitation of the infants' capacity to tune in to the feelings and needs of the mothers (Paul and Thomson-Salo 1997). This can be compared with what Stern describes as the infant's move from a sense of core-relatedness to a sense of inter-subjective relatedness, with an increasing affective attunement to the mother (Stern 1985).

Bibliography

Brazelton, T.B. and Als, H. (1979) 'Four early stages in the development of mother–infant interaction', *The PsychoAnalytic Study of the Child* 34: 349–370.

Christie, G.L. and Correia, A. (1987) 'Maternal ambivalence in a group analytic setting', *British Journal of Psychotherapy* 3, 3: 205–215.

Christie, G.L. and Morgan, A. (2000) 'Individual and group psychotherapy with infertile couples', *International Journal of Group Psychotherapy* 50, 2: 237–250.

Christie, G.L. and Pawson, M.E. (1987) 'The psychological and social management of the infertile couple', in R.J. Pepperell, B. Hudson and C. Wood (eds), *The Infertile Couple*, 2nd edn, London: Churchill Livingstone, pp. 313–338.

de Watteville, H. (1957) 'Psychologic factors in the treatment of sterility', *Fertility and Sterility* 3: 12–24.

Dick, R., Lessler, K. and Whiteside, J. (1980) 'A developmental framework for co-therapy', *International Journal of Group Psychotherapy* 30: 273–285.

Durkin, H.E. (1964) *The Group in Depth*, New York: International Universities Press.

Erikson, E.H. (1963) *Childhood and Society*, 2nd edn, New York: W.W. Norton, pp. 240–244.

Feder, L. (1980) 'Preconceptive ambivalence and external reality', *International Journal of Psychoanalysis* 61: 161–178.

Ford, E.S.C., Foreman, I., Willson, J.R. *et al.* (1953) 'A psychodynamic approach to the study of infertility', *Fertility and Sterility* 4: 456–465.

Gordon, R. (2000) *Dying and Creating*, London: Karnac Books, pp. 129–141.

McDougall, J. (1978) 'The psychosoma and the psychosomatic process', in *Plea for a Measure of Abnormality*, New York: International Universities Press, pp. 337–396.

MacLeod, A.W. (1964) 'Some psychogenic aspects of infertility', *Fertility and Sterility* 15: 124–134.

Parker, R. (1995) *Torn in Two: The Experience of Maternal Ambivalence*, London: Virago, p. 21.

Paul, C. and Thomson-Salo, F. (1997) 'Infant-led innovations in a mother–baby therapy group', *Journal of Child Psychotherapy* 23: 219–234.

Petersen, P. and Teichmann, A.T. (1984) 'Our attitude to fertilization and conception', *Journal of Psychosomatic Obstetrics and Gynaecology* 3: 59–66.

Pines, D. (1990) 'Emotional aspects of infertility and its remedies', *International Journal of Psychoanalysis* 71: 561–568.

Rodin, M. (1993) 'The Psychological Birth of the Mother', unpublished dissertation, Professional School of Psychology, San Francisco.

Rothman, D., Kaplan, A.H. and Nettles, E. (1962) 'Psychosomatic infertility', *American Journal of Obstetrics and Gynaecology* 83: 373–381.

Rubenstein, B.B. (1951) 'An emotional factor in infertility', *Fertility and Sterility* 2: 80–86.

Scheidlinger, S. (1974) 'On the concept of the "mother group"', *International Journal of Group Psychotherapy* 24, 4: 417–428.

Schindler, W. (1966) 'The role of mother in group psychotherapy', *International Journal of Group Psychotherapy* 16, 2: 198–202.

Stern, D.N. (1985) *The Interpersonal World of the Infant*, New York: Basic Books.

Winnicott, D.W. (1975) 'Hate in the countertransference', in *Through Paediatrics to Psychoanalysis*, London: Hogarth Press.

Changing patterns of kinship

Chapter 10

The story of Seth's egg

Emma Scrimgeour

Emma Scrimgeour is a painter and lives in London with her partner and two children.

Seth is my nephew, his mother is my sister and his father is my brother-in-law. Seth's conception took place in a Harley Street clinic Petri dish; the sperm was my brother-in-law's and the egg was mine. He looks very like his father and shares his dashing eccentric style in clothes and sense of humour; nevertheless he reminds us all of my son Peter when he was Seth's age.

My sister, Flora, asked me to give her an egg and I was pleased she did. She and my brother-in-law, Hugh, had experienced eight years of disappointment with fertility treatments which culminated in the devastating stillbirth of their naturally conceived daughter. By the time Flora and I had our first conversation about egg donation, Mark, my husband, and I had considered every way we might help them get a baby, including having one and giving it to them. Now that we had heard about egg donation it seemed a very simple and natural thing to do for my sister who, in a great many ways, had brought me up since I was fifteen.

She was a strikingly sharp child who delighted my father who called her his 'Queen'. Until I was born she was the only girl amongst three boys and her supremacy was unassailed. When she was told without any warning, aged five, that she had a sister upstairs she said, 'How nice for me'. This was much quoted by my father, and I always felt the ambivalence of the story. My sister guarded her position like a tiger and I turned out not to be very nice for any of them, sneaking on my siblings and throwing tantrums whenever they teased me.

Until I was fifteen I lived in the shadow of my sister's brilliant, rebellious school career and her powerful presence at home. We were opposites; physically I began by being tall and strong for my age (I was christened Tamara Press by my siblings after a Russian weightlifter who was caught taking steroids), whereas Flora was wraithlike and grew into a teenage beauty. I charged about on my pony and Flora read in her room, eschewing any form of physical activity. Whereas she was naughty and quick, I was eager to please, and if I hadn't later been 'saved' by her I may have ended up forever getting ready for my next gymkhana. I was both scared and immensely proud of her and I longed to be like her but would be seized by jealous rages, hurling her (and anybody else's) things out of the window or pouring mince into her boyfriend's boots. Sometimes I would sneak into her room to try on one of her beautiful, shoplifted dresses from Biba and get stuck, slightly wrecking them. At last, considered old enough to be part of my brothers' and sister's wild holidays camping by the sea in the Outer Hebrides, I ended up sharing a tent with Flora as she was forced out of hers by the unwelcome attentions of an amorous man with smelly socks. Throughout the rest of that summer we became devoted to one another.

Flora then took my education in hand; she gave me a copy of *The Female Eunuch*, introduced me to her radical Cambridge friends, and encouraged me in my sexual adventures. When our father died, we curled up in a bed together and slept through the wretched afternoon. After Dad's death we spent a long time together going over and over our parents' unhappy marriage and how it had affected us. I turned out to be a lackadaisical feminist; although committed in spirit, I was lazy. I slept through university lectures and arrived in London with no degree, or clue as to how I was to earn my living. By contrast Flora was working hard as a criminal defence barrister in radical chambers. Never without a man in her life, she swore she would never have children and certainly never get married. When I rang her to tell her I was going to have a baby her comment was, 'I expect you're going to make a career of this.' She was and is a fabulous aunt and our sons are extremely close to her and Hugh.

If I, Mark, Flora and Hugh had not remained so close through their long efforts to get pregnant, especially during their pregnancy and its terrible end with the prenatal death of their baby girl, Dora, Seth's story might have been less straight-forward. As it was, none of us could think of any reason to give the psychologist at the clinic as to why we shouldn't do it. Quite soon after we'd all agreed to give egg donation a try, Flora and Hugh looked into adoption and were given a three-month-old girl, Melody, to be their daughter. Her arrival was momentous and we were all ravished by her. The ghastliness of the death of Dora, Flora and Hugh's baby, and the awful years of unsuccessful fertility treatment were over, somehow Melody made sense of it all. Flora and Hugh's adoration of her was marvellous to see and they took to the nurturing of Melody with easy confidence and joy. When not long after Melody's arrival Flora suggested we go ahead with the egg donation, I reacted powerfully against it. Instead of feeling excited about the process, as I had done previously, it became unreasonably menacing. I found the prospect of the physical intrusion threatening, whereas before it had been insignificant. Also I became intractable over dates. It must have seemed very peculiar as I hadn't really got so much to do except a show of my paintings that was coming up. I had always been cavalier about my health, consuming anything going. I think I behaved like this because it was too soon to revisit the traumas that Melody had put behind us, but I didn't quite realise it at the time.

It was a good thing to have delayed it, for we all agreed later that Melody's place in the world would certainly have been undermined had Flora fallen pregnant shortly after Melody's arrival. Flora and Hugh accepted my contrariness with great understanding; they didn't mention eggs again until Melody became such an integral part of all our lives that we could barely remember life before her. This time the atmosphere was different; Flora and Hugh had Melody, we agreed

we were going to attempt one cycle to produce this baby and all desperation
disappeared. It was exciting. Our visits to the psychologist and the clinic were made
in this spirit. It felt as if we were watching ourselves in a Woody Allen movie as
the four of us sat in a row in front of the psychologist who tried to puzzle out
whether this was going to end in disaster. There was a sense of unreality about it;
it was hard to imagine that this process would work where so many others had
failed. I don't think any of us believed, or dared hope, it would result in a baby;
besides which the doctors made us feel as though we were part of an experiment
in eugenics and gave us frightful giggles. Though I hate needles, Mark got so good
at giving me injections in my bottom, I didn't mind at all, but I couldn't imagine
that it would work. The clinic made a mistake and over-stimulated my ovaries and
then wanted to scrap the procedure. I felt furious with them as it seemed to prove
their lack of humane interest in our case. It would have been very dispiriting for
everyone to have to begin again, so we insisted on carrying on. The day of the
beginning of Seth's conception was bizarre and very moving. As I staggered down
the corridor to the theatre where the eggs were to be harvested (by this time,
because of their miscalculation, I had so many in my ovaries it was uncomfortable
to walk or sit up), I turned back to wave at Flora in the hall and to Hugh who
was climbing the stairs, with great dignity, to the room where he was to produce
the sperm.

Three days later three fertilised eggs were placed in Flora's womb, five others
were put in a deep-freeze. Flora's pregnancy had the same wonder about it as the
Virgin Mary's except, unlike Mary, we never got over our disbelief, even when
we looked at the scan and could clearly see a boy. The closer it came to Seth's birth
the more incredible it became. Waiting at the hospital on the day of Seth's
birth, while Flora and Hugh were in the operating theatre (it was a Caesarian section
to minimise risk, so I was not allowed to be with them), was an agony of anxiety.
I had sat with them during the stillbirth of Dora in the same hospital and was fully
expecting to go through the same experience. I think we all were. It was impossible
to separate the happiness from relief when Hugh finally appeared to tell me that
Seth and Flora were safe and well.

Today our family have just got back from Seth's fourth birthday party. Flora
had cooked a delicious tea for Seth and his guests; she had made him a *Thunderbird
Two* cake. Seth is crazy about *Thunderbird Two*. Flora and Hugh made the party
fun, warm and hospitable for us all, and everyone, especially Seth, surrounded
by his friends and lovingly presided over by Melody, who is now six, had a
lovely time.

When Flora approached the clinic to carry out the donation the consultant was
anxious about our being siblings. For me it has made it beautifully simple; we
share the same genetic pool – the way Flora does things is familiar – her cooking
(which we both assimilated from our mother), the chaos we share in our separate
houses, ideas about a good day out – and I know her great sense of humour, her
outspokenness, her great pleasure in things. Both Mark and I and the boys love
Hugh very much and admire and respect him, not least for the incredible support

he gave Flora in her pursuit of children. (Hugh had mumps when he was nineteen and so wasn't figuring to have any children.) If I had any doubt that Seth or Melody were not being so fully loved and cared for in every way, I should be overwrought by it, and in Seth's case regretful and angry. But I was convinced that with Flora and Hugh this scenario would never happen. I am aware too that if I didn't love and respect Hugh I would have felt anxious about entering into our new relationship and then the joy of its success might be made awkward.

Flora and I have survived a quarrel since then and not a polite one either but a real fight in the style of our childhood; Flora torpedoing me with well-aimed missiles and then it ending up with me throwing her a punch. It was a bit shocking for everyone – especially Mark and Hugh – who had not witnessed us in our childhood roles before. We got over it though.

I don't feel any more maternal for Seth than I do for Melody but when I am with him I do feel very happy that I could help in his beginnings. While Flora was pregnant, the four of us had a conversation about whether Seth's biological mother should be an open issue, or whether it would contravene a basic right for Seth to be able to choose whether he wants his origins to be out in the open. It has become an open subject and it would have been strange had it been otherwise as it is a house without taboos. After Seth was born and for his first couple of years I stood back a little more than I might have done had I not thought there was a danger of Flora feeling I was hovering about too much. Now, Melody and Seth often come over to our house and spend the day with us and we spend weekends at their house in the country. One day I picked them up to bring them over to South London. We were driving through Hackney and Melody said from the back of the car, 'Emma, you know, Seth and I both have two mothers. I have my mother and Flora is my mother and Seth has you and Flora is his mother too.' It was said with absolute certainty and without a trace of confusion. I looked round and Seth was nodding his head and grinning.

If we hadn't gone ahead with this egg I would have regretted it for ever and who knows what sadnesses may have followed – but only now do I know how much we all would have missed.

Chapter 11

Seth

Flora Scrimgeour

Flora Scrimgeour is a barrister and lives in London with her partner and two children.

Seth doesn't seem a particularly inconceivable person. I suppose in our eyes he has left his strange beginnings behind, although when he was born I do remember other people's, not always well-disguised, shock that a Frankenstein's monster was so ordinary and sweet. I suppose from our point of view he was as ordinary as we could manage, the product of quite extreme pressures, great generosity and desperate improvisation.

In the 1970s my notion of women's liberation was that it would free women of the family ties and obligations that had suffocated so many of the mothers of my generation in the 1950s. It's been a strange spiritual journey through the 1990s, most of which I spent in a frantic quest for a family, any old family, just so long as it did entail all that suffocating obligation I so envied in all the parents I knew.

It may sound like a tall story coming from someone who went to the extremes that we did to have a baby, but although in the end we embarked on this genetic love story with my sister, for me it was not mainly a drama about a genetic inheritance, it was much more about a stake in the future, in the form of children to rear.

Emma, my sister, was born almost exactly five years after me, and I can remember the day of her birth. My memory is that it came as a complete surprise that our mum was going to have another baby, but I expect I just blanked out her earlier announcements in horror at the prospect of yet another rival. Emma was the last of five, and it was routine in our family for the existing siblings to attempt to kill the new one. I think we filled Emma's pram with earth, but that was later. I was happy on the day of her birth as someone had knitted a mustard-coloured garment for my doll, and I fancied that a sister would be a useful ally against three brothers. My unattractively regal reaction on the day was, 'What a treat for me', and so it proved, though not until we were both much older. In fact I was 20 before our sisterhood came good, but then it really did.

We are very different. Emma is creative, expansive, generous and sociable, whereas I chose to be a lawyer – for which I am sufficiently dogmatic, aggressive, and self-important. Emma had babies years before I contemplated it. I was very moved by her boys, and by her tigerish and selfless devotion to them, but I felt no twinge of envy when they were born. My then cohabitee was not a promising candidate for fatherhood, and the 1980s were an exciting time to be a dissident lawyer – a decade of protest, the futility of which was oddly not apparent to me at the time.

I recognised that my priorities had changed when I found myself in my early thirties gazing enviously at pregnant women, more or less at the same time as I started living with Hugh. He had mumps as a teenager and his sperm production was so hopeless that he used to get chucked out of andrology clinics and ordered not to come back. He was unselfpitying and practical. We used to go to the British Pregnancy Advisory Service (BPAS) in Charlotte Street where one floor was dedicated to the termination of pregnancy and the other to the generation of it. You could get a phial of donor sperm there in those days at a modest price and in an unpressurised atmosphere. It was a laugh, until after a year or so it became apparent that it wasn't working.

Shortly after panic set in, and BPAS had suggested that I give up for a while and try not to think about it, I was astonished to find that I was pregnant with Hugh's naturally conceived child. This is not a lie though I think most doctors who had seen the andrology reports thought it was.

I was deliriously happy and invested massively in the pregnancy. I think it probably did occur to Hugh that no pregnancy is a certainty, but it did not occur to me until our daughter was already dead. By that time she was post-term, and I was naturally utterly convinced that we were going to be parents. I felt some strange convulsive movements as the contractions were starting, and wondered immediately whether all our expectation was in vain. Nevertheless, when later the midwife couldn't find our daughter's heartbeat, I clung resolutely to the possibility that her implements were playing up, until the hospital machines confirmed it. I understood what had happened then, and held on to Hugh and demanded a Caesarian which I didn't get.

Emma and her family had been to supper the night before, and we had all had a happy time feeling Dora's pummelling hands and feet. Once Hugh and I had taken in what had happened, he rang Emma up, and with great courage and loyalty she came to the hospital and went through the melancholy business of Dora's birth with us.

I think that experience was probably worse for Emma and Hugh than it was for me. I was all buoyed up with natural birthing opiates, and I dealt with the shock by being inappropriately jocular and chatty. This must have been disconcerting for them. I told Emma my memories of the day of her birth, whilst we waited for Dora to make her brief appearance. Giving birth to a dead person was more bearable for me at the time than in retrospect, I suppose because at the time I had a job to do, however futile.

Dora was born early the next morning. I was frightened to see her when she first emerged, fearing that she would be some kind of horror, but she wasn't at all. She was just an ordinary little baby girl, remote and strange in her deadness, but with Hugh's mum's sumptuous mouth.

After Dora had been post-mortemed, we were encouraged to go and dress her for her funeral, and we did. We put her in a cardigan I'd knitted and embroidered with flowers, and then sat with her on our laps and chatted. Someone from the hospital took photographs of us sitting there with our dead daughter on our knees and tears streaming down our faces.

We had a little funeral for her in Suffolk where we had hoped that she would spend much of her time. There was a very nice vicar who overlooked our atheism and said a prayer of thanks for the pleasure Dora had given us. If we'd been less topsy-turvy I suppose we should have fixed up a humanist ceremony, but a baby's funeral without any sense of redemption would have been very hard.

The aftermath of Dora's death was a difficult time, made more endurable by a number of things. First, because we had no children we had no way at the time to know about the extent of our loss. We lost our hopes and expectations of a child, but we did not know her, nor what it would have been to be her parents. We recognised at the time that this made things easier, although we were acutely aware that Dora's conception was a much less likely event than her death, and that the chances of our conceiving a further child were indiscernible.

Our misfortune was easier to bear because no one was to blame for Dora's death. We did not have to get all knotted up in anger and recrimination and so it was easier to plod onwards. We both persuaded ourselves that whatever it was that Dora had died of, and the post mortem showed up nothing in particular, probably hadn't hurt or frightened her much or for long. We strove not to obsess about her loss of a chance at life. Most of all, most people around us were not scared or embarrassed by Dora's death, but were full of kindness and support, and we were well advised by courageous and sympathetic midwives.

In the days after Dora's death, I felt like I was stuck in a lift hurtling towards the ground. It got better in the end, but when Seth was born, I remembered that sensation and it felt as though I had escaped.

Dora's conception and death upped the stakes. In a rather spoilt way, I don't think I'd ever really contemplated the prospect that I would not be a parent, but once Dora died it became unthinkable. For a bit we dragged ourselves round Harley Street in search of more expensive ways to administer the donor sperm. I hated this. It was a ghastly round of intrusive procedures in sumptuous surroundings. About a year after Dora's death, when something wasn't going right as usual, I burst into tears. The doctor asked why I was crying and scuttled out of the room without waiting for an answer. I got dressed and paid the bill for the unsuccessful procedure still in tears. The only attention I got was from a cab driver who picked me up outside the clinic, and told me about his wife and their long-awaited son. The clinics were furtive (in contrast with the BPAS waiting room, no one ever chatted in Harley Street) and unfeeling and made me feel like a fanny with a chequebook attached.

The fertility treatment was fabulously expensive. We couldn't look for NHS help of any sort because if we applied to adopt it would be a blot on our escutcheon if it was known that we had recently been trying to make a baby. So we then led a double life: adoption training in an East End family centre at weekends and the leather sofas of Harley Street in the weeks.

We enjoyed the adoption training. Everybody was in the same boat and there was a desperate camaraderie between the applicants. The ethnic and cultural screening applied to adoption candidates was so minute that it was practically impossible to find yourself in contention with anyone else on the course for the same child. We were very lucky that our social worker didn't mind that we were middle-class, and felt that the squalor and chaos in our house suggested that we would cope all right with parenthood. In hindsight the period of our candidacy for adoption has a rosy glow, because it had such a joyous outcome, but it was awful at the time.

We were advised to get married to give some gloss to our adoption application and we did. Hugh's mum, Elaine, started to die of a brain tumour that summer. I felt terrible for him. It felt as though his hopes of a stake in the future and his ties to the past were all being hacked away together. By a grim coincidence the oncologist who diagnosed Elaine's terminal illness was married to the very decent gynaecologist who suggested that we should give up on conception as a route to parenthood.

After we got married and before Elaine died I realised I was pregnant again with Hugh. I think this is called a spontaneous pregnancy in Harley Street. We treated the pregnancy solemnly, and I believed in it. The miscarriage did not become apparent until after twelve weeks, but it was obvious from the scan then that the baby had never got beyond being a little broad bean. It felt like a horrible practical joke on all of us and one Elaine was just well enough to absorb. Again Emma bravely officiated at the hospital.

By spring Elaine was dead and social services had taken to coming round with polaroids of children which they waved solemnly under our noses before realising that they required cultural exotica in their adoptive homes which we could not provide. In the case of one little girl upon whose image we had dotingly gazed, we were by turns insufficiently Scottish, Italian, Iraqi, and Catholic! We started sending off to *Be My Parent* magazine for ready-made families of three. It was a bit like Emma's childhood attempts to extort freebies from cereal manufacturers: 'Dear Mr Frostie, I know 2 tokens isn't enough but I really do want the stickers, please.' Our supplications acknowledged the glaring inappropriateness of our household to the children in question and begged that it be overlooked. Our social worker was patiently deprecating about these letters, which never even met with a reply.

At some point in all of this we found some new Harley Street sofas to perch miserably on, this time so expensive that a bit of client care was thrown in. On our first visit it was suggested that if we were keen and happy to adopt, and therefore also unabashed by the thought of donated genetic material, we should consider seeking donated eggs. The age of the eggs was the most influential factor in conception, and mine were elderly. I recognised immediately that Emma was the crucial five years younger. We had put her through the wringer so much that I hesitated to ask, because I thought that she would feel she had no choice once I did. In the end I did tell her that we had been advised that donated eggs would provide us with a last chance to have a baby, and she immediately reacted with great generosity, offering to provide some.

We went through an initial ethical screen with a psychologist nominated by the clinic. This involved a joint encounter between her, Emma, and her husband Mark, Hugh, and me. It wasn't terribly searching really. I have a vague memory that she sternly warned us of the obvious genetic facts – that any resulting child would be a half-sibling to Emma's boys, my nephews, and would be my nephew or niece. To tell the truth, even writing this now, I am a bit shocked by the idea that Seth is my nephew, even though I am fully aware that he is Emma's son. Anyway, I think Hugh and I probably didn't worry or respond much at the time because we had lost all touch with the prospect of having a baby. Emma dealt sensitively and generously with the difficulty, by saying that the donated egg was ancestral, a common heritage, in her view, not an individual one.

This was selfless of her although there is some expression of common inheritance in our family. In the generations of it that we have both known it has been possible to spot bits of genetic inheritance leapfrogging generations, as well as great tracts of inheritance that are common to us; boot button eyes, thin fine hair, shortness and anxiety to please spring to mind.

There is one odd aspect to this which I can't begin to understand. Hugh has a brother who could have donated sperm. I think he indicated very early on that he was willing to do so. I absolutely didn't want to do this. It felt too much like I would have had sex with Hugh's brother. I recognise that this wasn't a much more peculiar idea than the arrangement we came to with Emma, although the obvious difference is that what we did was a three-way thing in which Hugh played a biological part.

Meanwhile we made a pilgrimage to America, where it was apparent that our advancing age might be less of a problem to our adoption application than it was here. We were asked by the lawyer in the States whether we had considered adopting an African American, which we hadn't at all because ethnicity was such a key factor in selecting adoptive parents in Britain that it had never arisen. We thought briefly about the number of households in our bit of London containing two white parents and mixed-race children and decided that we would be happy to do this and that such a child would not be out of place. When we said so, all the money, delay and red tape of which the lawyer had warned us melted away. Within a month the lawyer had found a mixed-race mother-to-be in California, who was happy with the idea of an English childhood for her fourth child, whom she could not afford to raise.

We were going to do this, until our social worker rang us with news of Melody's birth. She had mentioned Melody's mum's situation to us earlier but not in a way we had felt able to believe in. (In fact by this time we found it quite impossible to believe in any prospect of parenthood.) The call made it clear that Melody's very young mum felt unequal to the task of raising her, and that her social worker was interested in us as possible adopters. We knew that we could not reject Melody. She was alive. There was no guarantee that the American child's mother would in the end be able to stick to her bargain.

By the time we had been approved to adopt Melody she was 3 months old. I was told we'd been approved while on a train travelling back from a child abuse case with a whole lot of other lawyers. I was numb and shocked, and we all behaved in rather a barristerial way, celebrating this amazing, wondrous and life-changing news with champagne from the buffet. Hugh and I met in the East End to make a pilgrimage that same night to meet Melody in her tenderly loving foster home.

It was a strange meeting, with a fair-sized audience. When we got to Melody's foster home we found both her foster parents, two other foster children of theirs, our social worker, Melody's social worker and a range of cats and fishes all waiting to witness the encounter. Melody herself was lying serene and beautiful on her changing mat on the floor. We had some modest success with Melody, but then we couldn't for the life of us get her nappy tapes to stick – we kept oafishly smearing them with cream. Worse, Melody started to cry inconsolably, and we left in a state of agonised anticipation.

We had made practically no preparations at all for Melody's arrival. Partly we didn't need to because I had obstinately squirrelled away all the stuff we'd amassed from friends for Dora. Partly we were just completely incapable of serious investment in the prospect of becoming parents. Once Melody's arrival seemed imminent I did knit a very odd pink and green cardigan without a pattern.

The day after that, Melody came home with us. She looked round our kitchen and fell asleep. At the time I thought this was a sign that she was relaxed, but now I think it was probably her way of coping with anxiety. Her arrival mended almost all my broken bits. She was a delightful and on the whole accommodating person. She grew dozens of teeth in her first couple of months with us, never crawled again after she had learned to walk, and started earnestly acquiring speech at a year old.

When she first arrived she had been trained to sleep in a cot by her foster parents. She slept the first night for longer than they had said that she would and Hugh and I kept getting up to check if she was still alive. After a month or two with us, Melody made the decision to sleep with us in our bed, and there she remained till she was four and a half, all the way through Seth's babyhood, during which we were a foursome.

There was a piece on the radio about adoption shortly after Melody came to live with us which said that she was one of 250 healthy babies available for adoption in her year. I cried at our good luck.

Hugh and I, who had walked on eggshells with each other since Dora's death, got happy and normal enough to have a series of fierce babycare disagreements. It turned out that Hugh was a brilliant father, though the desperation to have a family had been mine, and not his. I, by contrast, was a slightly feckless mother. Bottles permitted fecklessness in a way that breastfeeding didn't.

Melody is a very particular person, and we bring her up in an oddly deferential way, not thinking that we know quite what to expect. She is intensely feminine, and gives me patient but weary lectures on make-up, dresses, ear-rings, high heels, etc. She is quite cautious and very pro-social. She has religious beliefs which neither of us share or have encouraged. If she didn't live with us I have a guilty suspicion that she would be tidy. She is beautiful and graceful and athletic beyond any dream we could have had for a biological child of ours. She is a deeply decent person, and chides us if we are unkind about other people (though our gossipiness is probably a lawyers' vice not a family trait).

I can't remember very well how in the midst of all this happiness and relief we came to organise Seth. Obviously I must have felt a strong continuing need to have a baby, even though Melody was a source of profound happiness and satisfaction to us both. The less selfish impulse was that we thought it would be nicer for her not to be an only child, but clearly that wasn't my only motive. It's a bit like those salacious readers' problems letters in the *News of the World*: 'I found myself in bed with my son-in-law.' I found myself back down Harley Street. The fertility doctor at this stage was a very nice young German woman, who couldn't quite believe that her arts could not bring about a conception. We were fond of each other and she wrongly encouraged me to have another couple of goes with my own elderly eggs after Melody's arrival, at a stage when I would have been prepared to call it a day.

When Dora died, Hugh's chances of begetting another baby were virtually nil, whereas mine of getting pregnant at 36 were not too bad. By the time we had adopted Melody there had been a huge development in andrology so that Hugh's few lively sperm could now be separated and injected into eggs (ICSI). Equally I was by then four years older so that my chances of successful fertility treatment would have been slim even if I hadn't had a long history of failing to respond.

Just when Emma probably thought that all the dramas were over, I began to want to take her up on her offer. I know that she was initially a bit shocked at my wanting to have another child which she rightly felt risked compromising Melody's happiness. I fear that really she was doing her best to say no, and that I simply and selfishly failed to understand that. I can remember going for a second four-person encounter with the ethics committee's psychologist. There we sorted out a time when Emma could fit the grisly business of having her ovaries stimulated into her work schedule. We both absconded briefly from my brother's wedding to go and see an embarrassed young doctor together at the clinic. By that time Emma had overcome her reservations.

We took Melody to Sicily at the end of the year, a dear little 18-month-old. She enchanted everybody and bustled up every set of steps she could find. We spent New Year in Agrigento, listening to bells and fireworks and holding on to each other and a sleeping Melody. This would have been all either of us wished for; but we came back and set about three-way techno sex.

I was doing a court martial during the early part of the year. This made a bizarre backdrop to the clinic visits. There was all sorts of grand ceremony and a lot of caper with people saluting each other during the trial, though the court was a decaying Nissen hut with buckets under the leaking holes in the roof. Rather like our family life, it seemed a charming testament to people's willingness to be content to improvise.

All the physical trauma of donation was poor Emma's. I had had no idea until I saw the effect of it on her how horrible fertility treatment was when it actually worked. Emma's pain and discomfort were profound. She took days to recover from the egg donation. In my case it had elicited so little bodily response that I had barely felt it physically.

My memories of our visits to the clinic are all of a particularly sinister young German doctor. He was tall and blond and had an unpleasantly commanding manner. He was given to wearing black leather trousers and a black polo neck. Emma and I both feared and disliked him, and I regret to say that we dubbed him Doctor Mengele. He always seemed to turn up whenever we did. It was a striking feature of this whole experience how few women were working as doctors in this area, and how much more sensitive the few of them were about it than most of the men.

After Emma's eggs had been 'harvested', there was a disgracefully ill-timed scene where she was asked to sign over all the eggs to us while she was in the early stages of recovery from the anaesthetic. I don't think this was a problem for her, but I have always wondered if the timing was a ruse of the clinic designed to catch donors at their most vulnerable and pliant. I suppose Hugh must have been around the same morning bravely playing his part by masturbating into a disposable cup, but I don't remember that bit. He was unfailingly good-humoured about doing this; in our early days he used to filch the porn provided by the clinic, as a souvenir of the conception, just in case it worked.

There were eight embryos. Emma and Mark were triumphant, feeling that they had provided us and several other people with the wherewithal to make families. Emma had a fantasy about the embryos turning up in donated families all over the world – a diaspora of boot-button-eyed people with short hairy legs.

The leather-trousered doctor put the best three back. Hugh and I had absolutely no expectations. Before we went back to the clinic for the pregnancy test I was absolutely convinced it hadn't worked and got cheesily drunk one night. Much more in despair than hope, we both shuffled along for the early blood test. Once the clinic had the blood, we both repaired to an old-fashioned Italian restaurant to await the inevitable thumbs down. We were completely shocked when the test was positive and rang Emma with the news in a state of awe.

I could not commit to this miracle pregnancy fully. I spent the time in a stupid mess, periodically committing all the crimes of pregnancy – heavy drinking, smoking, eating forbidden food, etc. This was a pathetic way to behave, but it was a reaction to our history. I had behaved immaculately during the Dora pregnancy and I was incapable of doing it again. I could not be doing with the twee birthing culture of North London. I knew the poor consultant – the same one as for the Dora pregnancy five years before – would extract our baby by Caesarean if we got that far. I found other women's serene and confident expectation smug. I couldn't share it and I suppose I envied them. Just before Seth was born my mum asked if I wasn't even a bit excited at the prospect of his birth. I told her truthfully that I would believe in him when I saw him. Emma coped understandingly with this alienated behaviour, only once gently remarking that my consumption of fags and whisky on a Hebridean holiday didn't seem quite appropriate to my heavily gravid state.

The consultant lost his nerve at week 37 of the pregnancy and I spent a week as an inpatient in the obstetric department of the hospital. Just as Dora had done, Seth twirled, twizzled and jumped around my womb, while twice a day the staff had to hunt around for a heartbeat to monitor. This was pretty agonising, but on the whole I enjoyed the dramas unfolding around me. I had a chatty neighbour who was pregnant with IVF twins and gently oozing amniotic fluid. We passed our days pleasantly, interfering in other women's birthing experiences, and gossiping about the day's events. One morning Rushida complained of backache and, very shortly after, her twins were born prematurely. She remained beside me at our joint request, but now with enhanced post-natal status, her days an anxious round of visits to the ICU and the breast-milking machine. She was extraordinarily brave and phlegmatic about her premature babies. I never saw her give way to self-pity, as I know I would have done in her situation.

Hugh and Melody came in every day. We had bought Melody a lovely book about having babies by Babette Cole, where the children have to explain to the parents how babies are made. Hugh and I used to read this book to her, and laugh about the fact that barely a word of it was true of Seth. We were in fact upfront with Melody about Seth's origins, just as we had been about hers. As a result, for years Melody believed that pregnancy was the result of a trip to the doctor.

Emma made her by-now-umpteenth trip to the hospital on the day of Seth's birth. We all three lurked around all day, reading and discussing *Hello* magazine, and assorted problem pages, passing the time of day, waiting for the Caesarean to happen, which it finally did in the late afternoon. Emma wasn't allowed to be there and we kissed her goodbye on the ward.

A lovely woman who had helped with Dora's delivery did the midwife part at Seth's extraction. It was a strange experience. As at our first encounter with Melody, there was a large audience, though this one was less enthusiastic. The consultant kept shouting 'not like that!' at the registrar who was doing the operation. There was a casual conversation going on between two of the bit-part players about their holiday destinations. Someone wanted some music so we had Jazz FM; first of all, some sub-Sinatra pumping out an aggressive number, then *I'm a Barbie Girl*. Meanwhile after a great deal of anxious rummaging Seth emerged, a little waxy white ghost, and cried with feeble surprise. So did Hugh and I, clutching him and each other. So did Emma when we all three reappeared on the ward.

Melody showed up that night with a person she'd made out of a wooden spoon and a J-cloth. She was pleased to see Seth and sat him seriously on her knee. Later she used to stump around the house using all her strength to carry him and clucking to him in a matronly way. Miraculously she loved him immediately and has never stopped. She was angry with me, though, and I felt absolutely terrible initially about what we'd done to her. I felt for a bit that we'd ruined her life, even though her devotion to Seth was so quickly apparent.

I was particularly guilty and anxious about breastfeeding. I felt that bottles had permitted Hugh and me to split Melody's care 50/50, and breasts now compelled me to give Seth 100 per cent. Oddly, after decades of being hopeless at getting pregnant, staying pregnant, and giving birth, I found that my breasts were well up to the challenge of sustaining life. This was very consolatory, and had the result that Seth continued to breastfeed until he was two and a half. Melody dealt with this phlegmatically by adopting a matron's role in Seth's early days. When he cried she used to bustle over and organise a breast for his consumption.

As a result of Seth's passion for the breast, I was 44 by the time I went back to the clinic to get Seth's siblings put back. We probably made stupid and sentimental decisions about this, but so far from making a diaspora, all Seth's brothers and sisters were melted at once after their long frozen spell. If any of them had been born they would have been well over four years younger than him. One embryo responded gallantly to its emergence from the professor's freezer and two others survived it. None of them stuck. I was sad about this but not disproportionately so. We'd had *two* bits of extraordinary luck by then.

I remained a bit like a Victorian parent with Seth, too stoical when he was ill, slightly fatalistic, although at the same time I was deeply moved by his arrival and thrilled at his existence. This static state was partly to do with anxiety for Melody and partly just being a bit deadened to risk by our many experiences of it. Seth was a delightfully mild baby, and I only really recognised his feebleness in hindsight, although when a GP suggested that he might have cystic fibrosis, and referred him for investigation, I recognised that he must be a bit off the map. He was sweet and uncomplaining and he didn't die, but he came close to it when he was 8 months old and got pneumonia after having chicken-pox. Huge doses of IV penicillin did him much more good it seemed than all my visits to the osteopathic centre – where his origins were sharply disapproved of – and after being almost dead for a few days he throve as never before and has not looked back.

He and Melody both know their stories. We have stressed the common ground between them, so they both think of themselves as having two mums. They told their Granny, Emma's and my mum, this recently, and she was tickled pink. Melody has begun to think about the fact that she has two dads as well. She thinks from time to time about how different her situation is from Seth's, and she grieves a bit for her absent family. She went through a phase of asking us to call her by her birth mum's surname, and from time to time she says to us that we aren't her real mum and dad. When she was younger she had lots of fantasies about her time with her birth mum. They were charming stories, and, at their most evolved, her birth mum would foster lots of baby wild animals in her garden, with which Melody helped her. Then the babies' parents came back to claim them, and Melody and her birth mum were invited to join them in the jungle.

We feel that Melody's ability to confront her heritage now is probably a sign of confidence, though time will tell. Recently she was gassing to someone, an adult, over the garden wall in Hackney and told them, 'I would have had a big sister but she died.' For obvious reasons we have never explained things to her in this way, and it seemed a cheerful view of her destiny.

Seth is very matter of fact. It isn't particularly clear that he understands how he came to be, and it is harder to explain his arrival to him because the biological detail is still difficult for him to grasp at his age. He has the modest advantage that he does not have to fantasise about his origins, as he is close to all three people who played a part in engendering him.

Melody and Seth know other adopted children, and at their school there are many other children who are products of donated genetic material, in particular many children of lesbian couples, so neither of them will ever feel especially unusual, I think. It is of course not clear whether the fact that Seth's life would have been unthinkable shortly before it became commonplace will matter to children like Seth or not. I expect we will be upbraided for bringing him about when he's an adolescent, and no doubt Melody will have much to say about our interference in her life, but I don't expect the invective to be much more poisonous than the things more routine children think and say of their parents in adolescence.

Perhaps when they are grown up they may have a stronger sense of loose threads and of regret than we do, of people unfound and ties unacknowledged. Melody will certainly look for her birth family and may not find them. At the moment I think I would be happy if I thought our kids' lifetimes might be dull enough to allow them to grieve over their antecedents when they are middle-aged in the way that we have had the luxury of doing in our generation.

Meanwhile, right now, in the dying days of 2001, I wonder if it was a mistake to make a life, and I treasure every moment with our kids.

Chapter 12

Gifts of life *in absentia*

Regenerative fertility and the puzzle of the 'missing genetrix'

Monica Konrad

Monica Konrad is a social anthropologist.

Bypassing: a side note on side routes

IVF practitioners and recipients of assisted reproduction will often refer to the new procreative technologies as pragmatic ways of bypassing childlessness rather than as effective treatments for the condition of infertility itself. Bypassing childlessness as technique is proffered in such contexts both as semantic guidance (the 'protocol' informing clinical instruction) and as a valid register of local explanation: here prospective parents and clinicians each *appear* to reinforce the other's interest through mutual engagement and agreement. And so it is that the standard story-line of assisted conception is itself conceived at the clinic as a potted account of human 'biology'. Should a couple be fortunate enough to achieve parenthood through the making of the euphemistic 'take-home' baby, this is generally attributable to an instrumental 'fix': to a view of one particular understanding of 'nature' working upon another such folk understanding of innate corporeal rhythms and bodily process.[1]

What precisely is at work, the critical bio-ethnographer may infer, is the trickery of 'nature' and its dependence on a mainly mechanised conception of the 'natural' physiological constitution of each ('individual') person so treated. The temporal illusions of synchronisation between hormonally stimulated 'cycling' women – evident for instance as the sharing of fertility between ova donors and recipients in their relational capacity as procreative 'partners' – can never be understood to stand in for a real treatment or 'cure'. Techniques of assistance are in this sense more than simply substitutive: technology may give nature a 'helping hand' but, like nature, facilitation is prone to error and fallibility.[2] And yet the extent to which reproductive technology itself can be recognised in the popular imagination as the cultivation of new relations of interdependence has remained variously elusive. The persistence of such elision, I would suggest, is an ethnographic curiosity of considerable cultural interest. The interest is not simply one easily confined to the analytical preoccupations of social anthropologists, who, one might add, are more routinely concerned with understanding how conception theories – as the organisation of sexual reproduction in a given context – underlie forms of power and social organisation across different cultures. It is also necessarily an interest of direct relevance to many 'applied' problems and contexts of decision-making:

to the work of health practitioners in the field of reproductive medicine, to the formulations of policy analysts and bioethicists; as well as to the general public more broadly, that is, to each person in their differential capacity to take certain decisions as potential reproductive agents.

This chapter is intended as a critical commentary on reproductive gifts of life that extend well beyond the entity of individual 'persons' as originally denoted by the classic Maussian formulation of the gift relationship.[3] Specifically, it is concerned with one aspect of such a puzzle of identification: the cultural valuing of the category of the 'missing genetrix', particularly the notion of reproduction *in absentia* as both symbolic and material conduit for the intergenerational transmission of forms of extensional life ('fertility'). I hope to show how an anthropological commentary on certain of these reproductive developments can speak to multiple (non-anthropological) audiences, and why it might be fruitful to take the time not to bypass the generative source of such insights. In the cut and thrust sensationalism of much contemporary media reportage, the function of technological taboo – typically encompassed through the fear-generating iconography of the 'slippery slope' – has its own cultural role to play in initiating (and simulating) questions of regulation and accountability, and notions of risk and progress. It is not the aim of this chapter to excite moral pronouncements and the following comments are not intended as a direct contribution to the field of 'bioethics'. Rather, my concern here is to facilitate the longview of reflexivity through various sites for comparison and thus to make possible the simultaneity (or holding constant) of plural perspectives. Opening up a small side route (as a culturally enhanced 'bypass'), the hope is that several interested parties will reflect on the terms of reference whereby contention is seen to create 'debate' as issues Westerners think they can most readily perceive as relevant to our own times.

Procreation *in absentia*: what is so 'new' about the new reproductive technologies?

One of the by-products of extra-corporeal reproductive techniques such as IVF – besides the material facilitation of new progeny – is the growing moral sentiment that the cultural elision between childlessness and infertility is itself an overly narrow homology for instructive comparison. Many of the ethical and social dilemmas relating to assisted reproduction may be perceived as cultural problems precisely because 'non-traditional' ways of bypassing maternity and paternity as intentional acts of parental self-actualisation have now come so explicitly to view as new 'facts of life'. To be childless is no longer simply a matter of subjective volition, nor necessarily an index of a patient's long-term reproductive health. More radical still, at least for the Euro-American imaginary – given the conventional assumption that the English feel they relate to one another when persons become visible as individuals – is the realisation that it is not possible to equate childlessness straightforwardly with a person who has not in some specific way 'conceived' a child.

The term 'genetrix' is generally and with good reason unfamiliar to clinicians and other health professionals working in the field of reproductive medicine. I import it deliberately into the debate from its traditional locus within a specific anthropological literature on kinship relations, and suggest that it can be pressed into service as a useful shorthand descriptive for a particular kinship eclipse evoked in real physical terms by the absent figure of 'mother-to-have-been'.

When the anthropologist John Barnes (1973) suggested in the early 1960s that the category of physical fatherhood be broken down analytically to discriminate between different notions of the 'physical', he drew important attention to the distinctions between the genetic father, the genitor and pater.[4] By shifting emphasis away from the primacy of so-called 'genetic kinship', Barnes showed how the Western assumption of a unique and necessarily male genitor (the monogenetic premise of 'one child, one genitor') could not be invoked straightforwardly as 'natural' fact (Barnes 1961: 298). What can be reconfigured today in the post-genome era as new pharmaceutical experiments or as predictive embodiments of 'genetic kinship' through genetic testing technology also take us back to old 'traditional' questions about substance and knowledge (see Strathern 2000). On the one hand, how the female equivalents of genetic mother, genetrix and mater are to be conceptualised has been largely overlooked in anthropological theory, in part quite legitimately so because we have no ethnographic record of a society for which the concept of maternity is entirely absent.[5] But, John Barnes and other kinship commentators on the parthenogenesis 'virgin birth' debates in the late-1960s were writing at a time when physical motherhood could be assumed as self-evident truths for all to see. Since then, the advent of the new life technologies has made knowledge about the status of maternity less 'macroscopic' – in Barnes's (1973: 68) terms. Not only do laboratory technicians and others work routinely with the aid of microscopes and other new optical instruments such as *in vivo* nanoscopes, but life itself has become miniaturised and the assumed connections between persons and body parts have become far less visible, far less ascertainable as certain knowledge. Whilst 'missing' knowledge about what counts as relatedness between persons could previously be pushed away as the ethnographic problem of distant others, safely attributed to particular peoples – as with Bronislaw Malinowski's claim, well-rehearsed by subsequent generations of anthropologists, that the Trobrianders of Papua New Guinea were simply 'ignorant' of physiological paternity[6] – now, it is simply easier to see (and directly sense) how body parts, removed from the person in whom they can be said to have 'originated', circulate extracorporeally in space and time across multiple bodies. However, there is very little public knowledge, outside of medico-scientific circles, about how these technologies entail the microprocessing of *ex vivo* substance as specific trajectories of time and temporality.

These points are germane to other forms of absence and particularly to the question of what can count in cultural terms as innovative about the 'new' reproductive technologies, in contrast to a previous generation of 'technologies' such as the contraceptive pill. One could offer many answers, prime amongst which would be the way that assisted forms of conception obviate the need for procreative partners, male and female, to be physically self-present as whole (gendered) persons in their own acts of human (genetic) reproduction. This separation of the person from his/her genetic substance as forms of 'irrelational kinship' – as the instantiation of relations of non-relations – transpired as a major theme of interest during the author's ethnographic field research on gamete and embryo donation in mid-1990s Britain. The experiences of anonymised ova donors and recipients, especially women's own idioms of assistance and how these departed from the wider biomedical rubric of altruistic 'gifts of life', imported from an earlier bio-ethics and social policy literature on organ and blood transplantation, became the subject of my doctoral research (Konrad 1996).[7] How women involved in procreative acts in which they need not be physically self-present make such reproductions culturally meaningful to themselves and engage as embodied moral agents raises issues of profound cultural importance. However, these are questions which none the less tend still to be overlooked in mainstream public policy debate. One might for instance point to the way that the centralised collection of archived 'pen portraits' that gamete donors are encouraged to write at the time of donation is not evoked *primarily* as bio-information to be read by genetic offspring as retrospective *testimonies of assistance*.[8]

The sociality of anonymity happens to be just one potent and rather obvious rubric for instancing why the dilemma of the 'missing genetrix' comes to constitute a cultural puzzle at all (Konrad 1996, 1998). When the editors of the volume suggested I might be interested to read the section on kinship, one observation above all caught my anthropological interest, in the chapters 10 and 11 'Seth' and 'The story of Seth's egg'. In explaining what it might mean for two biologically related sisters to 'share' a child as differently invested 'mothers', Flora Scrimgeour and Emma Scrimgeour were not just talking about how Seth came into being as an IVF-conceived baby. The sisters were also talking about how the child's genetic mother comes into being as a socially validated relative (kin person) and relation. Emma, Seth's genetic mother and the child's maternal aunt, is one step removed from direct social parentage and everyday care, yet simultaneously establishes degrees of relatedness as genetrix with a child that might otherwise be considered her (biological) 'own'. As Emma puts it, theirs is 'a house without taboos' (p. 108) in which children may appreciate with openness the multiple kinship of co-existing mothers within self-styled 'chosen families'.[9] Recalling comments made by the children during a car journey, Emma dispels views of necessarily maladjusted offspring as she repeats Melody's (Flora's adopted daughter) observations delivered from the back seat:

> 'Emma, you know, Seth and I both have two mothers. I have my mother and Flora is my mother and Seth has you and Flora is his mother too.' It was said with absolute certainty and without a trace of confusion. I looked round and Seth was nodding his head and grinning.

Yet it is Flora, as ova recipient and social mother, who brings to attention the fact that Emma's donated egg was seen foremost as part of a common heritage, rather than the specific biogenetic substance of a specific person (p. 113). In other words, Flora makes explicit as local kinship knowledge how Emma's own 'gift' of donation – enacted here as the subjective decision to transmit her capacity for fertility to her sibling – is not perceived as equivalent to a uniquely material substrate. The ova Emma subsequently donated to Flora (and which transform her into a sibling-validated genetrix) are not envisioned as entities bound to one woman's particular and singular genetic make-up and 'natural' physiological constitution. In this reckoning of relatedness Emma and Flora are both appealing to social memory and the importance of others as intergenerational relations: the gift of life here is part of a particular conception of consubstantiality about what it means to be 'related' ancestrally across genealogical time and space.

It is worth mentioning at this point that in the formalist genealogies of mid-twentieth century functional-structuralism, anthropological representations of idealised genealogical space-time used the trope (and method) of the pedigree and (genealogical) tree to depict the temporal passage of the generations.[10] Genealogy was seen to serve as metaphor for the spatial and temporal co-ordinates of territory and generational age-reckoning. But genealogies – even then – could be drawn upon as devices for the artificial compression of biological relatedness and the seeming preservation of social time. 'Telescoping genealogies' was a way of ensuring that the line of descent from the founding ancestor to the present generation remained a line that could be traced. As anthropologist Alfred Gell observes, the telescoping of family genealogy was about 'silently revising the content of accepted beliefs about the identities of ancestors, so that the line of descent from the founding ancestor to presently living individuals does not exceed a certain number of generations' (Gell 1992: 21).

In order both to foreground and to question how the assignment of social value to extracorporeal body parts has remained a culturally elusive task in public discourse on genetic donation, the following sections juxtapose various exemplars of reproduction *in absentia*. Each of these exemplars, as pieces of a contemporary reproductive puzzle, may be read or refracted as a genealogical re-reckoning of the kinship entity identifiable as 'mother-to-have-been'. As a succession of case studies they also show how the debates over different forms of genetic donation in Britain have been conducted around many genealogical 'silences' (*pace* Gell), rather than ideological revisions.

Pieces of the puzzle: juxtaposing different 'mothers-to-have-been'

Case study I: The 'foetal mother'

'It is in the nature of human beings to intervene to try to shape their world.' This declaration of human agency was made by the Human Fertilisation and Embryology

Authority (HFEA 1994a: 2) in the context of a public debate in mid-1990s Britain addressing the legal, social and moral implications of using ovarian tissue from adults, cadavers and aborted foetuses. After issuing a public consultation paper and inviting comments from the general public and professional bodies, the report was to conclude that only tissue from live donors would be acceptable for the treatment of female infertility. The use of tissue from foetuses, living women, and cadavers from girls or women who had died was however permitted in the case of embryo research.[11]

In the case of transplanting ovarian tissue from aborted foetuses, a key policy objection centred on the perception that the child's mother would not only have died *before* the child would have been conceived, but that 'she' herself would never actually have lived. In this sense, the notion of 'skipping' a generation (HFEA 1994a: 6) is seen to be tantamount to the paradox of 'breaking a natural law of biology'. Section 21 of the Public Consultation Document states:

A potential difficulty might be thought to be that *a generation of human development would be skipped* if foetal ovarian tissue were used in infertility treatment. Ovarian tissue or eggs from an aborted foetus have not been subjected to the pressures which govern survival and normal development to adulthood. This raises questions about the degree of risk of abnormality, at present unquantifiable, in embryos produced using such tissue. This might be seen as breaking a natural law of biology.

(emphasis added)

This concern with breaking a natural law of biology is an implicit reference to the evolutionary paradigm of social Darwinism which posits human nature as a continually evolving community of genealogical descent: the 'community in embryonic structure reveals community of descent', wrote Darwin in *The Origin of Species*.[12] In this consanguineal model of filiation by shared blood, to skip a generation would be tantamount to creating wilfully a missing link between persons and between the generations. The literary theorist Gillian Beer (1992) has suggested that the obsession with the missing link in the popular imagination of late Victorian Britain had as much to do with attempts to reinforce degrees of cultural distance as it did with seeking out ties for social connection. Man, she notes, was still just 'hypothetical' and so long as a 'gap' could be seen to remain between humans and animals, between races and species and between social classes, the supremacy of the image of the human could remain intact (Beer 1992: 22). By playing on this paradox of keeping what is cherished both distant and near, the project of man's hypothetical 'kinship' could be kept unfinished and could remain productively unresolved.

This Victorian paradox of wanting to locate the missing link in order to refute its very existence would seem to have several parallels more than a century later in 'high tech' Britain (as indeed elsewhere), where the fascination with skipping generations in reproductive discourse is also precisely the dread of being able to locate 'lost' links. On the one hand, biotechnology is seen to make 'persons' publicly visible as agents involved in the violation of their own (biological) mechanism of natural selection.[13] While, on the other, it is public knowledge (as the opening declaration of the HFEA report confirms) that it is part of the very 'nature' of human beings to make interventions. It is between these elisions of what counts as human nature that the notion of 'skipping' a generation can be seen to depend foremost on having *already* equated the value of the entity of the foetus with that of the category of the mother (see Hall 1994). According to this temporal sequencing of relations and events, the presumption of what constitutes the boundaries of the natural and the unnatural rests on the way that the figure of the 'mother', as the foetus, comes to be defined as an assumed presence whose identity would be known – or else could be surmised hypothetically – in terms of the establishment of links premised on specifically cultural ideas about *genetic* continuity. In other words, the cultural equation of the aborted foetus with 'mother' pertains to a way of thinking organised around the privileging of an ideology of biogenetic kinship. If it is thought that a generation is skipped, this is because the category of 'mother' breaks the rule of lineal descent reckoning, a reckoning whose prime imperative would be to trace back via genealogy from where this relation originated. 'She' – as the foetus/mother symbiosis – is symbolically homologous to the illicit act of having converted the blood tie into the disparity of a self-evident missing link, namely that which both uncomfortably connects and disconnects mother and offspring from each other. There is no natural selection here, only an 'organism' whose biological sequestration shows up a parentage of *obviously* indeterminate origins.

Recognising the theoretical inflexibility of the category 'generation' to incorporate change, Rodney Needham's (1974) scepticism towards the concept of human generation (albeit problematically set against what he saw as the malleability of genealogy to make adjustments to past events) was also an early voice wary of the synthesising pretensions of mid-century British kinship theory. The 'foetal mother' figure is perhaps one of the most graphic examples of the 'silent' reconfiguration of genealogy, territoriality and temporality, since 'she' shows how temporal relationships can no longer be expressed in the traditional genealogical idiom of natural biology. It is evident, at least in this context, that genealogical time can no longer be taken to 'stand in' for the succession of generations, and likewise that the contemporary concern with the genealogical mapping of the person as corporeal topology (witness the effects of the Human Genome Project with regard to both medical anatomy training and genetics research) is no longer simply interchangeable with concepts of territory or landscape as spatially bounded.

Case study II: Female posthumous reproduction

Following on from the 'death' of the foetus-mother as viable kinship entity in British statute, another instancing of the category of 'mother-to-have-been' is evident in those cases of clinically dead women whose bodies endure artificially sustained pregnancies in order to 'save' the life of (already gestating) embryos after fatal accidents. There have been a handful of such cases reported from Britain, America, Europe and Australia (Hunt 1992), though perhaps the most notable was the case of 'Marion P'. Marion Poch, an 18-year-old dental assistant from Erlangen in Germany, was at the time of her fatal car accident carrying a 14-week-old embryo of unknown paternity. Poch suffered massive injuries resulting in brain death and the formal issuing of her death certificate. As it happened, her gestating embryo was quite unharmed in the accident. Poch's parents, having professed they would go to any extent to save the life of their prospective grandchild, also pledged that they were prepared to adopt the baby. In the event they managed to persuade the medical authorities and their insurance company to keep Marion's corpse 'alive' in order that it could sustain the delivery by Caesarean section five months later. Marion as 'genetic mother' was kept 'alive' on artificial respiration, and during the course of the pregnancy an intravenous drip pumped her corpse with vital nutrients and hormones for the gestating embryo (Hunt 1992).

Tragic as such cases are, they are fascinating for the questions they raise about social agency, embodiment and reproduction. Who was doing and giving what to whom as the relational extension of one person's life? Who really gave birth to Marion's child and in what sense will Marion's kin remember her as a 'childless' daughter? Should we value life simply from the point of view of the pregnant mother, or should we draw on a wider perspective to take account of a broader range of implicated 'kin', including those not yet born? In Poch's case, her embryo as embryonic pre-life form, her embryo as potential child-to-be, her parents, her ex-boyfriend as genetic father (who incidentally it is claimed wanted no part as social father/pater) and the clinical team in charge of her 'care' can all be seen as playing their part in the 'birth' of Marion's child. The nurses and doctors, the ethical committee at the hospital, the lawyers, the insurance brokers were all 'assisting' as co-procreators. Here we can see clearly too that establishing claims over birth is more than a matter of which biological parent has contributed, and is recognised as having contributed, what kind of bodily substance and indeed what kind of nurturance.[14]

The case of Howard and Jean Garbner from California, USA, predeceased by their young daughter, Julie (1968–96), also received much press attention as a controversial 'case' of uncertain cultural resolution. Julie in fact had herself chosen to have her eggs cryopreserved after brain surgery and treatment for leukaemia, a decision which enabled her parents after her death to claim that they wished to 'recreate' their late daughter through a surrogate host pregnancy.[15] The press gave critical attention to the case, portraying Julie (and the out-surviving Garbner kinsfolk) as giving birth 'from beyond the grave'. The idea that 'old' persons might be regenerated through posthumous procreation takes us back again to the paradox of both simultaneously asserting and denying what can count culturally as the physical evidence of 'missing' links. Yet listening closely to what family members say about their kinship losses, these attempted reproductions do not appear to be about equating body parts with propertied selves, as is so commonly depicted in medico-legal debate. Rather they seem to be about the potential of biotechnology to help preserve and distribute social memory (of the deceased) across surviving kin.[16]

Here is Howard Garbner, Julie's father, on plans for his grandchild-to-be, whom he hopes will be a girl-child:

> We will call her Simcha, which was Julie's Hebrew name. It means happiness. It reflects what Julie's memory evokes for us . . . we [Howard and Jean] have never closed our minds to the idea of having more than one of Julie's embryos implanted in a surrogate mother. We [parents and Julie's sisters] would be willing to bring up several of her babies if that were possible . . . in a blink I can bring Julie back in my mind's eye. Within a year I want to hold a grandson or daughter who looks just like her.
>
> (Craig and Bourne 1996)

Case study III: Transplanting fertility and idioms of recycling (Delia and Fay)

Delia and Fay are busy mothers in their early thirties with young pre-school children who responded to advertisements in the local press; calling for anonymous donors to volunteer to help infertile women get pregnant.[17] By drawing parallels between various aspects of her social identity and domestic life to describe how 'things' can keep on being effective through different kinds of action, Delia is talking about how several aspects of her life – her household organisation, the kids' toys, events like car boot sales, as well as her own body parts – have no essential value as 'natural' property:

> When I found out that they could use me, that they could use my eggs, I was just really chuffed . . .'
>
> 'I was maybe a bit of use that I helped . . . we believe in recycling. We buy recycled paper, we keep all our newspapers separate and our tin cans – we're very much into that. It's the same sort of thing with my car boot sales – I'm just recycling my junk. I think it's a very good idea. They take on a new lease of life, I think. You've got things that are of no use to you anymore.'
>
> 'I bought that little rocking horse from a friend and yet it sat in her room collecting dust – it drives me mad now it's got a terrible squeak to it, but it's made a difference to the kids' lives – that's given a whole new . . . because the kids love it. And yet in my friend's house it just sat there. I think it's the same if I were dead, my heart wouldn't be doing me anything but it could give somebody else so much – a whole life, whereas if I'm lying dormant, it's no use to me . . . my eggs are just absorbed now – nothing happens to them. You think of all the women that ovulate and nothing comes new, whereas get them out of the womb and they could help people . . .
>
> (Delia)

What seems both self-evident and counter-intuitive in this narrative is the way in which Delia's comparisons are all of the same order irrespective of interiorised/exteriorised corporeal difference: a rocking horse is akin to her own reproductive eggs. It is about *doing* 'recycling'. And recycling seems a fitting idiom for her to pick since what she is talking about is practices like ova donation in which the self (and the effects produced by one's action) can be kept temporally indefinite as open relations. Recycling a part of herself – life just keeps on going: ova donation is about Delia extending and transforming herself in space and time through a corporeal agency. From whom the egg has come and to whom it is going as it 'journeys' *ex vivo* are not relevant here: the egg is non-filiative; it is not something of determinate origins (cf. Emma Scrimgeour mentioned above).

Fay, another anonymous ova donor in her mid-thirties, also develops a variant of this recycling discourse with her vivid imagery of 'continuous circles' that seem as though they are 'peopled' with life. People come afresh 'on to the horizon', an intersubjective space-time, which is continually expanding as these newly enacted relations. What Fay thinks of as her multiply divisible body (the social horizon) is in fact the site of conducting these social relations.

> You certainly realise that it's amazing machinery, in the fact that as fast as you remove one bit, another bit appears – particularly with that area. It certainly makes you think very hard about that bit of your body – when you consider what it does. No machinery can do that. Produce something out of nothing. They have to have something to start with. You're basically one large conveyor belt. As fast as something is chopped off the end, somebody else is coming over onto the top, like an escalator almost. As fast as it drops off one end, as soon as somebody gets off at the bottom, somebody else gets on at the top and it goes like a continuous cycle and until the day when it actually stops. . . . It was only really since doing this once and now going through it again that it's really struck home the fact that this is how it is, and that as fast as you remove it, another one appears, as fast as you cut your nails, they grow. As fast as you cut your hair, it grows. There's always something there to replace it. . . . As fast as one donor gives and receives, there's usually another donor on the horizon also waiting for somebody to receive. There will always be people waiting to receive . . . the world is made up of people giving and receiving. One company gives and then somebody gives back. And so it goes on . . . I am giving eggs, she's receiving them. Hopefully she's going to be giving life to the baby, and in return I'm receiving happiness for the fact that it all works out ok. It's all a case of giving something really. If somebody gives something, somebody has to take it, and vice versa. She takes an awful lot of risks. I am giving something to her. She takes risks, I basically take home the knowledge that I've done something to help somebody and hopefully she gives life to someone else. So it is always a continuous circle in that respect, not really around . . .
>
> (Fay)

As with Delia's narrative, Fay's reference to her interiorly active body and her person as someone involved in 'the world [as] made up of people giving and receiving' shows no switch of perspective between what is internal and external since social relations are 'seen' for the way that the body is composed of the (past and future-directed) actions of others. Fay's talk of unstoppable growth ties up with what she sees as the circulatory potential of continually renewable *re-circulations*: it is as fast as somebody gets off that somebody else gets on; it is as fast as you remove one thing that another thing appears; it is as fast as you cut your nails that they grow; it is as fast as one donor gives and someone receives that another donor will give and somebody else receive. Social transactions are the flows of 'a continuous cycle' in which everything must keep on going.

Since describing oneself and one's actions in terms of an embodied microcosm of social relations is hardly a usual feature of everyday conversation amongst women from any social class in any part of Britain, what is influencing and shaping her terms of reference? From where can we say Fay's discourse originates? One possibility is that media articles on the ethics of the intentional disposal of cryopreserved embryos and other related issues reach deep into contemporary consciousness and that headline-grabbing announcements such as 'A world of anguish in an inch of glass' (Moyes 1996) stir the imagination in profound ways. It could also be the case that various contemporary 'public understanding of science' initiatives are managing to take science out of the laboratory and into the home in genuinely effective and democratic ways. Both of these speculations raise a number of points about how, and the extent to which, science and culture intersect in the creation of popular imaginaries.[18]

Case study IV: Maternal connection as relational non-presence (Rita and Penny)

Rita is married, in her mid-thirties, the mother of two young children. It becomes clear over the course of our several meetings that certain aspects of her life history play a significant part in her experience of donation.

Rita was adopted as a young child and, though she has never met her birth mother, she says she has often wondered about her. She speaks of her affectionately, mentioning how hard she thinks it must have been for her mother as a single woman in the 1950s to have made the decision not to have a termination given the social stigma then of conceiving children out of wedlock. Also running through her account is some ambivalence about the status of her mother as an unknown, non-identifiable person. This seems, in part, to centre on what she knows to be the considerable difficulty of tracing her as a 'somebody' whom she can make into a 'known' relation.

> I just feel every now and again I would really like to see her . . . it's not a burning desire to come face to face with her. I'd like to. It doesn't matter. But I'd like to. It's a lot of hard work trying to trace her. . . . It must be hard to give

up a child and not to know where I was going . . . I don't know how much information she was given as to what the family was like that I was going to. I'm sure she was given some, but that's like with the egg donating . . . I'm doing the same sort of thing as my birth mother was doing and I am quite happy in one respect that the child, if there was one, would be alright . . . my mother gave me up for what she hoped was a better life and I'm giving a couple of my eggs to give them a better life, in the respect that they'll have children in it . . . I've given my eggs to somebody so hopefully their lives will be better . . .

(Rita)

In one sense, Rita appears to re-enact her birth mother's decision of many years ago when she chooses to give to another woman a part she has reproduced of herself. Though mother and daughter do not give away 'like' things of themselves in the genetic sense of identical body parts (as specific chromosomal alignments), they do enact similar kinds of relations in their capacity as social agents. They can both be seen as initiating and creating new relations. 'Through' a recipient who as untraceable 'stranger' stands in symbolically as the embodiment of her unknown 'lost' mother, Rita transforms the previously untraceable connections of the time of her birth into new kinds of continuities, new kinds of reproductions. In this way she makes a relatedness from out of the substance of her (as yet untraced) birth mother: she shares, as it were, in the substance of her mother through the symbolic, regenerative transformations she effects of the body parts her mother once 'gave' to her.

I would just like to say to my mother that everything is fine . . . that I've had a really good life and find out whether she had a good life as well . . . and I just feel closer to her now because I know what it would feel like to give children up – not that I have given a child up – but I felt closer to her even though I don't know her . . . because I have children and I know what she must have gone through to think . . . that I've got to have a better life without her . . . she couldn't give me the future that she obviously wanted to . . .

(Rita)

After donation, Rita is able to start the imaginative work that will make her 'like' her mother, a likeness that is independent of their consanguineal connection or genetic tie. Mother–daughter 'resemblance' is a non-genetical one constituted from out of the way that Rita, too, will never find out what happens to the reproductive part of herself she has given to somebody else. So the social person of 'Rita' may be seen as symbolising the relatedness that is the idea of a 'better life'. She enacts what it might have been like for her mother to transfer a baby that cannot be kept, and she also donates a way – a method – of making somebody else's life better – just like her mother, she imagines, once did for her. Rita's 'gift of life' to others is thus related to the 'life' her mother chose to give to her when she decided against the option of a termination. This becomes the unilateral activation of a 'relation'.

Comparisons with Penny, another donor in her early thirties, invite commentary too. Penny is unusual in the sense that she managed to get herself accepted on to the donation programme of one London clinic despite the fact that at the time of donation she did not already have children of her own and thus went against certain clinical criteria concerning desired donor eligibility. Adamant that donating ova is for her a kind of 'joint achievement' in which she gives her physical abilities for the financial abilities of others, she explains how she feels financially unable to bring up a child single-handedly and provide a materially comfortable environment.

> . . . and age being somewhat against me, I decided it would be a comfort to know that perhaps someone else could, well . . . the comfort of knowing there's a chance I may have a child through someone else who can give that child so much more than I could and who will cherish that child so much more due to the circumstances of his or her birth. If I ever do have a child of my own, the knowledge of the joy perhaps given to another woman which then has a ripple effect, touching other members of that family and friends . . . that's just great.
>
> (Penny)

When Penny refers to the possibility of herself having 'a [genetic] child of my own', she identifies herself as a culturally validated 'missing' genetrix in contrast to the conventional role of social mother. She goes on to qualify how her relation to motherhood revolves around her having provided and shared biogenetic substance, as well as being one that she can make meaningful without attributing to herself the 'fact' of biological ties (and followed up as the 'natural' expectations of mother–child uterine nurturance). It is these joint capacities, rather than biogenetic substances and physiological processes, that will be 'mixed' together, as it were, though these capacities are not envisaged by her as kinds of determinable value: body parts cannot be taken, or offered, for money. Her exteriorised fertility seems to accrue social value in the sense that it represents potential social relations that she might be prevented from activating, and in this sense her narrative concerns the way parts of herself are social relations already implicated in time: 'To me, donating eggs is a far more restricted donation than donating blood because of the limited productivity of a woman, so it's far more part of you, it's closer to me.'

Distinguishing between blood and reproductive organs in terms of what she sees as her finite biological capacity to reproduce, Penny donates not just a way for somebody else to have a child, but something that she will not be able to do a little later on. Her actions implicate her as another version of a 'missing genetrix' in the sense that she is none the less able to keep reproducing herself as a maternal identity in social space and time 'through' others (cf. Flora and Emma Scrimgeour, and Delia and Fay). But sweeping definitions of donations as altruistic behaviour miss the finer aspect of these kinds of embodied realities. When Penny conceives of the relations she makes from out of her body as kinds of continuing 'ripple effects', she is describing how she makes, or herself constitutes, certain kinship eventualities. 'Ripple effects' is the idiom she deploys to convey how body parts and persons circulate as value in social space and time; how a form of extensional relatedness is imagined as the shared substance of a regenerative fertility. She keeps making from out of herself 'new', that is, temporally infinite, relations; one person's body parts become bodies projected symbolically as persons forever expanding. And as with the other donors who participated in my study, the form her social agency takes is her anonymity: the way she embodies and gives cultural shape and meaning to the (common, non-propertied) body of 'anybody'.

Facilitating levels of comparison: turning the puzzle around

If a post-genealogical analysis pursues certain connections in terms of (past) traces of rupture and erasure, as well as prospective relations, what matters now in conceptual terms is through what kind of media it becomes possible to show that the former lines of filiation are shifting and being displaced. Certainly a critical response from cultural anthropology needs new instruments and new collaborations for tapping into the physicality of bodies, not for the purpose of revamping a physical kinship through a backdoor 'geneticisation' of medicine, but for tracking the embodied materiality of persons and body parts as temporally embedded and rehistoricised forms of 'nature'.

Taking aspects of technogenesis as the significant reproductive context here, I have attempted to trace the relation between the microprocessing of biology as new technique, and some of the cultural formations of a physical 'microkinship' in terms of a particular kinship eclipse: the social identity of the missing genetrix. But in the event this account has been caught in a seeming paradox. On the one hand, these examples show how it is no longer possible to address the 'becoming' of the human as a matter of the 'evolution' of an individuated biological organism. Just as the computer chip microprocesses vast amounts of data in infinitesimal amounts of time and changes our relationship to information, knowledge sourcing and management, so the infinitesimal replication of bio-substance in artificial 'growth' cultures temporally remodels life-forms and changes our knowledge of who we are and how we 'become' 'human', and thus what it means to factor in culturally notions of genealogy and genealogical reckoning. On the other hand, yet another effect of these technologies is to expose the limits of a non-materialist reading of biology and kinship. There is the danger that if analytical primacy is accorded to cultural kinship in terms of the *symbolism* of bodily substance alone (see Schneider 1968), a 'molecular' anthropology slips from view and the sheer materiality of 'engineered' or 'worked upon' substance is forgotten.

Yet there are other 'silent' paradoxes at work too that can get 'lost' in public debate. The genetically related sisters Emma Scrimgeour and Flora Scrimgeour, Marion Poch's parents from Germany, Howard and Jean Garbner from North America, and the British anonymous ova donors Delia, Fay, Rita and Penny all seem to be expressing sentiments about how they would like to extend and regenerate aspects of themselves and others in social time and space, whether to save an existing life or as the creation of new life.[19] Clearly, these kinds of sentiments, and the particularity of notions of 'assistance' they engender, are not getting incorporated into British legal statute, and it is questionable whether they are just starting to trickle through into some of the terms of debate on 'genetic altruism' informing the bioethics agenda on developments in biomedical technology (see, for example, Human Genetics Commission 2002: 37–38). When turning for comparative relief to the anthropological record, however, it is instructive to see how for other cultures the notion of a 'good' death can be conceived as a 'handing over of a vitality which can then be recycled' (Bloch and Parry 1982: 17).

A large body of Melanesian and Oceanic ethnography, for example, explores the symbolic linkages between images of birth, death and rebirth, portraying indigenous conceptions of the creation of social bonds in terms of local procreational idioms. Seen as cycles of exchange regulated by cycles of death, a key instancing of this regenerative reproduction of persons is the mortuary transactions marking the rites of the dead in which the deceased person is thought of as somebody 'taken apart' and reconstituted in new form during and after these transactions.[20] The so-called biological death of a person is seen to entail a redistribution of aspects of the deceased that are thought to reside subsequently in others (Weiner 1995: 135), such that 'the social person of the deceased (the aspect of a person that participates in the personae of others) is not diminished but *expanded to the limits of his or her social circle*' (Wagner 1989: 267; emphasis added). These ideas about extension all concern the belief that death brings with it the separation and release of valuable resources for use in new productive contexts, ideas that are enacted ritually in terms of the cultural attention paid to the deceased as the embodiment of – and crucially the temporality of – reordering new sets of social relations (or 'persons').[21]

Writing on the 'Aré 'Aré society of Malaita (Solomon Islands), for instance, Daniel de Coppet describes how it is the '*everlasting* work of mourning' which, as it were, 'feeds' the society and simultaneously is the substance of the 'Aré 'Aré person (de Coppet 1981: 179). The social management of death both creates the foundations of normative social order and is reflected in the internal composition of 'the person' as living substance made up from the three different elements of the 'body' (*rape*), the 'breath' (*manomano*) and the 'image' (*nunu*). This mutual interdependence of the social order in the power of the corporeal element, and vice versa, means that 'the society ['Aré 'Aré] builds up its own character of permanence through the repeated dissolution *into* the ritual and exchange process of the main elements composing each individual' (de Coppet 1981: 176). The 'image' of the dead person can only be completed as a part of previously sanctioned ancestors. It is by means of the *long-term* exchange of money between different kin groups that the 'image' enters ancestral life thereby cancelling out (in idiomatic terms taking the symbolic form of *eating* or *leaving to rot*) the 'images' of earlier ancestors and regenerating death as the life of new 'bodies' and new 'breaths'. In this way, the 'Aré 'Aré ensure that the complete dead person's 'image' is constituted out of pieces of money whose origins are the 'images' of other ancestors that have been displayed at one time or another at previous feasts. What this particular cultural system shows, then, is how the social circulation of the dead is achieved by the *continual transformative replacements of parts of the person* which become the simultaneous constitution of the person as a 'self-feeding process where nothing is ever lost' (de Coppet 1981: 192; and compare with the above case studies: I –IV).

If, by offsetting these Melanesian notions of life against Western practices of foetal tissue transplantation and genetic donation, the analytic effect is one that enables us to foreground how, upon the event of death, the possibilities for undoing and 'deconceiving' persons (Mosko 1983) defy a purely biological construction of the individual/body parts, then the ethnographic lens may be turned another few degrees or so to ask yet another set of questions. In what sense could one say that social anthropologists describing indigenous conceptions of the long-term regeneration of society – both as the legitimisation of an enduring socio-political order and as the continual re-embedding of ancestral spirits in the foetus of unborn clan members (see Poole 1984) – have drawn implicitly upon certain features of Western biological and philosophical theory such as epigenesis, recapitulation theory and the nature of unconscious organic memory? Further, how could these 'missing' features contribute to the shaping of our guiding theme of anonymous sociality and the 'puzzle' of making gifts of life *in absentia*?

Nineteenth-century European *Naturphilosophie* and *Völkerpsychologie* attracted a number of natural science and literary proponents of organic memory theory who both contributed to and departed from Darwin's theories of evolution in significant ways. The idea that memory was a fundamental reproductive capability of all living matter, and that the temporal linearity of direct descent ensured transmission beyond the individual life span, found expression for instance in Ernst Haeckel's attribution of a mnemonic faculty to individual cells and molecules, and was part of August Weismann's thesis (1893) of the non-changing property of the germ-plasm. An understanding of life as supra-individual in the specific sense that organisms and bodies could be constructed as the mere vehicles through which the continuity of life (conflated with genetic energy) could be transmitted also informed Haeckel's biogenetic law of recapitulation. Like Lamarck's law of the inheritance of acquired characters, Haeckel's thesis (1920) implied that the present organism contained its past within it, and that one could thus read ancestral and species development (phylogeny) by observing individual development (ontogeny). In other words, with his claim that the past development of society is 'recapitulated' in the development of the embryo, Haeckel and several other naturalists were advancing a view of the world compressed or telescoped into miniaturised form: 'a world order in miniature' (cf. case study III above).[22]

The idea that deep inside the invisible folds of 'primitive' tissue the embryo contains its yet-to-be realised human counterpart, the 'civilised' person, carries not only a future-directed pull, but one that links the embryo temporally to what is presumed to be its ostensibly shared evolutionary past. A belief that, in miniaturised form, the embryo condenses past stages of primitive development seems to replay the nineteenth-century European obsession with species differentiation, conjectures about the 'missing' link, and the 'recapitulating' relations between ontogeny and phylogeny.

Contemporary genome analysis also unravels itself as a version of organic memory theory. The knowledge that micro-organisms such as retroviruses (for example, HIV) insert their own DNA into the genome of the living cells they infect, so carrying with them 'past time', has given rise to the claim that as much as 1 per cent of the human genome is thought to be composed of fossil retroviruses that infected sperm and eggs millions of years ago.[23] Or consider the explanation of 'artificial cloning' techniques through recourse to time. Taking a single cell from an animal or human and persuading it to begin development again to produce the original organism's genetic twin may be explained in terms of asexual repro-duction, an intentional bypassing of procreative sex. Another interpretation, however, is that imprints from a previous generation have been 'borrowed'. The cloning of Dolly the sheep, from an udder cell of a ewe, has been described as making 'a mature, specialised gland cell "remember" its potential to generate a whole sheep'.[24] Further, the idea that *all* of past evolution can be read retro-spectively from the genome (a telescoping of past development) is also an implicit feature of the Human Genome Diversity Project: of the aim to gain insights into human origins, evolution, patterns of migration and reproduction and the global distribution of genetic disease. In just the same way that Haeckel's recapitulation theory posited a mythic simultaneity with primal 'archetypal' experience, belief in the substance of a truly global and transnational kinship – here encompassed by the ubiquitous techno-genome – fulfils a similar function in so far as it presumes the possibility of faultless transmission through past time.

It is also possible to see a modified version of Weismannian biophilosophy in debates about germ-line gene therapy and the immortalisation of life that is beyond, or not subject to, individual live human bodies. The insertion of engineered genes into the germ-cells of human embryos, for the purpose of eradicating major infectious diseases, would not only alter each treated person's genotype, as in the case of somatic-cell therapy, but would also impact upon the genetic constitution of all subsequent generations. As the geneticist Richard Lewontin puts it, 'future generations [who] would also have undergone the therapy *in absentia*' (Lewontin 1995: 55, emphasis original). Implicitly, future generations stand to 'inherit' their ancestors' morality and do so quite literally in the sense that physical changes to the germ-line are effects that get registered on everyone's body.

Such 'manipulations' of time also call for revised conceptions of human agency. When one turns to consult the anthropological record once more, the seemingly infinite regenerative capacities of the Melanesian/Oceanic agent look less certain than they did on first reading. This constitutes another twist or half-turn of our puzzle. Although de Coppet's analysis is concerned with the temporal aspect of a regenerative logic, and is particularly attentive to the theme of the symbolic conversion of loss as a positive resource, his account of 'Aré 'Aré society obviates the need for a theory of social agency by stressing the inevitability by which 'chains [of transformation] are not so much invented as rather blindly and faithfully followed' (de Coppet 1981: 201). One cannot help wondering from where de Coppet derived his imagery of 'chains'. Could the neo-Darwinian language of genes as blind and indifferent self-replicating entities have got mixed up here with the late-Victorian fascination with the Great Chain of Being and all the European arrogance of the white man's superiority contained in such models? That question is beyond the scope of the present chapter, but it is worth pointing out that there are important consequences with regard to how we proceed to interpret these ostensibly 'local' British notions of 'regeneration'.

I would like to draw to a close with a brief backtracking. Earlier, in the presentation of case study III, I left hanging a question about Fay, one of the British informants who participated in my egg donation study. What was it, I asked, that had influenced and shaped the key terms of her discourse? Was it not somewhat counterintuitive that she had conjured the world, as it were, into an egg? It would seem theoretically crude and misleading to say that she is like certain Melanesian agents who can draw the world effortlessly inside herself, just as it would to say that her miniaturised world view confirms the former European belief in ontogenetic/phylogenetic recapitulation. Both such possibilities are perhaps worth a moment's reflection, if only to question how and from where we, as reflective commentators on assisted conception practices, derive our own theoretical 'origins'. This chapter has attempted to foreground these kinds of 'origins' questions by way of different aspects or 'pieces' of a reproductive puzzle. Namely, I have been concerned to ask and to posit how our Western conceptualisation of the significance of the difference between the genetic mother and the 'missing genetrix' ironically enacts a certain cultural disappearance of 'self' as social 'death' and intergenerational transmission of 'life'. I hope others will see the merits of different kinds of bypassing activities and the prime importance of paying even greater attention to the real embodied experiences of procreative agents as multi-sourced persons.

Acknowledgements

My thanks are due to all the donors and recipients and their families who put up with my repeated enquiries; to consultant gynaecologists, nurse co-ordinators, counsellors and the staff at donor banks attached to assisted conception units; and to the staff of the Human Fertilisation and Embryology Authority for providing statistical information and guidance. Each has helped and contributed to the research in numerous and significant ways and I am most grateful for their support and various expertise.

Notes

1 Commentaries on the 'technological fix' in relation to beliefs about biology, the body and bodily substances as constructs of 'nature' in Western discourses of assisted reproductive medicine have continued to inform social critiques since the early publication of scholarly and activist responses in the 1980s on the 'new' reproductive

technologies. For a brief non-inclusive overview, see Stabile (1994); Overall (1987); Stanworth (1987); Franklin (1997). Much of this scholarship is strongly informed by feminist critiques of biological determinism and is also concerned to show that so-called sex differences in behaviour are gender-based differences; see for example classic statements in Hubbard (1990) and Fausto-Sterling (1985).

2 Edwards *et al.* (1999) pursue some of the susceptibilities from an anthropological vantage.

3 Outside of anthropology, it is worth emphasising that Mauss's (1990) insights have informed the Western reception of gift exchange theory in highly particularistic fashion.

4 The point being that each of these male identities may be assumed by different men as 'fathers'. The 'genetic father' being defined as the man who contributes male physiological substance; the 'genitor' as the man who is widely believed and thus culturally recognised by others as male progenitor; and 'pater' as the social father generally held responsible for the practicalities of childrearing. The 'genetrix', by logical association, is the woman who is culturally recognised in society as the person contributing female genetic substance. The complication generated by the new reproductive and genetic technologies (highlighted particularly, though not exclusively, in disputes over maternal surrogacy cases of claims to custodianship – see especially Fox (1993) and also Ragoné (1994)) is the 'fact' that the genetrix may not be interchangeable with the mother who gestates and gives birth to the baby. On possibilities and strategies for engendering reproductive identity as forms of 'collaborative reproduction', see for example Robertson (1994).

5 See Scheffler (1991: 372).

6 See Franklin's (1997: 29–37) overview of 'conception among the anthropologists'.

7 For example, in the field of bioethics see overviews on living donation by Lamb (1990) and Caplan (1997); classic social policy analysis relating to the UK is dealt with in Titmuss (1970) and updated in Oakley and Ashton (1997). See also Simmons *et al.* (1987).

8 At the time of writing the Human Fertilisation and Embryology Authority's (2001) ongoing public consultation in the UK on donor anonymity is considering the issue of confidentiality and the prospective provision of information to future generations of donor-conceived offspring.

9 On the diversity of form of 'chosen families' and 'stratified reproduction' more broadly, see Weston (1991) and Robertson (1994) respectively.

10 See Bouquet (1993) on the limitations of genealogy as bourgeois scientific method-ology.

11 An amendment to the Criminal Justice and Public Order Bill proposed by Dame Jill Knight was passed into law banning the use of foetal ova, or embryos derived from foetal ova, in fertility treatment. Given that the consultation was supposed to be a national inquiry into public opinion, it is worth mentioning some facts about the exercise. 25,000 copies of the consultation document were distributed by the HFEA. These contained structured questions on the use of ovarian tissue for research and fertility treatment and invited comments on issues which fell under the following headings: the psychological effects of 'donation' for future offspring, clinical and scientific issues, and moral, ethical and legal issues. It is of interest to note that several of the issues for consideration outlined in the consultative inquiry were structured in terms of the problem of 'consent'. Just under 9,000 replies were received from individuals and a range of groups, including sixth-form classes, religious groups, women's groups, village meetings, professional scientific, medical and nursing organisations and the education department of one of HM prisons. Though the final Report of the HFEA (1994b) does not break down in significant detail the reasoning behind respondents' objections, it does reveal tellingly that a quarter of replies came

from those opposed to abortion and that 16 per cent of responses (1,467 persons) were opposed to the use of foetal tissue. From the little that the Report does present as its findings, there would seem to be some discrepancy that does not get addressed by the HFEA analysts. This concerns the findings of three surveys carried out independently by three (unnamed) institutions and submitted as evidence to the Authority. Though it is not clear from the Report whether the surveys were inter-linked projects or carried out as separate studies, together these surveys focused exclusively on the views of some 1,500 women: those planning to have children and attending Family Planning Clinics, pregnant women attending antenatal clinics, women presenting for termination, and those attending infertility clinics. The significant finding from these studies, and the one that appears to challenge the consultation replies, confirms that '*Between one third and a half of all women approved the use of fetal tissue in infertility treatment*' HFEA (1994b: 8).

12 See further Darwin (1985: 427).

13 An outlawed vision typically depicted in press and policy reports as the 'monster' thesis of unnatural human deviation. On the 'unnatural' life of monsters, see Turney (1998) and Daston and Park (1998) in the context of Latour's (1993: 12) observation that we need 'to regulate the proliferation of monsters by representing their existence officially'.

14 Media reportage covering the Diane Blood case in the UK highlighted some of the problems a surviving partner faces in seeking to establish a right to claim legal possession of cryopreserved substance when prior consent for the collection of her husband's sperm had not been obtained from the deceased before his death (Cunningham 1996). I say 'reportage' because it is not, however, simply a matter of claims to proprietorial control over techno-legislated *ex vivo* substance that motivates people to make 'new' relatedness from out of old (see Simpson 2001).

15 See Usborne (1997) and Craig and Bourne (1996). Note there are differences between British and US law here. In the UK, a woman intending to have 'her' embryos frozen must forward written instructions on their intended use in the event of death. There were no such provisions in the Garber case.

16 In February 1997, the UK Court of Appeal finally ruled in favour of Diane Blood decreeing it legal for her to be inseminated with her late husband's cryopreserved sperm. Blood was now allowed to receive IVF treatment in a fertility clinic outside of the UK where contravention of the terms of the 1990 Human Fertilisation and Embryology Act would not apply. Upon hearing the ruling, Blood simply evoked a chain of links as social memory connecting her late husband to the prospect of her procreative embodiment of new life: 'It's Stephen's birthday today and I think it would have been a very nice birthday present for him and it's certainly very nice for me' (Wynn Davies 1997).

17 Pseudonyms are used in case studies III and IV to preserve donors' anonymity.

18 Another instance of bypassing. Even if we take Fay's ideas as representative of a folk philosophy of internal difference, I would suggest it is doubtful she was engrossed in contemporary complexity theory, systems of self-organisation or ideas about chaos, which would be – at least according to scientists, and as expressed (say) by authors such as Stuart Kauffman, James Gleick, Gerald Edelman, Francisco Varela and Ilya Prigogine – the obvious grounding for such ideas.

19 One might also in this regard consider as relevant some of the recent cases of sibling donations of genetically pre-selected embryos for tissue-matching by pre-implantation diagnosis, though this would involve a different mobilisation of the notion of the 'missing' (procreative) agent and his/her involvement in begetting/saving a life. Crucially what is seen to be problematic here in bioethical terms is the bypassing of an individual 'donor's' express consent (especially as violation of the ostensibly 'universalist'

principle of 'respect for the person'). Typically, the social valuing of these acts of genetic donation occasioned by stem cell transplantation technology has been conflated in media reportage with the creation of 'designer children'. On the controversy surrounding the case of the Hashmi family from Leeds (UK), see Shahana Hashmi's statements on genetically matching her existing pre-school son (suffering from thalassaemia beta) with regenerative tissue extracted from bone marrow as tissue enabled by the (prospective) birth of an IVF-conceived child. 'This is going to be a gift from nature, not a designer baby', *Sunday Telegraph*, 24 February 2002, p. 17.

20 See for example Damon and Wagner (1989); de Coppet (1981); Foster (1990).

21 Debbora Battaglia's work on Sabarl mortuary exchange, for instance, explores how memory is a 'productive' kind of forgetting where being 'held in mind' is tantamount to remaining symbolically vital through others' actions (Battaglia 1990: 12, 198; 1993). Others consider how local beliefs that the person remains an ongoing social context or trajectory, thereby transmuting the effects of loss, decay, deterioration and degeneration, relate to the value of death as a mechanism for the long-term regeneration of society. Much of this work has been theorised in terms of a simultaneous denial of and mastery over the arbitrary nature of biological death and individual distinction.

22 The above account is taken from Otis (1994). On distinctions in evolutionary theory between ontogeny and phylogeny, see further Gould (1977).

23 'Dangerous liaison', *New Scientist* 19/26 December 1998, p. 21.

24 'Cloning to be used to fight disease', *Guardian*, 9 December 1999, p. 11.

Bibliography

Barnes, John A. (1961) 'Physical and social kinship', *Philosophy of Science* 28: 296–9.

—— (1973) 'Genetrix: genitor: nature: culture', in J. Goody (ed.) *The Character of Kinship*, Cambridge: Cambridge University Press.

Battaglia, Debbora (1990) *On the Bones of the Serpent: Person, Memory, and Mortality in Sabarl Island Society*, Chicago: University of Chicago Press.

—— (1993) 'At play in the fields (and borders) of the imaginary: Melanesian transformations of forgetting', *Cultural Anthropology* 8(4): 430–42.

Beer, Gillian (1992) *Forging the Missing Link. Interdisciplinary Stories.* (Inaugural Lecture, University of Cambridge, 18 November 1991) Cambridge: Cambridge University Press.

Bloch, Maurice and Parry, Jonathan (eds) (1982) *Death and the Regeneration of Life*, Cambridge: Cambridge University Press.

Bouquet, Mary (1993) *Reclaiming English Kinship*, Manchester: Manchester University Press.

Caplan, Arthur L. (1997) *Am I my Brother's Keeper? The Ethical Frontiers of Biomedicine*, Indianapolis: Indiana University Press.

Craig, Olga and Bourne, Brendan (1996) 'Baby love', *The Sunday Times*, 29 December, p. 10.

Cunningham, John (1996) 'Pilloried by the public', *Guardian* 2, 29 October, p. 17.

Damon, Frederick and Wagner, Roy (eds) (1989) *Death Rituals and Life in the Societies of the Kula Ring*, DeKalb: Northern Illinois University Press.

Darwin, Charles (1985) [1859] *The Origin of Species*, Harmondsworth: Penguin.

Daston, Lorraine and Park, Katherine (1998) *Wonders and the Order of Nature 1150–1750*, New York: Zone Books.

de Coppet, Daniel (1981) 'The life giving death', in S.C. Humphreys and H. King (eds)

Mortality and Immortality: The Anthropology and Archaeology of Death, London: Academic Press.

Edwards, Jeanette, Franklin, Sarah, Hirsch, Eric, Price, Frances and Strathern, Marilyn (1999) *Technologies of Procreation: Kinship in the Age of Assisted Conception*, 2nd edn, London: Routledge.

Fausto-Sterling, Anne (1985) *Myths of Gender*, New York: Basic Books.

Foster, Robert J. (1990) 'Value without equivalence: exchange and replacement in a Melanesian society', *Man*, n s 25(1); 54–69.

Fox, Robin (1993) *Reproduction and Succession: Studies in Anthropology, Law and Society*, New Brunswick: Transaction Publishers.

Franklin, Sarah (1997) *Embodied Progress: A Cultural Account of Assisted Reproduction*, London: Routledge.

Gell, Alfred (1992) *The Anthropology of Time: Cultural Constructions of Temporal Maps and Images*, Oxford: Berg.

Gould, Stephen Jay (1977) *The Mismeasure of Man*, Harmondsworth: Penguin.

Haeckel, Ernst (1920) *The Evolution of Man*, 3rd edn, New York: Appleton.

Hall, Celia (1994) 'Fears of skipped generation raised by use of tissue', *The Independent*, 8 January, p. 2.

Hubbard, Ruth (1990) *The Politics of Women's Biology*, New Brunswick: Rutgers University Press.

Human Fertilisation and Embryology Authority (1994a) *Donated Ovarian Tissue in Embryo Research and Assisted Conception*, Public Consultation Document, London.

Human Fertilisation and Embryology Authority (1994b) *Donated Ovarian Tissue in Embryo Research and Assisted Conception*, Report, London.

Human Fertilisation and Embryology Authority (2001) *Donor Information Consultation*, London: HFEA.

Human Genetics Commission (2002) *Inside Information: Balancing Interests in the Use of Genetic Data,* London: Department of Health.

Hunt, Liz (1992) 'Marion the human incubator splits the conscience of a nation', *The Independent*, 1 November, p. 3.

Konrad, Monica (1996) 'Anonymous exchange relations: assisted conception between ova donors and recipients in the UK', unpublished PhD, London School of Economics and Political Science.

—— (1998) 'Ova donation and symbols of substance: some variations on the theme of sex, gender and the partible person', *Journal of the Royal Anthropological Institute* 4(4): 643–67.

Lamb, David (1990) *Organ Transplants and Ethics*, London: Routledge.

Latour, Bruno (1993) *We Have Never Been Modern*, Hemel Hempstead: Harvester Wheatsheaf.

Lewontin, Richard C. (1995) 'The dream of the human genome', in Jean Bethke Elshtain and J. Timothy Cloyd (eds) *Politics and the Human Body*, London: Vanderbilt University Press.

Mauss, Marcel (1990) [1925] *The Gift. The Form and Reason for Exchange in Archaic Societies*, trans. W.D. Halls, London: Routledge.

Mosko, Mark (1983) 'Conception, de-conception and social structure in Bush Mekeo culture', *Mankind* 14(1): 24–32.

Moyes, Jojo (1996) 'A world of anguish in an inch of glass', *The Independent*, 3 August, p. 1.

Needham, Rodney (1974) *Remarks and Inventions: Skeptical Essays about Kinship*, London: Tavistock Publications.

Oakley, Ann and Ashton, John (1997) *The Gift Relationship: From Human Blood to Social Policy*, London: London School of Economics and Political Science.

Otis, Laura (1994) *Organic Memory: History and the Body in the Late Nineteenth and Early Twentieth Centuries*, London: University of Nebraska Press.

Overall, Christine (1987) *Ethics and Human Reproduction: A Feminist Analysis*, Boston: Allen and Unwin.

Poole, Fitz John P. (1984) 'Symbols of substance: Bimin-Kuskusmin models of procreation, death and personhood', *Mankind* 14: 191–216.

Ragoné, Helena (1994) *Surrogate Motherhood: Conception in the Heart*, Boulder: Westview Press.

Robertson, John (1994) *Children of Choice: Freedom and the New Reproductive Technologies*, Princeton: Princeton University Press.

Scheffler, Harold W. (1991) 'Sexism and the naturalism in the study of kinship', in M. di Leonardo (ed.) *Gender at the Crossroads of Knowledge: Feminist Anthropology in the Postmodern Era*, Berkeley: University of California Press.

Schneider, David (1968) *American Kinship: A Cultural Account*, Englewood Cliffs, NJ: Prentice-Hall.

Simmons, Roberta G., Simmons, Richard L. and Marine, Susan Klein (1987) *Gift of Life: The Effect of Organ Transplantation on Individual, Family and Societal Dynamics*, 2nd edn, New Brunswick: Transaction Books.

Simpson, Robert (2001) 'Making "bad" deaths "good": the kinship consequences of posthumous reproduction', *Journal of the Royal Anthropological Institute* 7(1): 1–18.

Stabile, Carol A. (1994) *Feminism and the Technological Fix*, Manchester: Manchester University Press.

Stanworth, Michelle (ed.) (1987) *Reproductive Technologies. Gender, Motherhood and Medicine*, Cambridge: Polity Press.

Strathern, Marilyn (2000) 'Emergent properties: new technologies, new persons, new claims'. Rothschild lecture delivered to the Department of History of Science, Harvard University, April.

Titmuss, Richard M. (1970) *The Gift Relationship: From Human Blood to Social Policy*, London: Allen and Unwin.

Turney, Jon (1998) *Frankenstein's Footsteps: Science, Genetics and Popular Culture*, New Haven: Yale University Press.

Usborne, David (1997) 'Unease grows about baby from beyond the grave', *The Independent*, 2 December, p. 5.

Wagner, Roy (1989) 'Conclusion: the exchange context of the Kula', in F. Damon and R. Wagner (eds) *Death Rituals and Life in the Societies of the Kula Ring*, DeKalb: Northern Illinois University Press.

Weiner, James (1995) 'Beyond the possession principle: an energetics of Massim exchange', *Pacific Studies* 18(1): 128–37.

Weismann, August (1893) *The Germ-Plasm. A Theory of Heredity*, trans. W. Newton Parker and H. Ronnfeldt, London: Walter Scott.

Weston, Kath (1991) *Families We Choose: Lesbians, Gays, Kinship*, New York: Columbia University Press.

Wynn Davies, Patricia (1997) 'Widow wins right to have baby from her dead husband', *The Independent*, 7 February, p. 3.

Chapter 13

Women's work

The practice of donor insemination amongst some lesbian women

Jane Haynes

Jane Haynes is a psychotherapist and writer.

Amongst my friends and acquaintances who are lesbian, and who grew up, as I did, between the mid-1940s and early 1960s, I do not know any lesbians who became mothers except as a result of heterosexual relationships that, to begin with, were accompanied by marriage. Amongst these friends are those who would have liked to have children, but did not desire heterosexual relations, or were afraid of parental and/or social disapproval, who are now reconciling themselves to another loss – they are growing old without the company of their grandchildren. Some of these women now look upon the evolving generative mores in lesbian culture with envy and admiration for women who were determined not to allow society to sacrifice their wishes to become parents. Even in the world of psychoanalysis, supposedly a world in which we are trained to understand *difference*, until a few years ago, when the Institute of Psychoanalysis adopted an Equal Opportunities policy, lesbians reported difficulties in being accepted to train as psychoanalysts (Ellis 1994).

Attitudes to generativity, gender and the politics and kinship structures of families have changed as a result of feminist politics during the 1970s and 1980s, followed by the social and political activism of gay groups. Then the politics of AIDS cemented gay and lesbian society and thrust homosexuality into the collective imagination. Many lesbian women now feel able to become mothers, via donor insemination, without entering into a known relationship with a man. Donor insemination, which is one of the oldest techniques in reproductive medicine, was introduced into Britain about one hundred years ago, although it is probable that it has been practised surreptitiously throughout the history of civilisation.

The first known documented case of donor insemination occurred in 1884 when an American doctor who worked in Philadelphia, Dr William Pancoast, inseminated a sedated woman with a medical student's sperm without first obtaining her permission. It is exceptional in so far as, amongst assisted reproductive technology, it is a procedure that, despite dire warnings of the professionals, can be practised in a non-medicalised setting. (I shall return to a fuller discussion of the official status of donor insemination at the end of the chapter.)

With the development of the concept of single-parent families there have also been significant changes in the ways in which lesbian women now feel comfortable about becoming parents, either as single mothers, or in family units where one or both partners become birth mothers and share the parenting roles. In this chapter I interview two lesbian families in which three of the women are biological mothers. Debbie and Clare, who have been together as a couple for twenty years, have each given birth to a son, Josh aged 16 and Paul aged 11. Liz and Nicky, who have been together for twelve years, have a daughter called Rowan.

In the instance of my interviewees, who were not suffering from infertility, but were determined to pursue donor insemination as their preferred pathway to pregnancy, I found myself in the company of women who were aware of the complex consequences of their determination to have families and who were able to answer and inform their children's desires to know about their donor origins with frankness, honesty and gratitude to their donors. I also found myself talking to women whose devotion and responsibility to the varied gender needs of their children left me thinking that these children were privileged to have experienced the quality and refinements of their responsible parenting. The participants in these interviews, whose names have been changed for confidentiality, have retained full editorial control of the following texts.

Interview I

Interview 1 takes place between J.H. (Q), Clare and Debbie.

Q: Could we begin by discussing how you each assumed a lesbian identity, how that linked up with your ideas of femininity, and whether you always felt that having a child was going to be a priority for you. Maybe you could respond first Clare?

CLARE: Growing up, I guess I saw myself as heterosexual, not really being aware of any other alternatives. I had relationships with men until my early twenties, when I began to become aware of my attraction to women and through meeting lesbians and gay men realised that there was another possibility for me.

Q: Was there always a desire to become a mother?

CLARE: As I child I can remember that I always thought I'd have six children. I come from a family of six kids, and I always thought I'd have lots of children, just because that was the environment in which I grew up. It wasn't necessarily what I wanted, but I always thought that. And then from late teenage years, once I started having relationships with men, I was very clear that there was no way I was going to become wife, mother, whatever. I didn't want that model. At that point it was like: oh no, I don't want kids. Because of the role of being a woman in that context, and being a mother in a heterosexual relationship. I was very clear I didn't want that. And it was only after coming out and being with Debbie that I changed my mind.

Q: *When did you meet each other?*

CLARE: We met each other at the time we were both coming out. It was the first important lesbian relationship that either of us had had. The desire to have a child evolved within a couple of years of that, in the context of meeting other women who had children, and being involved with the care of other children. I don't think there was ever a conflict for me about having a child. I never thought I can't do it because I'm a lesbian. That was never an issue. We knew the possibility was there – we knew two women who'd each had a child and they became important role models for us.

DEBBIE: In the meantime we got to know a group of women who were supporting lesbians to become pregnant. It was all very much in a political context. They lived in a communal house and they took it upon themselves to support and help lesbians who wanted to get pregnant.

CLARE: They used to do things like arrange that women could use their house as a place to do inseminations – they were there as a kind of support network. They were very much committed to the politics of it, rather than it just being about friends doing it for each other. They were mainly straight women, but they were politically aware.

DEBBIE: I think what made it possible for us to think we could have a baby was because we could see that this was something that was already beginning to go on, and that we would get support.

Q: *When I think about my lesbian friends – well some of them are still afraid to come out professionally – I think it must have been much harder to struggle with a lesbian identity and motherhood in the sixties and seventies. It's easier, yet again, to be a single mother now than it was for you in 1985. It must have been almost impossible before the concept of single parenthood existed for many lesbians to risk having children outside the context of a heterosexual marriage. What was it like for you Debbie, realising that you were gay?*

DEBBIE: In my teens I used to have great crushes on girls, but the notion of homosexuality wasn't really OK for an Irish Catholic family. But neither was there a huge option in my head. I sort of knew that on one level, an unconscious level, that I wasn't heterosexual. I just knew it. I saw myself almost as bisexual. I didn't have that word then – those naming words. I went out with boys, but I also had sexual crushes on girlfriends. I went to university where I got very involved in the peace movement, and I began to meet a fantastic mix of people, and met lesbians for the first time. Then I met Clare and very soon we began to live together.

Q: *Which led to the decision to have your first child together. What seems to be quite unusual about your relationship, in my limited knowledge, is that you both decided to become biological mothers.*

CLARE: Well, we're just coming up to our twenty-year anniversary so it's very interesting to sit here and reflect on how things were, but I don't remember a point when we suddenly made a decision, we just knew it would always happen. But I remember we, together as a couple, decided we wanted to have a child, to have a baby. And it was quite circumstantial, actually, that I decided to do it, to become pregnant. Because I didn't have a very secure job and my family were easy with the idea of it.

DEBBIE: Yes, at that point your family were much more comfortable with the idea of you becoming pregnant. But it was very much a joint thing. It wasn't coming from, you know, great maternal desire, so much as expediency. I think the desire was much stronger on my part, wasn't it?

CLARE: I think Debbie very much wanted a child, but she knew that to be its biological mother was very much a no-no for her at that particular time.

Q: Why?

DEBBIE: Because I'd just come out – come out to my mother. Yes, it's changed now, but at that point it would have been too much for her if I had then got pregnant as well, it would have been pushing it.

Q: And careerwise you had just started work?

DEBBIE: I was just starting to qualify as a social worker, I was the one earning a salary.

Q: Did you have a good relationship with your family?

DEBBIE: I think that was why it was difficult, because out of all my sisters I probably had a quite close relationship with my mother. So I told her. I wanted to be honest with her because I loved her, but it was very difficult for a long time. For years. It was really until Clare gave birth to Josh and Mum came to visit us after the birth. And that really changed it. And then she died a few years ago, but in that time – after he was born – until she died, she became very, very involved. Her love for both the boys was very positive, so it all turned round completely. Now I always say to people who come to talk to us about their worries with getting pregnant, or when they're coming out to their parents, it's like, you don't know how it will be in ten years' time or fifteen years' time. People change as well, don't they? Parents change.

Q: At that time there was no possibility that you could be the biological mother?

DEBBIE: No it still wasn't possible. It was something I very much wanted to do, but it wasn't the right time. Also I had to get my qualification but I planned to have four or five kids then.

CLARE: When I became pregnant, I remember very clearly feeling, and saying this to Debbie, that if we split up, I'm not being left with the baby. I was very clear, we were twenty-five and I didn't want to become a single mum. We would have obviously made some kind of access arrangements. But I think in my head it was something we're doing together, and I'm not – I don't want to be left alone holding the baby – it's not only about my maternal fulfilment. It's about a project we're doing together; creating a family together. It was a different kind of motivation.

Q: So it wasn't a possessive feeling?

CLARE: No. No it wasn't.

Q: Did that change when Josh was born, or not?

CLARE: We've always been very, very equal in our feelings, I would say that right through we very consciously worked towards that goal. Just thinking about other friends who've had children, there's sometimes been the pattern that one of the women really, really wanted a child, and then their partner has been more ambivalent. But that's not how it's been for us.

DEBBIE: Maybe it's luck that we were both wanting similar things at the same time. It wasn't that Clare really wanted a child and I went along with the biology of it. It was very much like: let's do it. We're going to do this. We'll have more than one child. That was something we always thought – that Josh was going to have siblings. We felt that if we were having one child in the context of a lesbian household that it would be good for that child not to be an only child.

Q: Clare, were your parents supportive or not?

CLARE: Yes, my parents were always laid-back about me being a lesbian, it wasn't such an issue for them. My sexual identity was never a problem for them. They were delighted to have another member of their family. Although, I have since discovered that over the years, discussing it with my Mum, there were issues about her having to tell other people and so on. It was obviously something that as grandparents they had to come to terms with, which I didn't realise originally. But I never perceived it as an issue or a drama, or anything. I felt quite supported. They don't live locally. So the level of support was emotional as opposed to being involved on a day-to-day basis. The most stressful part of our situation was finding the right donor.

Q: Was it a known donor?

CLARE: Yes. A friend who agreed to donate. So that was fairly straightforward.

Q: You weren't worried about AIDS and sexually transmitted diseases?

CLARE: Yes, this was something we had considered but this was 1985 and before the AIDS epidemic had really developed in Britain.

DEBBIE: Well we did ask quite a few people to be Josh's donor. There was a process of selection, we had criteria that we wanted fulfilled, but in the end we chose a friend who had been a student with us. It was important for both of us to know the donor. I think we thought about that a lot and both Clare, and I wanted – you know, we were happy with him being known to us, but we were very clear that we did not want him, in any context, to become involved as a parent. We had many discussions about him not being involved but we do occasionally meet up with him and the boys and sort of keep in touch with birthday and Christmas cards.

CLARE: Yes, and this was all in the early days, people are a lot more ironed out now, with legal contracts and suchlike. But we discussed with him what his concerns were and we looked at worst case scenarios together. His worst case scenario was that if Debbie and I split up, and maybe the child was born with multiple disabilities, and one of us found ourselves in economic hardship – then we might put some claim back on him. And we talked a lot about that, about his anxiety. Then we decided it would be best not to draw up a legal document because that would name him. So we just went ahead and inseminated.

DEBBIE: I think it was the fourth month that Clare became pregnant.

Q: And did you collect the semen directly from the donor?

DEBBIE: Yes.

Q: It sounds very different from Liz's experience (interview 2) when a member of her support group acted as an anonymous intermediary. Your semen collection was more spontaneous, wasn't it?

CLARE: Yes. This was more personal – it was our own arrangement.

Q: You've stayed in contact with him?

CLARE: Yes.

DEBBIE: Yes, we're still in contact. We occasionally meet at various functions.

Q: Is he gay, did you say, or not?

CLARE: No. He is married.

Q: And has he met Josh?

CLARE: Yes. Yes, he's met, a few times. We've sort of crossed paths, over the years.

Q: And Josh knows he's his donor?

DEBBIE: Yes. He saw him when he was small, and then he saw him again towards eight or nine. So for the last few years it's been probably about once a year.

Q: I imagine the difference between knowing who your biological father is, and just having an abstract concept of having been fathered couldn't be more different. As a couple I know that you have experienced both of these situations. Can we turn to your experience of becoming Paul's biological mother, Debbie.

DEBBIE: We found ourselves looking for another donor.

I had to know what the donor looked like. I think there was that fundamental thing that I wanted to know something about the donor, characteristics about that person that I would recognise in the child. I had to know that they were alright. It was an emotional thing, it's not based on a genetic rationale – but intuitively knowing that somebody was an OK person. I couldn't go down an anonymous route. Although he was not a personal friend and we no longer have contact with him we did meet him and we got to know that he was a very decent, good person. It felt good to have him as our donor. That's actually quite important for Paul. We don't lie to our boys, we don't make anything up but we can tell him that we know his biological dad is a good and generous person.

Q: I agree, there is a fundamental difference between someone, your mother, knowing who your father is and creating a fantasy that has no reality base to it. I have spent hours on this subject with patients who have been adopted. Of course finding out and meeting with a parent later in life carries its own responsibilities and for the child there is always the risk that having initiated the meeting they may end up wishing they hadn't. Are you saying that mainly people's preference now is to go for anonymous donors?

CLARE: There's certainly a lot of women who are doing that. I think it's falling into two groups. There's the medicalised clinic-type route, which is completely anonymous. And then there are several male members of our network who are involved as co-parents – so that seems to be another new model of family groupings.

Q: There was no conflict in your minds about the type of donor?

DEBBIE: No, complete anonymity was never what either of us wanted.

Q: Most heterosexual women have no choice but to go down that route.

CLARE: Both of us had that gut feeling that that's not how we wanted to do it.

Q: Debbie, did you feel once Clare had had Josh that there was a growing biological desire in you for motherhood?

DEBBIE: I just adored and loved Josh so tremendously that I remember thinking that I desperately wanted another child to double this feeling that I had and for a sense of completeness to our family.

CLARE: I remember it being very much about you, as well. There was never a question that I would have the second child. It was always quite clear that this was what you would do. And you wanted that experience, didn't you?

DEBBIE: Yes.

Q: And to be able to breastfeed too?

CLARE: Yes, we breastfed both of them. And we both expressed our milk, so we both fed both of them, which was very important for us.

DEBBIE: We've often tried to encourage friends to do that, and people haven't always done it. So that you both get that feeding experience very early on.

Q: It seems heterosexual couples could learn a lot about the debate between donor anonymity and some degree of disclosure. In one way it's easier for you, as a couple, to address the matter with the boys because you couldn't provide the semen, it wasn't attached to the stigma of infertility. Some statistics quote as many as forty per cent of males have difficulty in fathering a child. Perhaps that means there's been more generosity, more thoughtfulness about the children's needs than usually occurs with donor insemination.

CLARE: The boys both have grown up – to see somebody who is a donor dad as a very generous person. Very, very kind, who wanted to help. What we try and stress, is that they have two very loving and adoring parents. It has been interesting watching the different developmental stages for them, in their questioning about it. At the age of three or four, it's like: 'Why haven't I got a Dad?' Someone else has got one, and they want one too, just like someone has got the latest toy, or whatever. They want to know why they haven't got one of them too. It's in that context, of trying to be the same as other children. And then, slightly older, at about eight, it becomes a real awareness of difference.

DEBBIE: Yes, the differences between them and other children. And the difference is about conception. And how they were actually born. Because he asked questions and we were honest with him, Josh was a fount of all knowledge to his friends, both from lesbian and heterosexual couples.

Q: Yes, up to about eight they prefer their own myths. My granddaughter Portia's just eight. We were sitting in Pizza Express one day and she suddenly said: 'I really want to know more about all those eggs. You keep saying that the Daddy just puts them into the Mummy's insides, but how?' And we both rushed off to Waterstones, and she was excited: 'Find me some proper pictures, Granny.' The brain becomes able to conceptualise more abstractly.

DEBBIE: And then it's the pre-teen thing, which Paul's just into now, which is much more about sex and sexuality than about being gay or lesbian. There are a whole set of other things which they bring onto it. For Josh, nobody is as important as his friends, and his band, for Paul it's still football. That's how it should be, isn't it?

Q: Yes, it's evident that they each have a secure base from which to form their own friendships.

CLARE: I can remember Josh once coming home from school and saying that the teacher had said something in a lesson about homework – the class was to interview all the members of their family, their mums, dads and brothers and sisters. And he came home very cross about this teacher's insensitivity. Not about him, because Josh had very much seen himself as having parents – in his head he translates Mum and Dad to parents. But one of his best friends was a single kid of a single mum. And Josh was cross that the teacher didn't think about how that must feel. And what I thought was interesting about that was that Josh didn't see himself as different – he felt he was in the norm of what was being said.

Interview 2

Interview 2 with Liz and Nicky. Liz is a training consultant and Nicky is a solicitor.

Q: Do you remember when you first wanted a baby?

LIZ: It was at least ten years before Rowan was born. Since my early twenties the thought had been growing into a physical pain in my head.

Q: When you discovered that you were lesbian, did you still take it for granted that you would have a child?

LIZ: I always took it for granted that I would have children. It wasn't just a split-second decision between now I'm heterosexual, now I'm lesbian. I had quite a few boyfriends, I won't go into numbers because it's embarrassing, before I met my first girlfriend, in my twenties. I come from a family of four, and my Mum always talked to me about having children because she wanted to be a grandmother. I was never a butch dyke who wouldn't touch a man with a bargepole. It never seemed to me that it would be a problem, I thought as long as I'm fertile I can have a baby.

Q: You didn't take on a secure lesbian identity until you were in your twenties?

LIZ: I had odd kinds of crushes. No, they weren't odd crushes, but nobody talked about the lesbian option. I didn't even think about it.

Q: So issues of gender identity weren't conscious during adolescence.

LIZ: No, but when you talk to Nicky she'll tell you a different story.

Q: How did your mother respond when she discovered she was going to be a grandmother to a lesbian partnership?

LIZ: I didn't – I mean, ooh, this is so hard. Because I didn't have a good relationship with her. I still don't. That was nothing to do with my lesbianism. It was to do with the way she behaved towards me. But I won't even go into that. She wasn't positive when she found out I was a lesbian. She said things like 'All your friends are very strange looking' but I think she was quite pleased in the end. She said 'There's nothing as special as your daughter having a daughter'. So she was happy about that. My father was outraged. He said 'But a child needs a father, who's the father?' I was furious with him. I said, 'Well, if you feel like that, you won't see your grandchild.' He was there the day after Rowan was born, totally besotted, taking video film. Whenever they see her they're very loving towards her.

Q.   When you met Nicky you were determined to become pregnant?

LIZ: Yes, I had a couple of relationships where I was with women for a few years that didn't want children. I knew those relationships wouldn't go much further. When I met Nicky and fell in love with her, I was delighted because she did want children. I just thought: 'Oh, God, you know, not only do I love her but she wants to have children. So this has got a future.' I read a book about lesbian families – and then we decided to go ahead with self-insemination.

Q: In terms of the donor . . .

LIZ: That was a major problem. It caused a load of difficulties. I became obsessed with finding a donor. I asked several friends to ask their male friends if they would consider being a donor. At least three or four men said no, they had girlfriends, and their girlfriends weren't happy with the idea. Then I asked a couple of men – I think they thought it was a bit strange, at that time – it was ten and a half years ago now – people thought it was a pretty weird thing to ask. Now it's a common occurrence. We didn't think of going to a clinic. It wasn't a financial problem, but at that time it was illegal to give sperm donations to lesbian women. You had to be married. I knew what we were doing was illegal, because you're not supposed to do donor insemination without it being registered. I belonged to a group which was set up by several women about twelve years ago, for lesbians who wanted to self-inseminate. We met at the Gay Centre, we put an advert for donors in a local paper and then we received all the letters and scanned them for nutters. We took it in turns to go and meet up with the ones who sounded all right, vet them and have them checked out. They seemed fairly decent people.

Q: Was there a big response?

LIZ: We got maybe twenty or thirty letters from that first advert but so many of them proved to be unsuitable. It did become extremely painful, and I thought: 'This is never going to happen; I'm not going to be able to do it.' At the time my sister was having her third abortion, I was furious with her, and I was thinking: you're getting rid of your baby, and I would look after and love a baby and can't. I was searching like crazy for someone. It did, briefly, cross my mind that if it went on much longer I might just go out and sleep with a bloke, you know, time it right.

Q: As you'd already had several heterosexual relationships that might have been a possibility. I imagine that there was a time when the only route available to broody lesbian women to become mothers was through a heterosexual marriage or relationship.

LIZ: Yes. I mean it wouldn't have been abhorrent. But I didn't want to do it like that; I wanted us to do it together.

Q: It would have been harder for Nicky?

LIZ: Yes, but she's pretty easygoing though.

Q: Was there huge disappointment each time you got your period?

LIZ: Yes, I felt awful. Felt desperate. I'd do things like go to work and I'd come out of work, and sit outside, thinking such nonsense, like I'd approach a stranger and get to know them and sleep with them or something, just odd things like that. I'd look at men and think 'Would he make a good father?' Do you know what I mean? Just bizarre things like that.

Q: Yes, I think so. Did you have fantasies about what kind of donor you'd like if you could choose?

LIZ: No, not really. I think everyone thinks the same thing. They want someone healthy, and not ugly, and hopefully with some intelligence. But in the end I didn't care. I didn't care. Once I'd found someone who said they'd do it, I just thought: right, I'll do it with him. Yes.

Q: Just to get a baby.

LIZ: Just to get a baby.

Q: I've had four miscarriages, so I know what that feeling is like . . . I couldn't have lived without having children, of course I would have survived but that's not the same thing . . . I just can't imagine being forced to make that adaptation in my life.

LIZ: I know. When we sorted through the letters, and agreed to help each other, I went and interviewed quite a few men for women in the group.

Q: You all wanted to be anonymous.

LIZ: It wasn't formally discussed, but quite a few women wanted anonymous donors and when it came to collecting sperm, it was one of the women from the group who collected it for me. I was afraid of any man having any involvement with our baby. She was going to be ours, and not belong to somebody else. If we'd had a close male friend who wanted a child and wanted to help us with it, I wouldn't have been separatist about it. I really wouldn't.

Q: You saw him once?

LIZ: Yes.

Q: And did you form any . . .

LIZ: – opinion of him? He just seemed ordinary – he seemed very nervous. He said he was doing it for altruistic reasons. He seemed genuine. He wasn't outstandingly good-looking. I didn't care.

Q: Did you want him to have an AIDS test?

LIZ: Yes, well, this is the awful thing – the whole thing was exploding in the media at the time, and that terrified me. But we had no way of knowing. I could have said to him, 'You must bring me the piece of paper that proves you've had that test.' But then I thought well, that's not worth the paper it's written on, it could be anybody's test, unless I'd gone into it like a detective. I was so desperate to get pregnant. I won't say I didn't care. I did care. I cared deeply, all the way through my pregnancy I was terrified something would go wrong, or that the baby might have a disease, but I suppose desperation makes you do strange things.

Q: But then women doing medicalised IVF take other sorts of risks all the time. Nothing matters once you decide you want the baby. I always think of Rumpelstiltskin, I would have given my soul to get my first child.

LIZ: Yes, one of Nicky's best friends had a kidney replaced four years ago. She's got all sorts of health problems. She's just become pregnant and the doctors are berating her about it. And she said 'I don't care. I really don't care.'

Q: No, it's not unusual. And did Nicky come and meet the donor with you?

LIZ: I don't think she saw him, I'll check that but no, I don't think she did. She was still living in Sheffield at that time, so it was more difficult for her.

Q: Do you remember the colour of your donor's eyes, or anything like that?

LIZ: Just pale, and blond hair, and very ordinary.

Q: Would you have considered someone of mixed race?

(At this point Nicky arrives home and we are briefly introduced but she doesn't join us.)

LIZ: No, not from any reasons of prejudice. But I don't think that would be fair on the child because one of us wasn't mixed race and I think it would have been even harder to explain. I have known women who've been mixed-race couples who have got a mixed-race baby. We met him once, and then one of the women from the group collected a semen donation – they met him in the city centre. He produced the sperm in a toilet. I was fraught with anxiety at home.

Q: Where did you get your instructions on how to preserve it?

LIZ: We just read about it in the Lisa Saffron book that our friends gave you as a reference. She recommended producing the sperm into a cup and then transferring it to a small plastic container, like a film container, and then keeping it warm under your arm, or in your hand. Some women put it down their bra.

Q: It must feel like you're in possession of the most precious of substances.

LIZ: Yes, there's this terrible feeling that your female messenger won't get there in time although, the sperm is fertile for a couple of hours. But you'd want them to get there in the first twenty minutes to make sure that it's as good as it can be. It was in a little plastic film container but the first time I got it, I was so paranoid about things like AIDS, that I was standing there with it in my hand thinking shall I use it? Shall I use it? And I just dumped it in the bin, because I couldn't cope with the idea that I might be introducing a virus to my body. And then a month later – and I know that sounded bizarre, because I'd been so desperate . . .

Q: No, it doesn't –

LIZ: – to have a baby. But, when it came to the point, I just thought: reason slightly has to take over here. What am I doing? I won't say I regretted it, because there's no point in regretting it. But by the next month Nicky made sure she was at home and we just took the donation upstairs. Our donor was really good-natured. A lot of the women who do self-insemination ask the donor not to have sex or masturbate for several days before, so they're highly fertile. You give a donation at the woman's most fertile time, and then miss a day and then do it again. So you've actually got four days in a month covered. He did it twice and Nicky used the syringe – just an ordinary syringe from Boots. He delivered it to my friend in the city centre, and then she drove back with it – fast! Then Nicky and I went upstairs, and she just got it out of the container with the syringe, and put it inside me. The very first time we tried it all slipped out again, because we just – we weren't sure what we were doing. And then there was a little bit left, so Nicky put some pillows underneath my bum and did it again, and we stayed still for twenty minutes, and yes. That was it really.

Q: It worked the first time?

LIZ: Oh God! When Nicky did it, my heart was banging, because I was thinking oh God, this is such a frightening thing to do. But she was calming me down, and stroking my hand, and saying 'It's all right. It's all right.' And it worked bloody first time! It worked first time. And I was so shocked. I came back from the chemist with the result, and I was streaming with tears. And Nicky said 'What's the matter?'

So I told her, and she was just saying 'Yes! Yes!' – really excited. But all I could think was: what have we done? What the hell have we done? Because, as I said, it was early days in our community, now it is quite common, and you just say, oh well, it's wonderful that so and so's pregnant, but then I was thinking – what an enormous responsibility. Have we done the right thing? What if the baby's going to be – you know – damaged in some way?

Q: Where you afraid that you'd be punished? Isn't it true that some doctors and midwives who disapprove of self-insemination try to threaten their antenatal patients with myths of self-insemination being unsafe because it's unsterile, as though intercourse could ever be sterile!

LIZ: I just thought, because we hadn't gone to a clinic, and hadn't had the donor screened, that he could have infections; at the point of being pregnant, I was too shocked to even be pleased. I thought how does this happen? I've wanted to be pregnant for ten years, and now at thirty-three I'm suddenly pregnant.

Q: Did you tell your Mum? Did you tell anyone? Once you'd got pregnant.

LIZ: Yes, then I told quite a few people. I think I had a scan, and then I told people. Because I didn't quite believe it, until I saw it. Even when I saw it on the screen I thought that's not in me. I mean, all the way through, right up to the point when we went to a National Childbirth class, I didn't believe it and I was hugely fat with Rowan. They had this grubby little doll, and they were pushing it through a plastic pelvis. I said to the woman 'That's not going to happen to me. I'm not having a baby.' I was totally in denial. I knew it was going to happen, but in my head I couldn't believe –

Q: You still couldn't believe it?

LIZ: No. No.

Q: When Nicky arrives I'll ask her what she felt.

LIZ: Oh yes, she's much more down to earth than me. She calls me a drama queen.

Q: Did you tell the hospital the truth?

LIZ: Yes. And they gave me hassle. One nurse in particular was very rude and abrupt, when I went for my examination. She asked me who the father was, and I said that it was an anonymous donor. And she went mad. She didn't shout, but she was really snotty with me, and said, 'What do you mean, an anonymous donor? And do you think that's fair on the child?' You know, asking me questions that were very nosy and invasive, that actually had nothing to do with her. And when I said that to her, she just said 'Oh, we've been trained now to deal with the whole person. We take the holistic approach.' She said it in a way that she didn't believe it, but she still used it as an excuse for her rude questioning.

Q: Was there a problem when it came to the delivery?

LIZ: No, because a couple of our friends had already been through this before, so they recommended a consultant at the hospital who, although he was bemused by the situation, had been quite nice to them, as lesbians. So I went, with Nicky, to him. And he was OK. Then I changed my own doctor because I found out that there was a woman – who would offer me a GP unit service – who had had lesbian patients. She was marvellous. . . .

Q: She looked after you during labour?

LIZ: Yes. She didn't really do anything. I said on my birth plan I didn't want anyone to interfere if possible. So her and the midwife just stood and chatted very quietly, and Nicky and me got on with it really. She examined me a couple of times. But I couldn't really hear anyone else's voice except Nicky's. Nicky was sitting against the wall – she was getting crushed behind me as I pushed. I didn't want to sit up, because I was on all fours I think. And then they said 'You have to turn over, because we can't see what's happening.'

(Nicky re-enters the room at this point and joins us)

So I sort of rested against you, and I was bearing down against you. And afterwards you couldn't breathe, I remember. Yes. And then, when Rowan came out, they put her on my tummy, and I was in terrible shock. And the doctor picked my arm up and put my arm round the baby.

Q: Nicky, when did you get to hold Rowan?

NICKY: Well, she was on you for a little bit, and then they wanted to weigh her and that, so I took her across to be weighed. It was only for a few minutes, really.

LIZ: I didn't know what to do with her. I didn't know how to hold her, but the interesting thing was, after you'd gone, in the evening, we lay awake, the pair of us, me and Rowan, all night. I don't think she – she hardly slept, and I certainly didn't. And I just stared at her, and she stared at me. And I thought oh my God, I'm in love! I bonded then, in the middle of the night.

Q: So when did Nicky bond?

LIZ: I think it was the moment she was born really.

NICKY: I got all emotional.

LIZ: You were crying your eyes out, weren't you?

NICKY: Yes, really. Very emotional.

LIZ: The next day we brought her home, didn't we?

NICKY: Yes, and it was really exciting. And your Dad came down. She was very sweet, you know, she was . . . tiny blue eyes . . . blonde – fine downy sort of hair . . . it was like feathers, wasn't it? Yes, it was very, very quick.

Q: Nicky, I get the impression that temperamentally you're very different from Liz who can be a little histrionic. (Laughter)

NICKY: Yes, we're very different. I've never been pregnant. I probably never will be, so I won't go through that sort of hormonal surge that I think all pregnant women go through. I mean, some women are sort of 'I'm having a baby' and they attune to it very quickly. And others find – find it more difficult to accustom themselves mentally and physically to the fact that they're pregnant, and they're going to have a baby.

LIZ: I found the whole pregnancy abhorrent really. I felt like I'd got an alien inside me. Once she started moving around, my first reaction was that I had an alien inside me. I wanted a baby –

Q: Do you know Doris Lessing's The Fifth Child?

LIZ: No.

Q: Maybe read it some time.

LIZ: But you were the one, Nicky, when I came home, saying, 'What have we done? What have we done?' You were saying, 'It'll be fine, don't worry.' You calmed me down.

NICKY: Yes, but I guess that's the difference in who we are as people, as well as parents. I am – I'm very content in my world. I work in a very difficult area of legal work, but I tend to absorb it quite well. I am used to coping with difficult situations and a demanding case load, I work with children and I tend to absorb a lot of powerful emotions. I get stressed, of course. That's human nature, but I have calmed down a lot, and I think for me it's been a really enriching experience to go through childhood again with Rowan in a second way. I think you need that balance, and I think that's why a relationship like ours probably works better than those who live in imbalance.

Q: Perhaps as a woman you were more able to understand the dramatic hormonal things that Liz was going through. Men tend to focus more on their differences.

NICKY: Well, if you've ever had bad period pains –

Q: Exactly.

LIZ: I can't forget the pain of childbirth though. I don't think – I expect you've heard this loads of times, you must have done. I don't think anyone prepares you for how desperately painful it can be, if you have no drugs. That's why I never wanted to do it again, apart from the fact I probably only wanted one child, but I thought I was going to die.

NICKY: Do you remember when we went to register Rowan, we saw twins had been born on the same day, but they'd both died.

LIZ: Yes, yes, really sad. But I think it's a myth that's perpetuated by women, that thing about forgetting the pain. Mum always said that it's not painful and you've got a lovely baby at the end of it. You'll forget the pain. And that is what you are told over and over again. And I don't think it's true. I don't think that you forget the pain, really – not unless you take drugs and things. But I was too scared of taking drugs. And I didn't have gas and air.

Q: You were too scared of the drugs, and yet you eventually managed to inseminate with an unknown substance. What did you think Nicky when Liz threw the first donation away?

NICKY: I respected her for making that decision. I knew that eventually Liz would want to go through the process. Maybe it's easier, in a gay relationship, to make the decision to throw it away. I didn't get angry. I just respected Liz for not – for not going through with it. Ultimately it also prepared me for the gravity of our *decision to be pregnant.*

Q: There's an anomaly – isn't there – between using unscreened semen, and refusing to put anything into your body during the birth process?

LIZ: Do you know what? It wasn't to do with polluting my body, at all. It was just the fear of drugs. I'm very susceptible to alcohol or any kind of drugs, and I don't like that feeling of being out of control, it's not that I'm a control freak, it's just that I don't want to become unconscious or have – you know – have something terrible happen to me and I was scared that a spinal injection was going to leave me paralysed or something, that they'd put it in the wrong place. The whole thing is perilous.

NICKY: Going back to that time when you were wanting to become pregnant, we – I think you were one of the few women who insisted that the donor should be screened for HIV and AIDS, even though we came to realise that there was no real proof. In the late eighties and early nineties, there was still a lot of fear amongst the gay community that had been generated by the politicians of the time. I mean, some gay men do choose to have unsafe sex, but they know there's a risk to that. But I think that we were reasonably reassured once we felt that Simon was tested regularly.

LIZ: It was only his word, wasn't it?

NICKY: Yes. But I think in this country, if you actually look at our statistics within

HIV and AIDS, you still have a relatively small number, in comparison to the States, or Russia. But I did meet Simon.

Q: You did meet Simon?

NICKY: I did meet Simon, and he –

Q: You didn't remember his name, did you Liz?

LIZ: No, I did remember his name, I just didn't want to say it.

NICKY: We met in a café bar, somewhere like that, in Leeds.

LIZ: Was I with you?

NICKY: Yes, you were talking to some of our friends but I don't know whether we'd actually picked him by then. But we were talking to him about – you know – we thanked him for wanting to do this. He was a smallish man, my sort of size, and with my sort of height, and hair. He seemed quite a shy man to me. Wore glasses. Wasn't anything special about him. But he seemed quite genuine, and that's what mattered to us.

Q: You never heard from him? He didn't want to know if you were pregnant?

NICKY: No.

Q: Have you told Rowan about him?

LIZ: Yes. She knows his first name. We told her that her donor was a good man who helped us to make her by giving us his sperm. She seemed to accept that and has never seemed especially interested. It's lucky because she knows lots of children, both at school and elsewhere, who have been made by artificial insemination.

Q: Did you offer Simon anything in return?

LIZ: No. Now I think it would have been nice to give him a present, you know, via another woman. But at that time the whole thing seemed very fraught, I suppose we didn't even think about it. I know that sounds awful, but we were just so focused on what we were doing.

NICKY: Yes, I was still commuting.

Q: So you didn't go to the insemination group Nicky?

NICKY: No, I never went to anything like that.

Q: Was there ever an issue about you wanting to become the biological mother?

NICKY: No, I think I was quite clear from early on that I was . . . I never really felt as though I've ever wanted to be pregnant. I think very briefly when Rowan was getting older that I got broody for about two weeks. But I never felt as though I physically wanted to go through pregnancy.

Q: I'd like to go back and ask you the same question that I asked Liz about how you became aware of your lesbian identity?

NICKY: I suppose I knew from about seven or eight that I was different. I had three brothers, and I was the youngest. And I was really quite influenced by my father and brothers. Although my Mum tried very hard, I guess there's a sense of – some lesbian women who come to it from very early on, around ten or eleven, like I did. I suppose growing up in the sixties and seventies it was still unusual for anyone to acknowledge it – I mean you did feel like you were the only one. It was a lonely time. Then I had a series of relationships with women from about seventeen. I never thought about becoming a mother. I didn't. I knew I wanted to have a good career, but I didn't know what. And so I just – I left school and I sort of bombed around a little bit. And I read books, but it wasn't really till I met the woman I had a relationship with before Liz. She really wanted a baby, and that's when I really started thinking about children.

Q: So you'd never thought of motherhood for yourself?

NICKY: No. No. I never felt really maternal or broody about getting pregnant, but parenting was different. I'm also a wimp in the pain department, and I have witnessed that pregnancy is very, very painful.

Q: And when you got your periods? What did that feel like?

NICKY: I think inconvenience. Well, I knew there was a reason, but primarily it was an inconvenience. But becoming a parent with Nicky to Rowan has been very, very important to me.

Q: And how have your parents responded to becoming grandparents?

LIZ: They're very loving with her. She sees them more than she sees my parents.

Conclusion

The history of assisted reproductive technology has followed a similar trajectory to the history of midwifery, whereby infertility, like obstetrics, has become a corporate and medicalised business dominated by men. It was not until the nineteenth century that childbirth became an exclusively medical process; traditionally it was the handy woman, or midwife, who was regarded by local communities as the official birth attendant, whose duties also included laying out the dead and women's matters were considered to be women's business. It was not until the early 1660s that the word 'man-midwife' was added to the English language. With the invention of the obstetric forceps by Dr Peter Chamberlen, Surgeon to the Queen, in the seventeenth century, all medical men were in agreement that midwives should not be permitted to use instruments and it was forbidden to instruct women in any life-saving procedures. In Thomas Dawke's *The Midwife Rightly Instructed* (1736) the surgeon refused to instruct the isolated rural midwife in his technique to deal with haemorrhages (Donnison 1998).

There is little recorded literature in the history of medicine on issues concerning infertility, although the wise women and midwives would be credited with most knowledge. In England the first formal arrangements for the control of midwives were made under Henry VIII's Act of 1512 and under this Act women midwives were subject to stringent secular and ecclesiastic conditions. Because of these women's associations with fertility, contraception and abortion there was much anxiety on the part of legislators. Provisions of the oath were directed at preventing the false attribution of paternity, the substitution of children, and the destruction of the foetus. It is interesting to note that, as discussed in Chapter 8 by Sammy Lee, one of the principal advantages of producing donor sperm by masturbation on official clinic premises is that it prevents substitution of sperm samples.

Seventeenth-century drama contains many references to impotence and infertility with their feared repercussions on hereditary issues. Secret acts of donor insemination were both acknowledged and feared. It was not uncommon, as reported in the dramas, for women who were desperate to produce an heir for a geriatric husband to consult a doctor for infertility and achieve an 'inconceivable conception' through the informal and secret provision of donor insemination – by the medical expert, quack, or a younger admirer. Cuckoldry was feared by one and all.

Today, any controversy about donor insemination – which is the only ART technique practised that can be accomplished outside of a clinic for assisted reproduction, and which does not require any specialised medical knowledge – is less likely to provoke anxieties about cuckoldry and more likely to raise them about a person's rights to have access to information about their genetic inheritance.

Inevitably there are many doctors, technicians and nurses who are not happy about losing control and their medicalised speciality being appropriated, and cautionary myths abound. It is not uncommon for women to be warned, even threatened, that it is dangerous to undertake self-insemination procedures outside of the clinic setting because of the inherent risks of infection and contamination, with the attendant risks of foetal damage, when the procedure is not undertaken in a sterile setting. The fact that we are born, as Freud reminded us, between urine and faeces, or that ironically 'Love has pitched his mansion in the place of excrement' (Yeats 1952: 295), has long been lost to obstetric professional consciousness. (Please refer to Sammy Lee's chapter for a description of insemination in a medical setting.)

It is a well-documented fact that the screening processes in registered clinics eliminate a large proportion of men who express an initial interest in donating semen, so that the initial number of men coming forward needs to be several times greater than the demand. Published reports suggest that between 60 and 80 per cent of donors are not accepted and it has been suggested that donors become increasingly difficult to recruit because of the antiseptic stringency of current screening procedures. Among donors it is interesting to note that the practical aspects of donating semen, which include having a urethal swab and also having to masturbate to the doctor's (who is often male) command, cause them the most anxiety.

There are no laws in Britain against self-insemination: the Human Fertilisation and Embryology Authority (HFEA) appertains only to clinics that provide ART services. Nor is it unlawful for a woman to advertise for donors, or to obtain fresh sperm to do self-insemination in the privacy of her home. Despite the homophobia revealed in parliamentary debate in 1990, the HFEA does not forbid its registered clinics to treat single or lesbian women, and the medical director of a clinic holds responsibility for deciding who the clinic should treat. Whilst the Authority's guidelines suggest that clinics should not adopt any discriminatory policies, it also states: 'A woman shall not be provided with treatment services unless account has been taken of the welfare of any child who may be born as a result of the treatment including the need of that child for a father.'

Most lesbians who self-inseminate do so because they do not want the biological father's presence to be a factor in the family they are seeking to create. Many women also prefer that the act of insemination is conducted in the intimacy of the couple's bedroom. However, Clare, Debbie and Liz, the biological mothers of their children, wanted to know something about their donors, and Nicky also had some additional social contact with Liz's donor. As discussed in the interviews, all the women felt it was important not only to know things about the donor but also to have seen what he looked like. Yet it was not the aesthetics of appearance which mattered most to them, but an intuitive sense of the decency of the man who was to become the biological father of their children. Since 1993 legislation in the United Kingdom has required the HFEA to keep a confidential register of those people born as a result of donor insemination; the donors are encouraged to provide a pen-picture of themselves. The anonymity of donor identity is protected by law. Section 31 of the 1990 Act requires that HFEA-licensed clinics collect and store confidential identifying information about egg and sperm donors which records their age, date of birth, height, weight, ethnic group, eye, hair and skin colour, and whether they have children of their own. It also requires that donors specify their occupation and interests, and a brief description of themselves as a person which could be passed on to their child or its parents. This is to make provision for the possibility that a future parliament will make a decision to allow this information to become available to a child resulting from anonymous donor insemination when they reach the age of 18. Present law does not allow donors to receive any information about their offspring.

Clinic donors are also informed by law that they are not the legal parent of the child that they father, and that they have relinquished all rights and legal claims over offspring that may result from donated eggs. Furthermore donors are warned that: 'The possibility that a child born disabled as a result of the donor's failure to disclose defects about which he knew, or could reasonably have known may be able to sue the donor for damages.' Donors can be pursued under the Congenital Disabilities Act of 1976 if they knowingly conceal a family history of genetic disorder.

For those women who undertake self-insemination outside of the registered clinic a different set of laws prevail, whereby the donor is considered to be the unmarried father. As such he has no legal rights but he may acquire parental responsibility by applying for a court order under Section 4 of the Children Act. If the court grants him parental responsibility he will share this with the biological mother. As discussed by Lisa Saffron, 'Most women do self-insemination in order not to share parental responsibility with the child's biological father. The possibility of a donor acquiring parental responsibility equal to the mother's and more than that of a co-parent is very threatening.' She also refers to the fact that:

> By law . . . a child has a right to make claim to inherit from the donor's estate if he dies when the child is in need of financial support. The donor should be advised to make a will stating why he shouldn't make financial provision for this child. You don't have to put the donor's name on the child's birth certificate; in fact you can only do this if the man agrees and signs the application form.
>
> (Saffron 1994: 147)

Clare and Debbie were unhappy that as the non-biological parent of each other's child they, like the biological fathers who are discussed above, had no legal parental responsibility for each other's birth child. So in 1995 they successfully applied for joint parental responsibility for both their sons under the Children Act 1989. They were among the first lesbian couples in the UK to use this legislation, which enables any 'significant adult' in a child's life to apply for a residence order, and a growing number of lesbian parents have been able to make similar legal arrangements since then.

It is of interest that amongst heterosexual couples who have conceived through donor insemination every survey reveals that a higher proportion of donor insemination parents than IVF parents decide not to disclose the donor origins to their child, and the incidence of secrecy is increased when conception occurs as a result of donor sperm rather than donor eggs. This would suggest that protection of the father and fears that his infertility – which may be perceived as synonymous with a lack of potency – will be unmasked, take precedence over a balanced consideration of a child's subsequent need to understand his or her origins. An increasing number of accounts are now being reported in the media of cases of identity crisis and even emotional breakdown, where children have discovered the nature of the anonymity of their conception – which unlike adoption is predominantly a mystery even to their mothers – and felt dispossessed of their identity. In the case of lesbian families total secrecy about origins is far less common.

There are a growing number of adults, conceived by donor insemination, who are demanding legal rights to receive 'non-identifying' information about their donors. In March 2002, Joanna Rose, who was conceived by donor insemination, and an unnamed 5-year-old claimant, were given leave by the High Court to act under the Human Rights Act to ask the court to order the setting up of a register that will allow all donors to provide identifying information on a voluntary basis.

On Friday July 26, 2002, their campaign won the first step in its legal battle in the High Court. Mr Justice Scott Baker said that the court had not yet decided if the government's stance – blocking access to any information about donor parents – breached the new Human Rights Act or the European Convention on Human Rights, on which it is based. Joanna Rose responded saying that this ruling had created 'a legal foothold on which to establish our rights and identities. This is an important and heartening event on a long road to recognition of us as people – just like everyone else, with social and genetic roots – rather than as products'.

Bibliography

Donnison, J. (1998) *Midwives and Medical Men – A History of the Struggle for the Control of Childbirth*, London: Historical Publications Ltd.

Ellis, M.L. (1994) 'Lesbians, gay men and psychoanalytic training', *Free Associations*, 4(32): 501–517.

Saffron, L. (1994) *Challenging Conceptions*, London: Cassell.

Yeats, W.B. (1952) *The Collected Poems*, London: Macmillan.

Chapter 14

Egg donation
The mission to have a child

Sue Stuart-Smith

Sue Stuart-Smith is Specialist Registrar in Psychotherapy at the Tavistock Clinic and the Royal Free Hospital.

> 'You have a mission to have a child and that's your absolute goal and so like any other mission you look at the ways you can achieve that, and you set about achieving it.'
>
> (Spoken by Caroline)

Embarking on egg donation treatment is for many women like Caroline a new phase in what has been a long and painful quest to have a child. Preceding this they have experienced years of infertility, with failed IVF (in vitro fertilisation) treatments using their own eggs, before reaching a point at which their capacity to produce viable eggs has diminished. For other women, egg donation is and always has been the only prospect they have of achieving a pregnancy. These are women who for a variety of reasons do not have functioning ovaries. For some it is due to a premature menopause or a genetic disorder. For others it is because their ovaries have been damaged as a result of treatment for cancer in childhood or early adulthood: the chemo- or radiotherapy which has ensured their survival has also left them sterile. Couples in any of these situations are faced with a choice of accepting childlessness or considering either egg donation or adoption. Unlike adoption, egg donation offers the possibility for the male partner of becoming a genetic father, and for the woman offers the experience of pregnancy and childbirth and thereby the possibility of being a biological if not genetic mother.

The clinical material presented in this chapter is taken from two cases, both of which are part of an ongoing research project which the author is carrying out. The research project is a qualitative study of women receiving IVF treatment using donated eggs. The study involves carrying out in-depth, semi-structured interviews with women after they have received counselling at the clinic where they are being treated and before the egg donation treatment commences. At a later date some of the women will be followed up. Because the qualitative analysis and the data collection are still taking place it is not possible in this contribution to present a systematic account of the women's experiences. Instead the discussion will focus on material from two women, Caroline and Sarah. These two have been chosen because they illustrate two different routes to egg donation treatment. In order to preserve their anonymity, names and any identifying information have been changed and publication consent has been granted.

Background

During the early 1980s technological developments such as the ability to cryopreserve embryos and to harvest oocytes (eggs) transvaginally meant that embryos could be successfully stored and donated eggs could be collected less invasively than before. This led to the setting up of a small number of egg donation treatment programmes in the mid- to late 1980s. Publication of successful results from these centres has led on to the practice becoming more widespread. Because egg donation is a relatively recent development the majority of the children created by this route have yet to reach adulthood. Sperm donation has a much longer history in the treatment of fertility problems and there is now a population of adult sperm-donor children. Comparisons are sometimes made between sperm donation and egg donation, although there are considerable differences in terms of the treatment process. Sperm donation is relatively straightforward and does not require medical intervention for the donor. Donating eggs involves hormonal stimulation to produce the number of eggs required and medical intervention to collect them, neither of which is without risk, so that it requires considerable motivation to be an egg donor. In certain countries, such as Sweden, Austria and Switzerland, egg donation is considered unnatural and whereas sperm donation is licensed, egg donation is not. Since the development of this reproductive technology it has become possible to separate biological motherhood (pregnancy and childbirth) and genetic motherhood.

In the UK most egg donation treatment takes place in the private sector, but even so the waiting lists for treatment are long and can be anything from eighteen months to four years. After a failed attempt it is often necessary to wait the same length of time again. The reason for the long waiting times is because of the shortage of donor eggs. Most donors donate altruistically, unlike in the USA where eggs can be bought and sold. Donors are also required to be under the age of 35 years because this reduces the risk of chromosomal abnormalities. Many clinics operate on the basis that if a couple can bring in a donor, either for themselves or who is willing to donate to the general pool, they can move up the waiting list and be treated much more quickly.

In order to address the problem of the shortage of donors some IVF clinics have implemented a practice called egg sharing. This involves a woman who is undergoing standard IVF treatment donating some of her surplus eggs in return for a reduction in the cost of her own treatment. There has been some controversy over this practice (Ahuja et al. 1997), mainly over the issue of financial gain and whether there is a risk of women with fertility problems passing future fertility problems on to any resultant children, although in most cases the fertility problems are not inheritable. One perceived advantage is that in egg sharing the woman who donates the eggs would be undergoing the medical interventions and hormonal stimulation, required as part of her own IVF treatment, anyway and not solely for the purpose of donating. Egg sharing is always carried out on an anonymous basis, which is important, because it would be possible for the recipient of an egg to conceive a child while the donor's own IVF treatments fail.

The main choice facing couples embarking on treatment is whether to use an egg donor who is known to them or not. A known donor, usually a sister, cousin or close friend, means that the couple have some knowledge of the genetic input into the child and if it is a family member it offers the possibility of continuing the genetic line. But this route also raises complications in terms of the future relationship of the donor to the child and whether it is openly acknowledged within the family or not. The alternative is an anonymous donor who will be matched to the recipient on basic features such as ethnicity, size and eye colour. Because of the shortage of donors in this country there is not much scope for selecting specific donor characteristics. The anonymity of donors is sometimes regarded as necessary in order to preserve the supply of donors, but research suggests that it is more important to recipients than to donors. Kirkland et al., in a study of oocyte donation, compared attitudes of donors and recipients and found that whilst 63 per cent of donors said they would donate if the recipient was told their name, only 26 per cent of recipients would accept if the donor was given their name. In addition, 90 per cent of recipients were strongly against the donor contacting the child later in life, but 54 per cent of donors had no objection to the child contacting them (Kirkland et al. 1992).

Current practice in the UK is that the Human Fertilisation and Embryology Authority stipulates provision of counselling for all couples receiving and donating gametes or embryos, prior to treatment, but there is little in the way of help following this (Human Fertilisation and Embryology Act 1990). Increasing numbers of couples turn to the Donor Conception Network, which is an important and growing self-help organisation.

It may seem surprising that the overall success rate of IVF on egg donation treatment programmes is higher that the overall rate for standard IVF treatments using the recipient's own eggs. The rates are 33.2 per cent pregnancy rate per embryo transfer for egg donation and 22.2 per cent pregnancy rate per embryo transfer for standard IVF (Lindheim 1998). These figures are less surprising when you consider that the success rate of IVF depends more on the age of the egg than on the age of the woman who receives the resulting embryo, and egg donors are almost always under the age of 35. It is not uncommon for an older woman with a history of recurrent failures of IVF to be offered the possibility of treatment using donated eggs as a way of maximising her chances of a pregnancy. Success rates in these cases may be as much as two to three times greater (Schover 1993). If treatment is successful, however, there is a higher rate of miscarriages in egg donation pregnancies (23 per cent) than in standard IVF (20.3 per cent) (Lindheim 1998). A study in the UK has also shown that egg donation mothers have a high incidence of obstetric complications such as hypertension and post-partum haemorrhage (Abdalla and Kan 1998). Infertility is often a relative, rather than an absolute, diagnosis and even in patients waiting on egg donation treatment programmes there is still scope for a spontaneous natural pregnancy rate. One study has measured this in the USA and found a spontaneous pregnancy rate of 2.5 per cent in 200 women waiting on an egg donation treatment programme over a five-year period (Sauer 1995).

In terms of the longer-term outcome, most of the existing research on the subject of egg donation is questionnaire-based and focuses on attitudes and general psycho-social outcome. Applegarth *et al.* sent questionnaires to fifty-nine couples who had a child or children (age range 12 weeks to 7 years) born as a result of egg donation. They found that 81 per cent of the births had been by Caesarian section and that 84 per cent of the mothers had breastfed their babies. The children's health and development were described as within normal limits. The only area in which the couples' responses were inconsistent with each other was over the question of which (if any) family members were aware of their use of egg donation (Applegarth *et al.* 1995). Golombok *et al.* have followed up families with children created as a result of egg and sperm donation and found no evidence to date that the children (average age 6 years) are at increased risk for psychological problems (Golombok *et al.* 1996, 1999).

Although all this is reassuring it is also important to remember that some of the issues which arise from gamete (egg or sperm) donation may only become relevant as a child matures into an adult with his or her own reproductive capacity. Experience from work with adopted children has shown that, for many, knowledge of their biological or genetic origins is important and that this is particularly the case when they themselves enter adulthood (Hoopes 1990). It is still too early to know to what extent the experience of children born as a result of gamete donation will resemble this. It is known that the majority of couples (up to 80 per cent) who receive donated sperm opt not to tell the child about the nature of his or her conception (Cooper 1997). It appears that the figures in oocyte donation are not likely to be as high as this. A questionnaire survey carried out in the UK, of parents with a baby conceived through egg donation, indicated that 48 per cent intended to tell the child, with a similar number wanting to keep it secret (Kirkland *et al.* 1992). Cultural differences may also influence this decision: for example, in the USA a study of oocyte donation has found that 74 per cent intended to tell the child (Pettee and Weckstein 1993); a Finnish study found that 38 per cent intended to tell (Soderstrom-Anttila *et al.* 1998); and a French study has shown that the majority intended not to tell the child (Raoul-Duval *et al.* 1992).

But what about the mothers themselves? In terms of more detailed research, at present very little is known about these mothers' hopes, anxieties and fears, in relation to the pregnancy and the baby. One account of a case suggests that it can be difficult for a woman to turn down this form of treatment if she feels that she is depriving her partner of his only chance to have a genetic child (Cramond 1998). Another suggests that the first sight of the baby may be particularly charged with meaning because of anxieties over bonding and that the sex of the baby might affect how the mother feels about her lack of genetic relation to the child

(Rosenthal 1998). All these impressions are based on clinical anecdotes. The experience of infertility itself gives rise to powerful feelings such as loss, anger, shame, envy and powerlessness, in alternating cycles of hope and despair which have been well documented (Raphael-Leff 1992, Daniluk 1996, Williams 1997). Sandelowski's work on 'relinquishing infertility' has shown that the experience of infertility exerts an important influence on the process of an IVF pregnancy. Couples in Sandelowski's study (who were not using donated gametes) had difficulty in normalising the pregnancy, tending to regard it either as special or more fragile than a naturally occurring non-IVF pregnancy. Feelings of fragility were particularly likely when there were also obstetric complications. This study suggests that the process of pregnancy can represent a continuation of certain features of infertility treatment rather than an immediate release from it. Many women receiving donated eggs will have a previous history of treatments for conditions such as cancer or premature menopause as well as earlier IVF treatments and pregnancy losses, and they are also at high risk for obstetric complications. Sandelowski's work suggests that these experiences may well influence their perception of pregnancy and early motherhood (Sandelowski *et al.* 1992).

Case material

In this section, apart from the women's accounts themselves, I have set out to offer some preliminary thoughts about what is communicated both consciously and at times unconsciously by them. My understanding is based on thinking in psychodynamic terms about the impact of receiving a donated egg on the internal world of the recipient. This can only be a beginning – both in terms of this research project and also more widely in terms of our general understanding of the implications of this new technology for both the individual and collective psyche. It is worth remembering that by virtue of agreeing to take part in a study like this these women are more likely to be psychologically minded and are inevitably interested in being open with those around them about the egg donation.

Caroline

Caroline is a professional woman in her early forties who has been married for nearly ten years. Her 'mission to have a child' has grown in intensity and complexity over the eight years she and her husband have been trying. They underwent fertility investigations after several years of not conceiving naturally. All the investigations on her were normal but her husband was found to have a very low sperm count which necessitated IVF treatment using ICSI (intracytoplasmic sperm injection). At this point, Caroline was able to produce her own eggs but none of the embryos implanted in her during four years of IVF treatment resulted in a pregnancy. Recently she has been told that her capacity to produce eggs has declined to a point where in order to go ahead with any further IVF treatment they will need to use a donated egg. What started out as her husband's fertility problem has now become hers as well, although they will continue to be able to use his sperm. Looking back she is aware that earlier in her life she might have had a child if she had been with a different partner but she is also clear that her husband is the only man that she has ever wanted to have a child with. She thinks that the fact that they both now have fertility problems makes them better able to support each other and that neither of them feels it is exclusively his or her 'fault'.

Sarah

Sarah is in her early thirties and has known from the age of 17 that she would be unable to have children naturally because of undergoing treatment for a life-threatening cancer in her late teens. The treatment was successful but left her sterile and needing to take hormone replacements to maintain her oestrogen levels. She thinks that she could not have coped during her years of illness without her mother's unfailing support. She feels close to her mother and comes from a large extended family, growing up surrounded by younger nephews and nieces. From an early age, her main aim in life was to have a family of her own. In her twenties, the impact of surviving the cancer but being unable to fulfil her aim led to intermittent episodes of depression during which she continued to work but felt unable to sustain a close relationship with any of her partners. She sought help through counselling and psychotherapy as well as taking antidepressants for a time. Now in her thirties, she is more settled and has been in a relationship with her current partner for the last four years.

Thinking about the treatment

The prospect of fertility treatment with a donor egg inevitably gives rise to a new surge of hope, partly because it is a relatively successful treatment. Sarah describes feeling excited and energised as her hopes are raised: 'The day I've imagined since I was seventeen is almost there and that's quite a big thing for me.' At the same time she is confronted with a loss that will never be made good even if the treatment is successful: 'Loss, I think from never being able to have my own child and grief from the children, the baby that I will never have, that would be mine.'

Caroline, however, is also preoccupied by the specialist's words to her and her husband about their very slim chances of success using her own eggs. They were told that there was '"a less than a one per cent chance" – but even then of course, it means that there is one per cent chance – you clutch onto that, tiny one per cent'.

They are still considering whether to risk having one last IVF treatment before embarking on treatment with donor eggs:

> 'I don't really want to say okay that's it, we're not going to try any more and it's not even as if it can happen randomly with us – you know that we have a lot of sex and suddenly I'm pregnant because it just can't happen. So the day we say we're not doing another IVF is the day that's *it*. I'm keen to try one more go.'

Unlike Sarah who knows that she has no chance at all of ever having a genetic child, Caroline is struggling to relinquish her hope, however slim it is.

So far, Caroline and her husband have adopted a pragmatic approach of researching as much as possible themselves about possible fertility treatments and have always had the next treatment option in mind, so that when a treatment fails they know what to do next. For Caroline this has been essential in order to ward off the despair that she would otherwise feel at these moments. For a time egg donation was a next possible step on the horizon, but now that she is confronted with it more closely she describes her growing realisation of how much it differs from other steps in the IVF treatment ladder which they have already taken:

> 'It's not just a matter of delivering a solution, suddenly the emotional bit sort of kicks in and you think oh, there's a biological thing here where I'm saying goodbye to my biological links and when you get to that point, it will always be there.'

Receiving counselling about the implications of egg donation at the clinic where she is waiting for treatment has been the stimulus to her and her husband thinking about some of the wider issues both for them as a couple and for any child they might conceive. She speaks of how much it helps them that neither of them is to 'blame' and that they share the 'fault'. Feelings of blame and shame are commonly described by patients with fertility problems, and the concept of fault, with both its meanings of defect and culpability, is a powerful one. Although Caroline draws solace from the shared difficulty, she is also clearly struggling with the fact that, unlike her husband, her part of the fault will persist in the genetic fault-line that egg donation represents. She refers to the lack of genetic link as 'severance of the biological continuity'. Her own family have always taken an interest in their genealogy and she feels this makes it harder.

> 'I do feel it strongly. And of course it's pure vanity, but it's that thing in your life where you want to see what you can produce and what it will be like. Of course that wouldn't stop because it's not biologically your child, obviously it's still about nurturing, and carrying and giving the child opportunities.'

Sarah, although full of hope and enthusiasm, has some anxieties about the treatment. She describes a conversation with an old friend about some of her concerns:

'We were talking about the fact that it is somebody else's egg and he said, "Well, if your heart goes wrong, you'll have a bypass." Obviously it's a completely different thing, but in a way it's a similar kind of thing, in that if your body doesn't work properly for some reason you try and get by as you can.'

The analogy is an apt one because a bypass is not only about body-parts that fail but is also an alternative route, which is what this treatment offers – egg donation cannot overcome a fertility problem but provides a possible way round it.

Sarah longs for resolution and this extends to more than her lack of fertility:

'What I've found quite difficult since I was ill with the cancer was that I never felt I could leave it behind me because of the consequences, i.e. I am infertile, I found that very difficult, because I really wanted to move on with my life and I felt like the further away it got behind me, the closer I was to getting into the real repercussions which are that I couldn't have children. So I guess maybe I've always been so keen to have children because I thought that eventually when I did have a child, all of it would finish, it would end.'

She communicates a powerful, partly unconscious, wish for a baby to repair the whole traumatic experience of her cancer: 'I think, probably, in my head, somewhere, I have this ideal fantasy kind of world, where I'm married with kids and my whole life is brilliant and I think that's gone on since I was sixteen or seventeen.' However much she wishes to be able to put the experience of cancer behind her, as the interview progresses, it also becomes clear that she feels that she never will be able to do this entirely because it will always confront her in some way because of the fact of the missing genetic link.

Whilst the treatment represents an important source of hope for Caroline, she is much more concerned than Sarah by what she calls the 'biological severance' and focuses less on thoughts of repair. To an extent, egg donation contains within it the possibility of both. It is striking how the two women with their very different histories each focus on different aspects.

Thinking about the pregnancy

Sarah is concerned about whether, if she becomes pregnant, she will feel that the foetus is an alien thing inside her: 'I've just recently had feelings of, would I feel like I had somebody else's child growing inside of me?' At the same time she has a friend who is not in fertility treatment but who is frightened of becoming pregnant: 'She feels like she is going to have some alien thing growing inside her and that is nothing to do with egg donation, that's to do with growing a little person inside you.' Every pregnancy inevitably has an element of *me* and *not me* about it and therefore the scope for the pregnancy to seem alien. The struggle for egg donation recipients at this stage may be about how to identify a *me* part, which they would be contributing to the process. Sarah is preoccupied by this: 'It wouldn't be growing if it wasn't for me, you know, it wouldn't develop and it's only developing because of me, so in that sense it would be me making its blood and its bones, it's only the cell that's donated.'

Caroline describes how her husband

'feels very much that with donation, there is the kind of osmosis, you know, because, the baby is physically nurtured by you and obviously that's a huge thing. The fact that you go through the whole process and you deliver a baby which is pretty much yours, he sort of takes that on board and that means more – how do I describe it, he doesn't see the biological severance as such a big thing as I do.'

However, her reservations are outweighed by the fact that it will be her husband's genetic child and that they can both contribute to the influence of nurture.

All this highlights how little we still know about the role of the uterine environment. In being a biological (but not genetic) mother, the mother is still creating an internal environment for the foetus and providing the basic materials from which it grows and develops. In terms of the relative role of genes and environment we now know that far from being a straightforward split they are closely interwoven and mutually interactive processes. For example it is recognised that some aspects of genetically programmed postnatal brain development only take place in the presence of specific environmentally stimulated neurochemicals. Likewise the foetal environment is recognised to be more than a passive support system – but just how much more, we do not yet know. There is much to be discovered about the way a donor egg recipient mother might affect both the physiological and psychological development of the foetus.

Thinking about the donor

Both women think about possible donors by imagining how they would feel if they were to donate an egg. Caroline considers that if she could donate an egg she would want to understand a bit about the environment in which 'the child, the egg bit of the child would be being brought up'. She and Sarah both regard it as one of the most generous and altruistic things a woman could possibly do and that perhaps a motivation might be that they have some knowledge and understanding of the pain of infertility, either from their own experience or that of someone close to them. This is Sarah speaking: 'I think that the difference between women and men is that men donating sperm don't have this kind of psychological image of all their children running round and women do.' It seems that in these women's minds the thought of this single cell already represents a fantasy child and they feel that this is probably the case for a donor too. Inevitably this makes the giving and receiving of such a donation all the more complex and powerful.

Sarah had imagined up until recently that she might ask one of her sisters to donate an egg to her 'because then it would have both my mum's and my dad's genes', but she is moving away from this idea. She wonders how she would feel if she had 'a little girl who looked identical to one of my nieces'. In addition she thinks that 'for the child to know who their genetic mother is, I just think that would be more difficult than having an anonymous donor'. As a result she and her partner have decided to opt for an anonymous donation. She feels this will also allow them to preserve a stronger sense of themselves as a couple and that a known donor would intrude on them: 'I just want it to be, to do with me and Mark, if it was a known donor, there would always be somebody, a third party there who is to do with our child and I don't want that.'

Caroline has a close friend who she has considered asking to donate directly to her because she likes her and her children so much. However she is afraid that the friend or the friend's husband would think of the child as her friend's child because: 'If I gave somebody my egg I would spend the first part of that child's life looking at it and thinking, oh yes it is like mum or dad or me or whoever and not I hope in any negative way but it would just be curiosity.' Although she and her husband have decided to pursue anonymous donation she would ideally prefer to know more about the donor: 'The ideal would be your absolutely best friend who was totally wonderful and has wonderful children, donating an egg and then going to live in Australia. So it's just not there, just not on your doorstep.' Like Sarah, she is concerned about the link between the donor and a child and its potential to undermine her sense of being a mother: 'I don't want to run the risk of somebody ever turning round to me and saying "That's my child".' Sarah and Caroline both feel that anonymous donation might protect them to some extent from this and would give them a more secure basis from which to embark on their motherhood.

Because of the shortage of egg donors there is inevitably not much scope for choice about donor characteristics. At present, information about a potential donor is provided on a form that documents the donor's ethnic origin, employment, their interests or hobbies and basic physical attributes such as size and eye colour. Both Sarah and Caroline say that they also care about qualities such as sense of humour and intellect but know that they cannot have access to this kind of knowledge of their donor.

Because of the long waiting list for treatment Caroline and Sarah are trying to recruit a donor who would be prepared to donate to the general egg bank so that they can receive treatment more quickly. Apart from approaching friends and relatives the clinics often suggest other strategies such as putting up a notice in the GP's surgery and advertising in magazines and newspapers. This is Caroline speaking:

> 'We'll try putting up notices and probably some ads, hopefully in some magazines. But I find that slightly random, in that there is a reference number they ask people to quote, which is the identifier and you sort of think well what if they don't get the right number or they miss the reference and then we don't know who it is and then I lose my donor.'

Along with all the other random things that she has experienced Caroline is anxious that she will miss out again and lose a donor. It is as if all the losses involved in the treatment so far have produced in her a state in which she has become sensitised to loss and is fearful of any further losses.

Thinking about the child

Caroline and Sarah both envisage telling a child they might conceive about the fact that they have been created from a donated egg. They have also told their respective parents and parents-in-law that they are embarking on the treatment. Sarah is clear that, because of her complex medical history, it would not be possible for her to keep the egg donation a secret even if she wanted to:

> 'I hope that if we had a child it would always view me as its mother, but know that it, genetically had another mother . . . I just think that it's the right thing to do and I hope it wouldn't change the way the child felt about me, which is why I think it's important that they know from a very early age, so it's not a sudden realisation or shock.'

The counselling that is provided on egg donation treatment programmes helps recipients to think about issues that might arise in the future but is not directive about issues such as whether a child should know about its origins. Caroline has started to think more about this since she and her partner attended counselling:

> 'We had assumed there was no question of telling the child. Not that we had thought about it much, but on my part the assumption was, that once you got the egg, that's it. But, you know, having thought about it, it makes sense, that the child should know more. But like all those things I suppose it's the fear that the child will go, "Oh god you're not my real mother, I'm going. I'm going to go and find my real mother."'

Both women are afraid that in being open with a child about his or her origins they will lay themselves open to being rejected or regarded as less significant. Sarah, however, rather as with her fears about the pregnancy, links to a more ordinary experience of being a mother:

> 'I think you have to not be shocked if they turn round and say vile things to you like "you're not my real mother". Because I think children can be vile anyway, they can say things that are just as hurtful whether you're their biological or genetic mother or not, like "Why did you bother having me?"'

Caroline is also concerned about whether she might, in turn, experience rejecting feelings:

'In the back of your mind you're thinking what if I have this completely ghastly, terrible child, who I just don't like? Now I'm sure Mother Nature would never let you not like your child but it's not a conversation I would ever have with my mother because she would pick it up and run with it, and take it all the way. One thing you don't want to reinforce is any feeling you might have that somehow you haven't got a connection with this child, it's the sort of nightmare scenario if you look at your child doing something horrible and you think oh, that must have come from the mother.'

She invokes Mother Nature as a benign force to counteract her fears. The other two mothers who appear here are less benign. It appears that she feels separated from her own mother through being unable to conceive naturally and that the genetic mother can loom in her mind as a potentially bad taint. Whilst the anonymity of the donor may be felt in most ways to be protective it might also have the potential to heighten anxieties about 'bad blood'.

These two women have described how the potential donor is felt as a possible intruder both into the marital/couple relationship and the mother–child relationship. In addition, the treatment process of IVF is itself physically and psychologically intrusive. It undermines a couple's sexual intimacy and introduces a third person into the reproductive process in the form of the treating doctor. In gamete donation, a different third figure, that of the donor, will persist far beyond the treatment process for both the couple and the child. At a deeper level, especially for the recipient, the existence of such a third figure carries the potential to stir up oedipal anxieties to do with rivalry, dependency and feelings of inadequacy. Where there is a known donor, the complexities of the relationship will be grappled with externally as well as internally. In anonymous donation, where there is often very little information about the donor, the donor figure will still occupy a place in the inner world of the recipient mother and, later on, within the child as well. The donor appears from the accounts given here to be a figure of potential dual aspect within the internal world. On the one hand she is felt to be a generous and beneficent figure who donates the gift of life, and on the other she appears as an excluded figure who might return later on with adverse consequences. These kinds of fears lie deep within the human psyche. They feature strongly in families who adopt a child as well as in certain age-old fairy tales in which a figure returns to reclaim a child. It seems that even in the face of the most sophisticated technology, what we, as humans, have to manage psychologically are still some of the most basic and primitive forms of anxiety.

Bibliography

Abdalla, H.I. and Kan, A.K.S. (1998) Outcome of ovum donation pregnancies. *Contemporary Reviews in Obstetrics and Gynaecology* 10(3): 165–170.

Ahuja, K.K., Mostyn, B.J. and Simons, E.G. (1997) Egg sharing and egg donation: attitudes of British egg donors and recipients. *Human Reproduction* 12(12): 2845–2852.

Applegarth, L., Goldberg, N.C., Cholst, I. *et al.* (1995) Families created through ovum donation: a preliminary investigation of obstetric outcome and psychosocial adjustment. *Journal of Assisted Reproduction and Genetics* 12(9): 574–580.

Cooper, S. (1997) Ethical issues associated with the new reproductive technologies. In *Infertility, Psychological Issues and Counselling Strategies*, ed. S.R. Leiblum, Wiley, New York, pp. 41–66.

Cramond, J. (1998) Counselling needs of patients receiving treatment with gamete donation. *Journal of Community and Applied Social Psychology* 8: 313–321.

Daniluk, J.C. (1996) When treatment fails: the transition to biological childlessness for infertile women. *Women and Therapy* 19(2): 81–98.

Golombok, S., Brewaeys, A., Cook, R. *et al.* (1996) The European Study of Assisted Reproduction Families. *Human Reproduction* 11: 2324–2331.

Golombok, S., Murray, M., Brinsden, P. and Abdalla, H. (1999) Social versus biological parenting: family functioning and the socio-emotional development of children conceived by egg or sperm donation. *Journal of Child Psychology and Psychiatry* 40: 519–527.

Hoopes, J.L. (1990) Adoption and identity formation. In *The Psychology of Adoption*, ed. D.M. Brodzinsky and M.D. Schechter, Oxford University Press, Oxford, pp. 127–145.

Human Fertilisation and Embryology Act (1990) HMSO, London.

Kirkland, A., Power, M., Burton, G. *et al.* (1992) Comparison of attitudes of donors and recipients to oocyte donation. *Human Reproduction* 7(3): 355–357.

Lindheim, S.R. (1998) Indications, success rates and outcomes. In *Principles of Oocyte and Embryo Donation*, ed. M.V. Sauer, Springer, New York, pp. 167–208.

Pettee, D. and Weckstein, N. (1993) A survey of parental attitudes toward oocyte donation. *Human Reproduction* 8(11): 1963–1965.

Raoul-Duval, A., Letur-Konirsch, H. and Frydman, R. (1992) Anonymous oocyte donation: a psychological study of recipients, donors and children. *Human Reproduction* 7(1): 51–54.

Raphael-Leff, J. (1992) The Baby Makers: psychological sequelae of technological intervention for fertility. *British Journal of Psychotherapy* 7: 239–294.

Rosenthal, J.L. (1998) Psychological aspects of care. In *Principles of Oocyte and Embryo Donation*, ed. M.V. Sauer, Springer, New York, pp. 167–208.

Sandelowski, M., Harris, B.G. and Black, B.P. (1992) Relinquishing infertility: the work of pregnancy for infertile couples. *Qualitative Health Research* 2(3): 282–301.

Sauer, M.V. (1995) Spontaneous pregnancy in women awaiting oocyte donation. *Journal of Reproductive Medicine* 40(9): 630–632.

Schover, L.R. (1993) Psychological aspects of oocyte donation. *Infertility and Reproductive Clinics of North America* 4(3): 483–501.

Soderstrom-Anttila, V., Sajaniemi N., Tiitinen, A. and Hovatta, O. (1998) Health and development of children born after in-vitro fertilization and parents' attitudes regarding secrecy. *Human Reproduction* 13(7): 2009–2015.

Williams, M.E. (1997) Toward a greater understanding of the psychological effects of infertility on women. *Psychotherapy in Private Practice* 16(3): 7–26.

The shadow

Chapter 15

Dark reflections

The shadow side of assisted reproductive techniques

Diane Finiello Zervas

Diane Finiello Zervas is a Jungian psychoanalyst.

Dark annunciation

The air was hot and humid as I walked down the winding road that led from Bellosguardo into Florence in late July 1966. After a blissful two months as a student on the Sarah Lawrence Summer School Programme, I was entering the city to take leave of my favourite monuments before returning to America to complete my last year at university. I had adored my stay, and learned much about the works of art with which I had first fallen in love some four years earlier, on a trip that determined my future career: the history of the art of Renaissance Florence. Now, my suitcases stuffed with Italian clothes and shoes, I was eager to return home. My future appeared limpid and secure as perhaps it could only to the baby-boomer generation to which I belonged: graduation, marriage to my Yale boyfriend, to whom I'd written all summer, eschewing the persistent attentions of numerous Italian *papagalli* (persistent male followers best handled, we were told, by ignoring their existence), and graduate school, with its promise of a career, to be indulged in before settling down to raise a family.

Musing on these certainties, I reached my destination, the vast, barn-like church of S. Croce, determined to see Giotto's Bardi Chapel, with its scenes from the life of St Francis, founder of the Franciscan order. There could have been no greater contrast between the path of worldly and material renunciation deliberately chosen by this young aristocrat, who had dedicated himself to God and Lady Poverty, and the one I envisioned for myself. I made my way down the right-hand side of the cool nave, stopping along the way to admire Donatello's Cavalcanti *Annunciation*, with its monumental sculpted *Virgin* recoiling in fear and self-protection from the *Angel* on her right, who bowed before her with his incomprehensible message: 'And, behold, thou shalt conceive in thy womb, and bring forth a son, and shalt call his name Jesus' (Luke 1: 31).

As I stood before this work, contemplating the particular circumstances that both separated the Mother of God from all her worldly sisters, and yet united her with us, all daughters of Eve, I became aware that I was no longer alone. Lingering nearby, and intruding rudely on my aesthetic reveries, stood a dark, swarthy man. 'Not a *papagallo*, but a Gypsy', I thought, annoyed at this abrupt intrusion into my space. Ignoring his presence, I walked on, climbing the few steps that separate the nave from the chancel and its side chapels, into the narrow and magical space of the Bardi Chapel. He followed me. 'How dare he!' I muttered, staring fixedly at *St Francis's Trial by Fire before the Soldan* on the right wall. To no avail. He moved closer and closer, until I could sense his unfamiliar bodily odour and breath. 'Leave me alone', I ordered, pushing him away with disgust. He paid no attention. Instead, like some angry demon, he backed me into the right corner of the chapel, his face distorted with anger. Frightened, I cowered as he spat out his words, the antithesis of Gabriel's message. 'I curse you', he exclaimed, 'I curse you and your unborn children! May you remain barren; may your children never live to see the light of day!' Then he was gone, departing as mysteriously as he had appeared.

Optimistic child of my era, and Protestant by upbringing, I shrugged off this extraordinary archetypal experience, which then merely cast a shadow over my last day in Florence. In reality, however, it was an annunciation of changes that I could not possibly have imagined. Within three months of my return, Florence was severely damaged by the flood of November 1966. Within another two years, my life with my fiancé was in tatters. My art historical career became a necessity, not a luxury. My first marriage, turbulent and short-lived, produced my first miscarriage. By the time I was 37 I had had two more, the last a heartbreaking end, at six months, to an unplanned but lovingly accepted pregnancy.

My mind hovered uneasily around the events in the Bardi Chapel some fifteen years earlier, as my husband and I tried again, unsuccessfully, to begin our family. When I was 39 I decided to seek medical help. My feelings were ambivalent; my older husband and I had successful professional careers, and I feared the risks of another late pregnancy. But surely it was our right to have a child, the tangible product of a stable relationship after previous disappointments? My female gynae-cologist agreed, and referred us to a Harley Street fertility expert. He was, to be fair, realistically pessimistic as he guided us through our initial examinations. Ours was not a case of unexplained infertility, as my husband had also fathered a son in a previous marriage, but of age-related infertility. In order to 'assist nature', my husband and I underwent a course of artificial insemination. But the Gypsy's words continued to echo in my mind, heightening my fear about the possible conse-quences of such an unnatural pregnancy: suppose the foetus was abnormal, or I miscarried yet again? Worse still, suppose we were to dislike the child we had worked so hard to create? The Gypsy had appeared to speak a truth; what would happen if I consciously attempted to negate it? If I could not accept his dark annunciation – my reproductive fate – perhaps I would remain caught in his spell. I decided that if this first attempt failed, I would not try again. Nor would I consider any other methods of assisted reproductive technology (ART), especially in vitro fertilisation (IVF), as I knew of at least one acquaintance whose IVF treatment in the late 1970s had resulted not in a much-wanted child, but rather in ovarian cancer and death.

I did fail to conceive, and have had to live with the ever-present sorrow and loss that childlessness, for me, has brought, despite life's other successes. My decision to accept the Gypsy's dark annunciation has made me particularly sensitive to the shadow aspects of ART, those unexpected or negative possibilities that are often downplayed, ignored or suppressed in a couple's (or individual's) unrelenting determination to produce offspring at whatever cost. This chapter is not meant to belittle the precious lives that have been created by ART, but rather to look, physically, psychologically and archetypically, at the shadow dimensions of this remarkable process, particularly for older women.

Psychological attitudes before and during ART treatments

If, as women, we assume that the passage from partner to mother will occur naturally (if that is what we desire, or even if we remain ambivalent), the seeming inability or, worse yet, failure to conceive can be deeply upsetting, often leading to a lowered state of self-esteem. Long before a decision is made to seek help, the potentially infertile woman may become frustrated, anxious, angry, stressed and depressed, feeling that her basic femininity is threatened.

Not surprisingly, those women who identify most strongly with the traditional role of partner–mother (and with their own mothers) are the ones most severely affected by the threat of infertility (Cook 1993; Van Balen and Trimbos-Kemper 1995). Because of their difficulties in imagining a different feminine role for themselves, this particular sub-group of women is more likely to suffer from anxiety and depression before initiating medical investigations, to become compulsively/obsessively addicted to ART procedures, and to suffer psychosomatic and psychological disorders after failed treatment (Kemeter 1988; Hynes et al. 1992). Medical and psychological research has confirmed that women with a history of depressive symptoms are twice as likely to report infertility as those with no previous history, which suggests that depressive symptoms and the use of antidepressant medication may be significant factors in the pathogenesis of infertility (probably by means of various psychoendocrinological, psychoimmunological and behavioural mechanisms (Lapane et al. 1995)). It is important that depressed women who perceive themselves to be threatened by infertility should, if possible, have an opportunity for counselling and therapy before undergoing the arduous medical investigations and treatment associated with ART, particularly as the successful pregnancy rate is also significantly lower (less than half) for seriously depressed women compared with their non-depressed counterparts, in the twelve months following ART procedures (Thiering et al. 1994).

Similarly, medical reports made during the 1970s and 1980s found that infertility, whether or not medically diagnosed, and some aspects of infertility testing and treatment often led to emotional stress and marital problems.[1] Not surprisingly, a pilot study carried out in 1985 found that 71 per cent of women awaiting IVF treatment experienced decreased sexual enjoyment while undergoing infertility investigations (Dennerstein and Morse 1985), and another report found that 74 per cent of women with primary infertility feared that negative results of investigations would cause their partners to devalue them as women (Wallace 1985). Many infertile women, whether diagnosed or not, employ avoidance-coping strategies before treatment, such as limiting contact with friends who have children (Raval *et al*. 1987). Evidence also suggests that marital and sexual problems appear to peak in the period before infertility investigations begin, with a significant drop during treatment; women, however, experience the lowest level of marital happiness before any medical investigation, in contrast with men, for whom the nadir occurred while awaiting diagnosis (Van Keep and Schmidt-Elemdorff 1975). Recent research confirms that both partners embarking on IVF and donor insemination (DI) are likely to experience high levels of anxiety (Cook *et al*. 1989: 91), whereas depression, more often associated with loss and mourning, is likely to occur after unsuccessful treatment (Slade *et al*. 1997; Eugster and Vingerhoets 1999), possibly as a result of unrealistic expectations, but also because of their failure to achieve the much-desired role of parent.

Not surprisingly, women who prove to be infertile become more depressed the longer fertility treatment continues (Chiba *et al*. 1997). The psychological symptoms associated with female infertility, moreover, continue long after the final diagnosis. Both the raised rate and the intensity of depression in infertile women are similar to those experienced by patients diagnosed with cancer, or hypertension, or who are undergoing cardiac rehabilitation, and in many cases the depression may endure up to six years following fertility treatment.[2] Long-term effects of infertility on women have been found to include lowered confidence and self-esteem, hostility, and more health complaints; in one study a third of the long-term infertile women interviewed continued to have serious well-being problems (Van Balen and Trimbos-Kemper 1993).

Thus, in order to survive both the experience of infertility and the often long-term investigative procedures and treatments, couples need to have experienced a stable and mutually supportive partnership. From the view of evolutionary psychology, this is understandable, as a diagnosis of infertility thwarts the primary reproductive urge that forms the deep instinctual substratum of couple-making, thereby inhibiting the maternal and paternal archetypes from unfolding naturally, and threatening both partners with the possibility of rejection and abandonment if reproductive goals are not sufficiently countered by more differentiated life goals.

The shadow body

The woman who seeks treatment for infertility needs to consider any potential short- or long-term physical effects. These may include the possible risks of infertility drugs to herself, although a recent study suggests that most infertile women are prepared to endure a significant amount of physical discomfort and the possibility of potential long-term physical risks to themselves in order to conceive a much-desired baby.[3] There are several areas of concern for the prospective ART mother. These include hyperstimulation of the ovaries, which can sometimes be fatal (Smith and Cooke 1991; Pawson 2001); the risks associated with a multiple pregnancy, and the increased age-related risks of pregnancy; the possible side effects of the ovulation-inducing drug clomiphene citrate (CC)[4] and human meno-pausal gonadotropin (hGM); the risks of laparoscopy, used for egg extraction, and the related risks of surgery and anaesthesia; and any potential uterine infection caused by the sometimes painful hysterosalpingography, used for radiography of the interior of the uterus and fallopian tubes, or by intra-uterine implantation.

Over the last decade, there has also been increased media coverage about potential links between fertility drugs and ovarian and breast cancers. In Britain, two high-profile cases underscored such concerns. In 1997, the 33-year-old journalist Ruth Picardie died of breast cancer almost two years after conceiving her twins by IVF treatment, having written about her terminal illness in the *Observer* magazine *Life*.[5] The following year, Liz Tilberis, editor-in-chief of *Harper's Bazaar*, published her autobiography *No Time to Die*, which chronicled her five-year struggle with ovarian cancer. Tilberis, whose primary infertility had been caused by undiagnosed pelvic inflammatory disease, linked her cancer with the fertility drugs she had taken for three months before and during her nine cycles of IVF treatment at a leading London infertility clinic in the early 1980s (Tilberis 1998: 5–7, 33–44, 102ff., 241ff.). She died in April 1999, aged 51.

Do such cases provide evidence of fertility drugs' potential to constellate a cancerous shadow body, provoking the conception or stimulation of a malignant growth rather than, or in addition to, a much-wanted child? And how has the medical profession evaluated and interpreted such risks over the last decade, as enough data became available for preliminary analyses?

To begin with, such concerns must be placed in their proper context. Both ovarian and breast cancers are still rare. In the United States, for example, there is an overall lifetime risk of 1.8 per cent for ovarian cancer and 12 per cent for breast cancer (Whittemore 1994). As all the most recent medical studies emphasise, the aetiologies of these cancers are multifactorial, including various genetic, environ-mental and endocrinologic factors. Moreover, their incidence in the general population is age-linked, so that older recipients of fertility drugs automatically fall within the higher-risk categories. Furthermore, oral contraceptive use, preg-nancy and breastfeeding are known to lower the risks of both diseases.

Nevertheless, retrospective studies published during the early 1990s did appear to find significant links between fertility drugs and reproductive cancers. In 1992, a threefold increased risk of ovarian cancer was reported among infertile women who had used ovarian-stimulating fertility drugs, and a twenty-sevenfold increased risk for women who had not been pregnant before (Whittemore et al. 1992b). In 1994 an increased risk (11.1 per cent) of ovarian cancer was observed among women who had been prescribed CC for twelve months or more (like Liz Tilberis), compared with those who had taken it less frequently.[6] Use of hGM was also linked with a ninefold increased risk of low-risk borderline ovarian tumours in a 1996 report (Shushan et al. 1996). Two other retrospective studies from this early period of research found no substantive links between fertility drugs and ovarian cancer (Ron et al. 1987; Venn et al. 1995). By 1996, the overall lifetime risk of ovarian cancer for women who had taken fertility medication was estimated as between 4 and 5 per cent.[7]

Now, however, a different pattern appears to be emerging, one of serious concern for a particular sub-group of women seeking treatment for infertility. For although studies published between 1996 and 2000 indicate that ovulation-inducing fertility drugs do not appear to be *causally* linked with ovarian cancer among *fertile* women, there are significant links between *infertile* women, ovarian cancer, and certain fertility drugs (Bristow and Karlan 1996), a possibility that had received scant attention in the earlier literature.[8] In one study, for example, women who had given birth were found to have a 61 per cent lower risk of ovarian cancer in general than women who had opted to remain childless or had been unable to conceive, and this risk was lowered with each successive full-term pregnancy. By contrast, there was a 50 per cent increased risk of ovarian cancer among involuntarily infertile and nulliparous women compared to age-matched controls, certainly a matter of great concern both for women with unexplained infertility and for those who have postponed childbearing to the end of their reproductive careers.[9]

In addition, it has been argued that infertile women who used certain fertility drugs, in particular CC, had between 2.5 and 2.8 times the risk of ovarian cancer compared with women without a history of infertility.[10] According to three of those studies, those who took the drug and became pregnant did not share this risk, while those who failed to conceive after treatment incurred a twenty-sevenfold increased risk of ovarian cancer.[11] The fourth study, moreover, found that nearly three-quarters of the women who developed ovarian tumours had used CC, and that stronger or prolonged doses of this drug (1000 mg or more) significantly increased risk.[12] Finally, evidence also suggests that fertility drugs may stimulate or hasten the growth of pre-existent or undiagnosed ovarian cancers, or act as possible mutagenic agents of benign to cancerous tumours, although this may again be related to the sub-group of women with particularly refractory infertility (Bristow and Karlan 1996; Salle *et al.* 1997). Thus, women who do not remain childless by choice appear to constitute a high-risk group in which infertility is a symptom of an underlying factor that predisposes them both to decreased fertility and ovarian cancer.[13]

Opinions regarding the potential effects of fertility drugs on the subsequent development of breast cancer appear mixed. In one study, the use of CC was associated with a reduced risk of contracting the disease (Rossing *et al.* 1996b). Another recent retrospective report noted a slightly higher risk for women exposed to CC or hMG (1.65 per cent, increasing to 2.6 per cent and 2.52 per cent for women associated with one to two CC treatments and doses of 1000 mg or less), although it concluded that there appears to be no excessive risk of developing breast cancer among infertile women treated with CC or hMG as compared with the general population, and that CC may in fact reduce the risk of breast cancer in infertile women (Potashnik *et al.* 1999). As in the case of ovarian cancer, however, infertility is also associated with an increased risk of breast cancer.[14] Recent research indicates an increased risk of breast cancer among women with fertility problems plus late age at first birth, and it seems possible that future research may uncover a common underlying factor for all three complaints (Weiss *et al.* 1998).

In conclusion, any woman concerned about the possibility of the cancerous shadow effects of ovulation-induction fertility treatment must be prepared to consider the potential risks in terms of her family and personal medical history, oral-contraceptive use, previous (if any) pregnancies, type of infertility, and present age, tempered by the knowledge that fertility treatment, like hormone-replacement therapy, is still a relatively new and developing technique, and thus it is still too early to ascertain the full extent of any long-term outcome. The woman who has remained involuntarily infertile, however, is faced by an additional dilemma: whether it is in her best interest, physically, to attempt conception in order to lower her risk of ovarian and breast cancers, in other words to attempt a pregnancy that would possibly protect herself in addition to creating the previously inconceivable child, regardless of the potential personal, psychological and social consequences.

Shadow babies? Potential effects of treatment on ART-conceived children

Despite increasing public familiarity with ART and its growing success rates, there is no doubt that these new techniques have created a 'Brave New World' whose territory is still largely unexplored, with many potential benefits, pitfalls and challenges to our traditional notions of reproduction and families. The processes used to create ART children (particularly by egg donation, donor insemination, embryo transfer, GIFT-related procedures, IVF and surrogacy) do set them apart from naturally conceived children, as is evident from the growing body of research about them in the last two decades. From a Jungian perspective, these previously inconceivable children are the modern-day counterparts of the mythical hero, who often experienced an unusual or traumatic conception or birth, a difficult childhood (orphaned, raised by one or more sets of parents, and in some cases overprotected), and had to overcome considerable challenges in order to reach his full potential. Having made the decision to enter this unfamiliar realm of ART, what are the potential risks – the shadow aspects of the process – that women and their partners might encounter during the conception, gestation and development – the 'heroic' journey – of the ART-created child?

Shadow eggs, sperm and embryos

Most fertility experts would argue that the potential risks to the ART-produced embryo and foetus are no greater than the ones encountered in a normal pregnancy, with the added proviso that they are often working with a 'high-risk' group of women (Winston 2000: 16–24). Because (at the present time) the quality of the embryo is directly related to the egg and sperm that have created it, and egg quality is inversely related to a woman's age, the older she is when she attempts a pregnancy, the greater the chances that she may produce defective eggs. When fertility drugs are used to stimulate ovulation or multiple follicle production in older pre-menopausal women, more defective eggs may be produced, lowering the chances for a healthy embryo and pregnancy, and increasing the possibility of non-fertilisation, non-implantation, a defective foetus, and early miscarriage. If clomiphene, the standard fertility pill, is used to stimulate follicle production, it is apparently difficult to predict when the LH surge – necessary for egg maturation – will occur, and thus eggs may be released (and harvested for GIFT-related or IVF use) before they are mature enough to be successfully fertilised; moreover up to half of clomiphene-induced eggs have been found to have chromosomal anomalies (Lee 2001). Concern has also been voiced about any eventual patho-logical effects on children created from gametes that have been exposed to the high levels of oestrogen produced during multiple ovulation in certain ART procedures, given that exo-oestrogens used to prevent miscarriages in the 1950s sometimes produced abnormal malignant vaginal changes in women in their late-teens or early twenties. Similarly, what might be the impact on the eventual fertility of male ART children, given the suggested links between environmentally produced oestrogens and male infertility (Lee 1996: xii–xiv)?

There are also potential problems with the use of frozen semen, known to be less fertile than fresh semen, and with the delicate procedure of intracytoplasmic sperm injection (ICSI), which may cause physical or short- or long-term genetic damage to the sperm or egg (Winston 2000: 10, 66–82). Similarly, embryos may become physically or genetically damaged in the freezing/thawing processes, and the chances of producing a live baby from a previously frozen embryo are about half (11.6 per cent) those of employing a fresh one (Winston 2000: 114, 126–7). The use of frozen eggs also involves risks and carries a very low success rate, but the United Kingdom Human Fertilisation and Embryology Authority has recently decided to license their use in fertility treatment (HFEA Policy Update and Issues 2000).

Claims have also been made that IVF pregnancies may carry a higher incidence of physical and mental retardation, and of abnormalities including defective cytokinesis (last stage of cell division), skeletal and growth problems, heart and lung disorders, brain disorders, kidney problems, digestive system disorders, ear, nose and throat problems, gland and genital disorders, and a risk of Siamese twins (Dyson 1995). In the case of IVF treatment, preimplantation genetic diagnosis (PGN) may be used to screen embryos for inherited genetic diseases before implantation, although the procedure itself involves some risks, including possible contamination, diagnostic error or failure, cell damage, and, because two embryos are usually transferred to the uterus, the possibility of twins (Winston 2000: 83–101). Finally, the antenatal anxiety, worry and stress experienced by many women attempting ART-conceived pregnancies (augmented by a diagnosis of a multiple pregnancy or a decision to selectively reduce the number of foetuses) may well have negative physiological effects on the gestating child.

As with any other medical procedure, there is always a possibility of human error. In October 2001, a leading fertility expert was accused of allegedly implanting many more than the legal number of eggs into the wrong fallopian tube of a GIFT patient (Van Guens and Morris 2001). In 2000 there was panic after two fertility clinics in Hampshire, England alerted forty women that their stored embryos had gone missing and that they might therefore have been implanted with the wrong embryos and given birth to babies that were not their biological children, a modern-day version of maternity ward error (Booth and Syal 2000; Hawkes 2000).

Media coverage has also highlighted another growing area of controversy and litigation: the custodianship, use and/or disposal of frozen embryos produced by a couple who subsequently divorce. In one recent case, the divorced biological mother wished to use the embryos herself; in another, the divorced biological father wished them to be donated or preserved for implantation in a future partner. In both instances the American courts ruled that preserved embryos should not be used against an ex-partner's will, thereby avoiding unwanted biological parenthood and legal responsibility for any future offspring.[15]

Shadow babies/children

Accumulating evidence suggests that ART-produced babies and children differ little from their naturally conceived or adopted counterparts (Levy-Shiff et al. 1998; Bruinsma et al. 2000). In the early 1990s, one study noted more mother–infant relational problems in the post-partum period in IVF- and infertility-conceived children compared with two control groups (children born to infertile women who had undergone ovulation-induction treatment but no medically assisted procreation, and children born by natural procreation); at nine months, there was a greater frequency of sleep disturbances in the children and maternal depressive syndromes in the IVF and infertility groups than in the controls. However, these disturbances gradually decreased, and by the age of 3 there was little difference among the three groups (Raoul-Duval et al. 1993). Another report suggested that, despite their good developmental progress, young IVF children displayed a 'higher incidence of behavioural and emotional difficulties than a normal population sample' (Golombok and Cook 1990). Most later research found little significant evidence to sustain this earlier hypothesis,[16] although an Israeli report on IVF and embryo-transfer (ET) school-age children found lower socio-emotional adjustment in school, increased susceptibility to anxiety, aggression and depression, and greater risk of emotional disturbances, particularly among boys and the children of older parents (Levy-Shiff et al. 1998). Similarly, a 1997 survey of Dutch children conceived by DI revealed 'more emotional/behavioural problems . . . than children who were naturally conceived', a result possibly related to the lower socio-economic status of their parents. In addition, many of these DI children perceived themselves to be cognitively superior to their fathers (although they had not been told that they were genetically unrelated), whether or not they were genetically related to their mothers, a trend that may reflect a real difference between the cognitive competence of their biological fathers (as a high proportion of sperm donors are university or medical students), and their social fathers (Brewaeys et al. 1997; Golombok et al. 1999).

Although the above results provide reassuring evidence for the parents of younger ART-conceived offspring, there are several outstanding issues that can only be evaluated when these children are significantly older. Research has confirmed that parents appear to bond more strongly with their ART-conceived offspring than the parents of naturally conceived children, providing them with a higher level of nurturing care during their early years. IVF and other previously infertile mothers appear to be more emotionally involved with their offspring, and to provide a greater level of parental competence compared with fertile mothers (Van Balen 1996). Will these parents be able to let them go as they become adolescents and young adults? Or, like the parents in the fairy tale *Rapunzel*, 'who had long in vain wished for a child', will they unwittingly consign their child to the enchantress whose herb, rapion, satisfies the wife's cravings and helps to produce their baby child. The 'witch-mother' takes away the newly born Rapunzel and, when the child is 12 years old, shuts her away in a tower in order to keep her to herself. Psychologically, the fairy tale provides us with an image of an overly possessive, formerly infertile, mother who may unconsciously imprison her child for her own needs.

The possible psychological effects of sibling loss could also become a problem for the surviving children of multiple ART conception. A sensitive child might feel sad or guilty if they learned that they were selected and their sibling embryos rejected, frozen, discarded or used for stem-cell research. And there may well be cases of 'surviving twin syndrome' experienced by children whose sibling embryos/foetuses either died or were selectively 'reduced' in utero.[17] Similarly, DI children might wish to learn if they had any other siblings.

Such future possibilities among ART-created children only serve to confirm the cautionary words of Peter Ellison (2001: 247): 'Paradoxically, it seems we are gaining the ability to artificially control the very shape and limits of our reproductive lives before we fully understand what it is we are controlling.'

The shadow feminine

The generations of women who reached maturity during the last four decades have lived through a sexual revolution, as feminists continue to remind us. Birth control has given us sexual freedom, allowing us to experiment with relationships and to plan our families. Reproductive 'choice' has permitted more of us to occupy respected positions in the workplace, and enabled us to combine family and career. The hubristic belief that we can 'have it all' in this material age – and the increasing success rate of many ART techniques – are tempters, often causing us to ignore our 'reproductive biological clocks', postponing the decision to have children until our thirties or forties. Whereas pregnancies used to occur (or not) 'with God's will' (*Deo concedente*), we now expect them to happen 'according to our will'; with modern technology, all things are possible.

When, as daughters of this revolutionary period, we experience unexpected difficulties in what we assume to be our natural ability and prerogative to conceive and give birth to living children – in short, to become mothers – we experience a violent shock. Whether we are young, old, housewives or career women, our consciously held assumptions that we 'can have it all' are profoundly challenged. Potentially deprived of reproductive choice, we are thrown back into the instinctual feminine world – the archetypal realm of the Mothers – where, for millennia, infertility has been perceived as failure or, worse yet, a curse, often accompanied by family isolation or ostracism.

Today, the medically male-dominated world of ART offers previously unimaginable rays of hope to some women threatened by a diagnosis of infertility. Faced with the inconceivably painful sentence of undesired childlessness, it is both understandable and admirable that they summon the courage to undergo such invasive, unpleasant and sometimes risky procedures, often against great odds, in order to attempt to produce a child. The fertility experts often describe them as 'desperate' to have children, and argue that the new procedures have been designed to meet these women's specific needs. This position has been challenged by Pfeffer, who argues convincingly that basic questions about the possible social causes of infertility are rarely addressed. Instead, infertile individuals are viewed as stigmatised victims who have been 'struck down by a spontaneous idiopathic condition', with pregnancy as the only treatment that will relieve their 'unremitting desperation', thereby placing fertility experts in a powerful, lucrative, and God-like position (Pfeffer 1987).

Viewed from a Jungian psychological perspective, it is imperative to explore the inner, archetypal impulses that appear to compel this particular group of women to seek motherhood 'at all costs'. How do they differ from other women, who, faced with the same dilemma, choose, most reluctantly, to accept their childless fate? What does the 'child' mean to them? And, in their determined pursuit of motherhood, what are the unknown, unexplored, or repressed dimensions – the dark shadow aspects of their attitudes or situations – that may be unexpectedly encountered by ART-created mothers and their offspring?

The Mother and Child archetypes

In Jungian psychology, the archetype is a concept that defines 'an *a priori* factor in all human activities, namely the inborn, preconscious and unconscious individual structure of the psyche'. Thus, like a newly-hatched bird, a newly-born infant 'possesses a preformed psyche which breeds true to his species', and the child's behaviour results from patterns of functioning, which Jung describes as 'images'. The term 'image' is intended to express not only the form of the activity taking place, but the typical situation in which the activity is released. Such images are 'primordial' in so far as they are peculiar to the whole species, and must have come into being when the species was created (Jung 1938: pars 151–5).

Jung first developed the psychological concept of the Mother archetype in 1911–12, when he was writing the *Psychology of the Unconscious*. In this work, Jung expanded Freud's definition of libido, arguing that it was not limited merely to the sexual drive, but was rather an 'essential life energy' which included the opposites of biological and psychological, concrete and general, natural and spiritual, and which could find expression in affect, love and sexuality, as well as in intellectual and spiritual ideas. As Jung emphasised, this essential life force underwent various transformations in the individual's life, according to his archetypal needs. Accordingly, he reinterpreted the Oedipus myth, emphasising its symbolic and transformative meaning; it became the hero's journey, marked with his successful or unsuccessful attempts to escape the mother, do battle with his father, establish an independent existence, find his beloved and meet his fate.

For Jung, the hero's journey was a symbol of the individual's struggle for maturity, and he related it to the process of striving to reach one's fullest potential or Self – which in analysis is called the individuation process (Jung 1911). In contrast to the modern cult of individualism, which is characterised by the ego's hubristic refusal to face limits or change direction, the attempt to individuate often involves sacrifice and surrender by the ego in order to understand and experience the deeper and often painful meanings of what it is to be human. As Jung noted: 'All those moments of individual life, when the universal laws of human fate break in upon the purposes, expectations, and opinions of personal consciousness, are stations along the road of the individuation process' (1945: par. 557).

The Mother archetype is one of the most important concepts in Jungian psychology. By its very nature, the Mother archetype is the first that we experience in our early lives. It is the matrix of all others, and stands behind our personal experiences of being nurtured and of nurturing. As infants, we participate in the archetypal dyad of Mother–Infant, and the type of personal mothering we receive – good or bad – will determine whether we experience the Mother archetype in its positive or negative aspect, on one end of the pole as the Great Good Mother and on the opposite end as the Devouring Terrible Mother. Our psychic encounters with one or the other pole of maternity will in turn influence the way we relate to each other, to the world around us, and to any children we may bear.

As with all archetypes, that of the Mother has a number of characteristic aspects. Those most relevant to our discussion include, on the personal level, the mother, grandmother, stepmother, mother-in-law, or other woman with whom a relationship exists, such as a nurse, governess or remote ancestress. On the mythological level, they manifest themselves in the Great Mother and the Goddess, especially in her triple guise as maiden/matron/crone. Among the Mother archetype's relevant positive symbols are the objects and places that stand for fertility and fruitfulness, such as the cornucopia, the ploughed field, garden, cave, spring, various hollow objects, and the uterus. On the opposite pole, important negative symbols include the witch, dragon, grave, sarcophagus, deep water and death.

Such images give us an idea of the qualities that are associated with the loving and terrible sides of the ambivalent Mother archetype. In her positive guise, her attributes include maternal solicitude and sympathy, helpful instincts and impulses, and all that cherishes, sustains and fosters growth and fertility. Opposed to these are her negative attributes: all that is secret, hidden, or dark, the abyss, anything that devours, seduces, poisons, or that is terrifying and inescapable, like fate. In psychological terms, the Mother archetype refers to the unconscious (the progenitor of consciousness), particularly in its maternal aspect, which involves the body and the mystery of matter in general (Birkhäuser-Oeri 1988: 14).

According to evolutionary psychiatry, the positive qualities associated with the Mother archetype were well established before the emergence of *Homo sapiens*. They enabled our female ancestors to survive and reproduce, and they still influence the behavioural, emotional and symbolic lives of modern women (Stevens and Price 1996). Although the role of mother is no longer the primary one for many of today's women, it remains one of four possible structures of the feminine psyche as described by Jungian analyst Toni Wolff. Composed of two pairs, these include the Mother (represented in Greek mythology by goddesses such as Hera and Demeter) and its opposite, the Love Goddess (Aphrodite), and the Amazon (Artemis and Athene) and the Medium (Pythia and Hestia).[18] The qualities associated with the 'Mother' pole of the feminine psyche, which include motherly cherishing, nursing, helping, charitable activities, and teaching, *are not confined to her own offspring*, but reach out to strengthen and protect whatever needs protection, help and development. The negative aspects of the Mother pole, related to those of the Mother archetype, include inappropriate mothering, anxious nursing, interference with the natural process of development, and the projection of unaccepted aspects of the personality on to children, students, or clients. In the individual woman, one of these structural forms will dominate; another may function as an auxiliary, while the remaining two 'can be made conscious and integrated only with difficulty and during the later part of life'. Thus, if the feminine psyche is healthy, a 'Mother' woman will also have an auxiliary mode of functioning that enables her to become more Amazon-like or more medial (relating intuitively to the unconscious: Wolff 1956: 4).

As daughters, our relationship to our personal mother will colour our experience of the Mother archetype, thus producing different kinds of mother complexes (feeling-toned groups of images and ideas in the unconscious grouped around a core derived from an archetype). Jung identified four types of mother complexes related to different types of mother–daughter relationships; in some, the feminine is exaggerated, while in others the feminine is neglected or atrophied. One is particularly relevant for this chapter: the mother complex characterised by an overdevelopment of the maternal instinct. An exaggeration of Wolff's Mother pole of the female psyche, in its positive guise this type of mother complex is 'identical with the well-known image of mother glorified in all ages and all tongues . . . the mother-love which is one of the most moving and unforgettable memories of our lives, the mysterious root of all growth and change' (Jung 1938: par. 172). But in its negative or pathological aspect, it manifests itself in the woman whose only goal is childbirth:

> To her the husband is obviously of secondary importance; he is first and foremost the instrument of procreation. . . . Even her own personality is of

secondary importance; she often remains entirely unconscious of it, for her life is lived in and through others, in more or less complete identification with all the objects of her care. First she gives birth to the children, and from then on she clings to them, for without them she has no existence whatsoever. Like Demeter, she compels the gods by her stubborn persistence to grant her the right of possession over her daughter. Her Eros develops exclusively as a maternal relationship while remaining unconscious as a personal one. . . . Women of this type, though continually 'living for others,' are, as a matter of fact, unable to make any real sacrifice.

(Jung 1938: par. 167)

This type of mother complex is related to the findings of recent psychological studies, which confirm that many women who decide to undergo ART treatment come from traditional backgrounds, with an emphasis on the roles of wife and mother, and often identify themselves strongly with their own mothers (Cook 1993). Viewed from a Jungian perspective, they remain caught in an over-feminised mother-complex, identifying themselves with the positive elementary aspects of the Mother archetype and unconscious of its negative qualities.

Under such conditions, psychological obsession may distort biological instinct to produce the so-called state of 'desperation' often described by ART fertility experts. There may be a number of conscious and unconscious factors fuelling this situation: the desire to repair a damaged body- and self-image; to make reparation to one's mother by producing a grandchild; to achieve status in the family and society; to give something to her husband; to give birth to herself again, or to repair her own unhappy childhood through her children (Ulanov 1993: 27).

As Eva Pattis Zoja points out, such unconscious needs are also exaggerated in today's society, where the transition from maiden to mother remains the one great initiatory event in women's lives:

Pregnancy is charged with the archaic power to make [a woman] feel new and renewed. . . . Such a way of experiencing one's womanly identification is a surrogate for a no longer extant rite of passage [from childhood into puberty]. . . . A woman who has never been pregnant has no clear awareness of . . . this, but she can none the less possess an inarticulate 'knowledge' of it. The more her life is charged with conflict, the greater her nostalgia for such a state will be.

(Pattis Zoja 1997: 34–9)

For the potentially infertile woman imprisoned by an exaggerated maternal complex, the 'child' remains a concrete object, limited to a biological or narcissistic extension of herself (and/or her partner). Under such circumstances, she remains cut off from her imagination. Because she identifies 'child' with her conscious longings for a baby, she is unable to relate symbolically to the archetype of the Child. As an image of future potential, the Child archetype is meant to 'compensate or correct, in a meaningful manner, the inevitable one sidedness and extravagances of the conscious mind' (Jung 1938: par. 278). Caught in the collective cult of the 'child', the ART-obsessed woman may be unable to realise that the image of the Child is also an archetypal symbol of her own future development and creativity, a herald of healing and wholeness that may enable her to experience the Mother archetype without becoming a biological mother.

The symbolic and spiritual potential of the Child archetype is well illustrated in Queen Maya's dream of the Buddha's conception. Having participated in the Midsummer festival for six days, on the seventh day the elderly, childless queen prepared herself and performed the required rituals and holy vows. She then entered her bedchamber, fell asleep and had the following dream:

> The four guardians of the world [gods] lifted her on her couch and carried her to the Himalaya mountains and placed her under a great sala tree. . . . Then their queens bathed her . . . dressed her in heavenly garments, anointed her with perfumes and put garlands of heavenly flowers on her. . . . They laid her on a heavenly couch, with its head towards the east. The Bodhisattva, wandering as a superb white elephant . . . approached her from the north. Holding a white lotus flower in his trunk, he circumambulated her three times. Then he gently struck her right side, and entered her womb.
>
> (Young 1999: 22)

Paradoxically, for the potentially infertile woman who is unable to connect with the creative and spiritual potential of the Child archetype, the process of ART treatment may be a necessary experience. If successful, it enables her to experience the initiatory journey of childbirth, hopefully transforming her into a caring mother. If unsuccessful, ART itself will be the initiatory experience, forcing her into the feminine realm beyond motherhood where the 'child' must finally be abandoned, thereby allowing her to mourn and move on. In either case, awareness of her own shadow, and the compelling aspects of the Mother archetype, will help her on her journey.

Dark Eros

Couples who have not been able to conceive easily are aware that, in the successively more conscious and controlled attempts to produce a baby, the first deity to flee their bed may be Eros, the god of passion and relationship, who was Aphrodite's constant companion. Eros is not ruled by temperature charts or the 'right days of the month', and, as male partners will attest, he is often singularly absent when procreation is exclusively directed towards childbearing. There is no place for him in the intrusive and demanding world of ART/IVF, where women often need to make frequent journeys to hospitals at inconvenient times, accompanied by partners who must ejaculate to order. Here, the poison of his arrow remains, but Eros has been replaced by Pan, the god of panic, masturbation and instinctual compulsion (Hillman 2000). This is confirmed in a study of 'fertility problem stress' in infertile couples, where researchers found an increase of marital conflict, and a decrease of sexual self-esteem, satisfaction with sexual performance, and frequency of sexual intercourse, leading to significantly decreased satisfaction with life-as-a-whole, self-efficacy, marriage, intimacy and health (Andrews *et al.* 1991).

Does Eros reappear after ART treatment? In the case of a successful outcome, he may, although, as the ancients remind us, Eros and Aphrodite are not deities associated with marriage; that is the preserve of Hera (*Mythologies* 1991: 395–400). For the majority of unsuccessful couples, however, Eros remains absent. Research on the long-term effects of infertility in couples has found that sexual behaviour is often still ruled by the constraints of procreation (Van Balen and Trimbos-Kemper 1993). Viewed psychologically, such couples remain in thrall to Pan. Erotic imagination has disappeared, replaced by a fixed, inappropriate image of procreation only as means-to-an-end. In the myth of Eros and Psyche, Eros flees when Psyche wounds him in her compulsion to 'see' him (when she cannot live with mystery). To regain him, she must undergo an arduous series of tasks imposed by Venus. Aided by the animals (instinctual energies), she eventually succeeds, and she is reunited with Eros. The couple who remain infertile after ART treatment face a similar undertaking; they must face the difficult task of mourning and use their released instinctual energies to create a new erotic (related) world to inhabit as they move forward in life.

APPENDIX

Mythological examples

Classical mythology includes a number of goddesses whose births, attributes, or behaviour provide useful archetypal examples for the woman who may be contemplating ART treatment. It is surely significant that ancient women called upon the two Virgin goddesses, Athene and Artemis, for help in conception and childbirth, as if to remind them that, once over the threshold of motherhood, there nevertheless remained other modes of feminine consciousness.

Artemis' mother Leto was one of Zeus' great spouses. When she became pregnant, she was forced by jealous Hera to give birth in a place where the sun never shone, and she fled to the island of Delos. There, in a darkened cave, she gave birth to twins. Artemis was born first, without travail. The Moirai immediately appointed her to act as her mother's midwife, and thus she helped to deliver her brother Apollo. Goddess of the hunt and all that was wild, she always appeared as a maiden, and was never addressed as 'mother'. When she was a child she had asked her father for the company of the sixty nine-year-old daughters of Okeanos as playmates. Artemis became the special protectress of this age group of young girls, who, as *arktoi* or she-bears, remained in her service until they became nubile, dedicating their waistbands and toys to her. In Attica, for example, before marriage maidens between the ages of 5 and 10 were consecrated to Artemis of Brauron or Munichia. During this time of *parthenia*, they were allowed to hunt and slaughter sacrificial beasts, affording them a chance to explore their Artemisian strength and aggressiveness before it was tempered by marriage. Later, as matrons, when they first became pregnant they loosened their girdles and dedicated them in Artemis' temple.[19] According to Homer, Zeus made Artemis a lioness towards children in childbirth, allowing her to kill whomever she pleased. At the shrine of Artemis of Brauron on the Acropolis, those women who had successfully survived the ordeal of childbirth left her their garments as votive offerings.[20] Thus Artemis is an archetypal feminine image as savage as nature herself, untouched by, but intimately involved with, women's initiatory experiences.

The goddess Athene symbolises a different kind of female energy. An example of an inconceivable birth, she sprang full-grown and clad in armour from the head of her father Zeus, who had swallowed her pregnant Amazon mother Metis in an attempt to prevent the birth of a future son-usurper. Called 'Virgin', she is also invoked as Meter, 'Mother'. According to one story, the blacksmith-god Hephaistos attempted to lie with her, but she vanished, and his semen spilled on to the earth, which (as the goddess Gaia) bore Erichthonios, and then gave the newly-born child to Athene to rear. Athene displays the severed head of the Gorgon Medusa (a negative image of the Mother archetype) on her breast, a trophy from the hero Perseus, whom she had instructed and protected during his fight with the monster. Thus Athene's Gorgon head is a symbol of the masculine energy in the female psyche necessary to overcome the negative mother complex, and alludes to the creative energy released by the 'beheading', symbolised in the myth by the winged horse Pegasus and the hero Chrysaor, who sprang up from Medusa's spilt blood. Amongst her many functions, Athene presided over the woman's transition from maiden to wife. In one area of Greece, women left their virginal girdles at her shrine before marriage, while in Athens, parents took their daughters to the Acropolis before their marriage to give offerings to Athene, who was meant to protect the wedding and ensure conception.[21]

Hera, Zeus' consort, was the goddess of marriage, whose role it was to ensure that the young bride, inflamed with desire for her groom by Aphrodite, would later come to identify herself with the childbed in which she would bear her legitimate children. As such, she is perhaps also an apt goddess of the ART process. In the name of her daughter Eileithyia, Hera (like Artemis) could be invoked by women in labour. But she also provides an example of 'motherhood-gone-mad'. Incensed by Zeus' ability to give birth to Athene from his head, Hera decided to equal his feat by creating a child without him, but also without dishonouring their marriage bed. She left the gods' abode, prayed and struck the earth (Gaia), imploring the gods' ancestors to give her a son 'who shall not be weaker than Zeus himself'. A year later, her wish was fulfilled, but the creature she brought forth was the dragon Typhaon. Another tale relates that Hera went to Gaia's garden of plants, where the goddess (in the guise of Flora) gave her the magic herb 'simple', whose touch cured infertility. From her contact with this fertility herb, Hera conceived the war-god Ares. But not all her parthenogenetically created children were as troublesome; she conceived her ever-youthful daughter Hebe, cup-bearer to the gods and later wife of Heracles, by eating a head of lettuce.[22]

Notes

1 Bullock 1974; Elstein 1975; Drake and Grunert 1979; Bell 1981; De Vries *et al*. 1984.
2 Domar *et al*. 1992 and 1993; Van Balen and Trimbos-Kemper 1993.
3 Rosen *et al*. 1997: 90–4 found that, of the fifty-two women seeking infertility treatment who were interviewed, 79 per cent were willing to accept an increased risk of ovarian cancer, although only 24 per cent of that group understood that treatment for ovarian cancer was usually not curative.
4 These include severe headaches, blurred vision, nausea, uterine bleeding, weight gain, hair loss, constipation, dizziness, insomnia, hyperthyroidism, rashes, abdominal distension and pain, ovarian cysts, and links with gastrointestinal symptoms and disorders, haemoconcentration, renal failure and coagulation disorders, as well as abnormalities in the ova: Dyson 1995: 38.
5 Republished posthumously with e-mail correspondence in Picardie 1998.
6 Rossing *et al*. 1994; Whittemore 1994 provides an appraisal of Rossing *et al*.'s study. On the other hand, CC was reported to reduce the risk of cervical and breast cancer: Rossing *et al*. 1996a and 1996b.
7 Whittemore 1994. Rossing and Daling 1999 suggest that increased detection of such cancers may also reflect increased surveillance before, during and after fertility treatment.
8 Escobedo *et al*. 1991; Harris *et al*. 1992; Whittemore *et al*. 1992b.
9 Risch *et al*. 1994; Nieto *et al*. 1999. See also Mosgaard *et al*. 1997, where nulliparity was found to incur a 1.5- to 2-fold increased risk of ovarian cancer; infertile nulliparity without medical treatment increased this risk further; treatment among parous and nulliparous women did not increase the risk of ovarian cancer compared with non-treated infertile women, but women who remained nulliparous after treatment had a slightly higher risk of ovarian cancer than those successfully treated.
10 Whittemore *et al*. 1992a and 1992b; Harris *et al*. 1992; Rossing *et al*. 1994. See Bristow and Karlan 1996: 500–1 for a critical review of Whittemore *et al*. and Harris *et al*.
11 Whittemore *et al*. 1992a and 1992b; Harris *et al*. 1992.
12 Rossing *et al*. 1994; see also Franco *et al*. 2000 who note that between 1982 and 1997, among women treated with ovulation-induction for infertility, at least forty-three cases of ovarian cancer have been published, and that the mean age of those women, at 30.3 years, is approximately twenty years younger than the normal patient population for such tumours. On the other hand, Rossing *et al*. 1996a reported that infertility-related use of CC may reduce the risk of cervical cancers relative to the general population.
13 Venn *et al*. 1999; Rossing and Daling 1999; Nieto *et al*. 1999.
14 Cowan *et al*. 1981; Ron *et al*. 1987; Brezezinski *et al*. 1994.
15 Coles 1999; *Herald Tribune* (Reuters), 15 August 2001.
16 Golombok *et al*. 1993, 1995 and 1996.
17 See Bryan 1992, pp. 98–105, for the 'surviving twin syndrome' in naturally conceived twins.
18 Ulanov 1971, pp. 193–211; Stevens 1998, pp. 309–10; Gordon 2001.
19 Dilling 1914, p. 407.
20 See Kerenyi 1979, pp. 130–48; Hillman 1980, pp. 39–45; *Mythologies* 1991, Vol. I, pp. 445–9, 395–7; Pattis Zoja 1997, pp. 64–6.

21 See Kerenyi 1979, pp. 118–29; Hillman 1980, pp. 26–32; Pattis Zoja 1997, pp. 66–8; Shearer 1996, pp. 23–40.
22 See Kerenyi 1979, pp. 95–8; *Mythologies* 1991, Vol. I, pp. 399–400.

Bibliography

Andrews, F.M., Abbey, A. and Halman, L.J. (1991) 'Stress from infertility, marriage factors, and subjective well-being of wives and husbands', *Journal of Health and Social Behavior* 32: 238–53.

Bell, J.S. (1981) 'Psychological problems among patients attending an infertility clinic', *Journal of Psychosomatic Research* 25: 1–3.

Birkhäuser-Oeri, S. (1988) *The Mother Archetypal Image in Fairy Tales*, Toronto: Inner City Books.

Booth, J. and Syal, R. (2000) 'Baby mix-up scare after blunders at IVF clinics', *Sunday Telegraph*, 24 September 2000: 4.

Brewaeys, A., Golombok, S., Naaktgeboren, J.K. and van Hall, E.V. (1997) 'Donor insemination: Dutch parents' opinions about confidentiality and donor anonymity and the emotional adjustment of their children', *Human Reproduction* 12: 1591–7.

Brezezinski, A., Peretz, T., Mor-Yosef, S. and Schenker, J.G. (1994) 'Ovarian stimulation and breast cancer. Is there a link?' *Gynecological Oncology* 52: 292–5.

Bristow, R.E. and Karlan, B.Y. (1996) 'Ovulation induction, infertility, and ovarian cancer risk', *Fertility and Sterility* 66: 499–507.

Bruinsma, F., Venn, A., Lancaster, P., Spiers, A. and Healy, D. (2000) 'Incidence of cancer in children born after in-vitro fertilization', *Human Reproduction* 15: 604–7.

Bryan, E. (1992) *Twins, Triplets and More*, London: Penguin.

Bullock, J.L. (1974) 'Iatrogenic impotence in an infertility clinic: illustrative case', *American Journal of Obstetrics and Gynecology* 120: 476–8.

Chiba, H., Mori, E., Morioka, Y., Kashiwakura, M., Nadaoka, T., Saito, H. and Hiroi, M. (1997) 'Stress of female infertility: relations to length of treatment', *Gynecologic and Obstetric Investigation* 43: 171–7.

Coles, J. (1999) 'The custody battle for an embryo', *The Times*, 1 December 1999: 37.

Cook, R. (1993) 'The relationship between sex role and emotional functioning in patients undergoing assisted conception', *Journal of Psychosomatic Obstetrics and Gynaecology* 14, Special Edition: 31–40.

Cook, R., Parsons, J., Mason, B. and Golombok, S. (1989) 'Emotional, marital and sexual functioning in patients embarking upon IVF and AID treatment for infertility', *Journal of Reproductive and Infant Psychology* 7: 87–93.

Cowan, L.D., Gordis, L., Tonascia, J.A. and Seegar-Jones, G. (1981) 'Breast cancer incidence in women with a history of progesterone deficiency', *American Journal of Epidemiology* 114: 209–17.

Dennerstein, L. and Morse, C. (1985) 'Psychological issues in IVF', *Clinics in Obstetrics and Gynaecology* 56: 316–22.

De Vries, K., Degani, S., Eibschitz, I., Oettinger, M., Zilberman, A. and Sharf, M. (1984) 'The influence of the postcoital test on the sexual function of infertile women', *Journal of Psychosomatic Obstetrics and Gynaecology* 3: 101–6.

Dilling, W.J. (1914) 'Girdles: their origin and development, particularly with regard to their use as charms in medicine, marriage, and midwifery', *The Caledonian Medical Journal* 9: 403–25.

Domar, A.D., Broome, A., Zuttermeister, P.C., Seibel, M. and Friedman, R. (1992) 'The prevalence and predictability of depression in infertile women', *Fertility and Sterility* 58: 1158–63.

Domar, A.D., Zuttermeister, P.C. and Friedman, R. (1993) 'The psychological impact of infertility: a comparison with patients with other medical conditions', *Journal of Psychosomatic Obstetrics and Gynaecology* 14, Special Edition: 45–52.

Drake, T.S. and Grunert, M. (1979) 'A cyclic pattern of sexual dysfunction in the infertility investigations', *Fertility and Sterility* 32: 542–5.

Dyson, A. (1995) *The Ethics of IVF*, London: Mowbray.

Ellison, P.T. (2001) *On Fertile Ground*, Cambridge, Mass.: Harvard University Press.

Elstein, M. (1975) 'Effect of infertility on psychosexual function', *British Medical Journal* 3: 296–9.

Escobedo, G., Lee, N.C., Peterson, H.B. and Wingo, P.A. (1991) 'Infertility-associated endometrial cancer risk may be limited to specific subgroups of infertile women', *Obstetric Gynecology* 77: 124–8.

Eugster, A. and Vingerhoets, A.J. (1999) 'Psychological aspects of in-vitro fertilization: a review', *Social Science and Medicine* 48: 575–89.

Franco, C., Coppola, S., Prosperi Porta, R. and Patella, A. (2000) 'Induzione dell'ovulazione e rischio di neoplasie ovariche', *Minerva Ginecologica* 52: 103–9.

Golombok, S. (1997) 'Parenting and secrecy issues related to children of assisted reproduction', *Journal of Assisted Reproduction and Genetics* 14: 375–8.

Golombok, S. and Cook, R. (1990) 'The impact of successful and unsuccessful IVF in infertility patients', *Journal of Reproductive and Infant Psychology* 8: 214.

Golombok, S., Cook, R., Bish, A. and Murray, C. (1993) 'Quality of parenting in families created by the new reproductive technologies: a brief report of preliminary findings', *Journal of Psychosomatic Obstetrics and Gynaecology* 14, Special Edition: 17–22.

Golombok, S., Cook, R., Bish, A. and Murray, C. (1995) 'Families created by the new reproductive technologies: quality of parenting and social and emotional development of the children', *Child Development* 66: 285–98.

Golombok, S., Brewaeys, A., Cook, R., Giavazzi, M.T., Guerra, D., Mantovani, A., van Hall, E., Crosignani, P.G. and Dexeus, S. (1996) 'The European study of assisted reproduction families: family functioning and child development', *Human Reproduction* 11: 2324–31.

Golombok, S., Murray, C., Brinsden, P. and Abdalla, H. (1999) 'Social versus biological parenting: family functioning and the socioemotional development of children conceived by egg or sperm donation', *Journal of Child Psychology and Psychiatry* 40: 519–27.

Gordon, E. (2001) Personal communication.

Harris, R. Whittemore, A.S. and Itnyre, U. (1992) 'Characteristics relating to ovarian cancer risk: collaborative analysis of 12 US case-control studies. III. Epithelial tumors of low malignant potential in white women. Collaborative Ovarian Cancer Group', *American Journal of Epidemiology* 136: 1204–11.

Hawkes, N. (2000) 'Tests offered in embryo mix-up', *The Times*, 25 September 2000.

HFEA Policy Update and Issues (2000) 'Policy update and issues for the coming year', Chapter 6, *HFEA Annual Report 2000*. Online. Available: http://www.hfea.gov.uk/annrep2000/chapt6.htm

Hillman, J. (1980) *Facing the Gods*, Dallas: Spring Publications.

—— (2000) *Pan and the Nightmare*, Woodstock: Spring Publications.

Hynes, J.C., Callan, V.J., Terry, D.J. and Gallois, C. (1992) 'The psychological well-being of infertile women after a failed IVF attempt: the effects of coping', *British Journal of Medical Psychology* 65: 269–78.

Jung, C.G. (1911) 'Symbols of Transformation. An Analysis of the Prelude to a Case of Schizophrenia', *Collected Works* 5, London: Routledge & Kegan Paul, 2nd edn 1986.

—— (1938) 'Psychological Aspects of the Mother Archetype', *Collected Works* 9i: 75–110, London: Routledge & Kegan Paul, 1968.

—— (1945) 'On the Nature of Dreams', *Collected Works* 8: 281–97, London: Routledge & Kegan Paul, 1969.

Kemeter, P. (1988) 'Studies on psychosomatic implications of infertility – effects of emotional stress on fertilization and implantation in in-vitro fertilization', *Human Reproduction* 3: 341–52.

Kerenyi, C. (1979) *The Gods of the Greeks*, New York: Thames and Hudson.

Lapane, K., Zierler, S., Lasater, T., Stein, M., Barbour, M. and Hume, A.L. (1995) 'Is a history of depressive symptoms associated with an increased risk of infertility in women?' *Psychosomatic Medicine* 57: 509–13.

Lee, S. (1996) *Counselling in Male Infertility*, Oxford: Blackwell Science.

—— (2001) Personal communication.

Levy-Shiff, R., Vakil, E., Dimitrovsky, L., Abramovitz, M., Shakar, N., Har-Evan, D., Gross, S., Lerman, M., Levy, I., Sirota, L. and Fish, B. (1998) 'Medical, cognitive, emotional, and behavioral outcomes in school-age children conceived by in-vitro fertilization', *Journal of Clinical Child Psychology* 27: 320–9.

Mosgaard, B.J., Lidegaard, O., Kjaer, S.K., Schou, G. and Anderson, A.N. (1997) 'Infertility, fertility drugs, and invasive ovarian cancer: a case-control study', *Fertility and Sterility* 69: 168–9.

Mythologies (1991) ed. Y. Bonnefoy and W. Doniger, Vol. 1, Chicago and London: University of Chicago Press.

Nieto, J.J., Rolfe, K.J., MacLean, A.B. and Hardiman, P. (1999) 'Ovarian cancer and infertility: a genetic link?' *Lancet* 354: 649.

Pattis Zoja, E. (1997) *Abortion. Loss and Renewal in the Search for Identity*, London and New York: Routledge.

Pawson, M. (2001) Personal communication.

Pfeffer, N. (1987) 'Artificial insemination, in-vitro fertilization and the stigma of infertility', in M. Stanworth (ed.) *Reproductive Technologies. Gender, Motherhood and Medicine*, Cambridge: Polity Press.

Picardie, R. (1998) *Before I Say Goodbye*, London: Penguin.

Potashnik, G., Lerner-Geva, L., Genkin, L., Chetrit, A., Lunenfeld, E. and Porath, A. (1999) 'Fertility drugs and the risk of breast and ovarian cancers: results of a long-term follow-up study', *Fertility and Sterility* 71: 853–9.

Raoul-Duval, A., Bertrand-Servais, M. and Frydman, R. (1993) 'Comparative prospective study of the psychological development of children born by in-vitro fertilization and their mothers', *Journal of Psychosomatic Obstetrics and Gynaecology* 14, Special Edition: 117–26.

Raval, H., Slade, P., Buck, P. and Lieberman, B.E. (1987) 'The impact of infertility on emotions and the marital and sexual relationship', *Journal of Reproductive and Infant Psychology* 5: 221–34.

Risch, H.A., Marrett, L.D. and Howe, G.R. (1994) 'Parity, contraception, infertility and the risk of epithelial ovarian cancer', *American Journal of Epidemiology* 140: 585–97.

Ron, E., Lunenfeld, B., Menczer, J., Blumstein, T., Katz, L., Oelsner, G. and Serr, D. (1987) 'Cancer incidence in a cohort of infertile women', *American Journal of Epidemiology* 125: 780–90.

Rosen, B., Irving, J., Ritvo, P., Shapiro, H., Steward, D., Reynolds, K., Robinson, G., Thomas, J., Neuman, J. and Murphy, J. (1997) 'The feasibility of assessing women's perceptions of the risks and benefits of fertility drug therapy in relation to ovarian cancer risk', *Fertility and Sterility* 68: 90–4.

Rossing, M.A. and Daling, J.D. (1999) 'Complexity of surveillance for cancer risk associated with in-vitro fertilisation', *Lancet* 354: 1573–4.

Rossing, M.A., Daling, J.R., Weiss, N.S., Moore, D.E. and Self, S.G. (1994) 'Ovarian tumors in a cohort of infertile women', *New England Journal of Medicine* 331: 771–6.

Rossing, M.A., Daling, J.R., Weiss, N.S., Moore, D.E. and Self, S.G. (1996a) 'In situ and invasive cervical carcinoma in a cohort of infertile women', *Fertility and Sterility* 65: 19–22.

Rossing, M.A., Daling, J.R., Weiss, N.S., Moore, D.E. and Self, S.G. (1996b) 'Risk of breast cancer in a cohort of infertile women', *Gynecological Oncology* 60: 3–7.

Salle, B., de Saint Hilaire, P., Devouassoux, M., Gaucherand, P. and Rudigoz, C. (1997) 'Another two cases of ovarian tumours in women who had undergone multiple ovulation induction cycles', *Human Reproduction* 12: 1732–5.

Shearer, A. (1996) *Athene. Image and Energy*, London: Viking Arkana.

Shushan, A., Paltiel, O., Iscovich, J., Elchalal, U., Peretz, T. and Schenker, J.G. (1996) 'Human menopausal gonadotropin and the risk of epithelial ovarian cancer', *Fertility and Sterility* 65: 13–18.

Slade, P., Emery, J. and Lieberman, B.A. (1997) 'A prospective, longitudinal study of emotions and relationships in in-vitro fertilization treatment', *Human Reproduction* 12: 183–90.

Smith, R.H. and Cooke, I.D. (1991) 'Ovarian hyperstimulation: actual and theoretical risks', *British Medical Journal* 302: 127–8.

Stevens, A. (1998) *Ariadne's Clue. A Guide to the Symbols of Humankind*, Princeton: Princeton University Press.

Stevens, A. and Price, J. (1996) *Evolutionary Psychiatry. A New Beginning*, London and New York: Routledge.

Thiering, P., Beaurepaire, J., Jones, M., Saunders, D. and Tennant, C. (1994) 'Mood state as a predictor of treatment outcome after in-vitro fertilization/embryo transfer technology (IVF/ET)', *Journal of Psychosomatic Research* 37: 481–91.

Tilberis, L. (1998) *No Time to Die*, London: Orion.

Ulanov, A.B. (1971) *The Feminine in Jungian Psychology and in Christian Theology*, Chicago: Northwestern University Press.

——— (1993) *The Female Ancestors of Christ*, Boston and London: Shambhala Press.

Van Balen, F. (1996) 'Child-rearing following in-vitro fertilization', *Journal of Child Psychology and Psychiatry* 37: 687–93.

Van Balen, F. and Trimbos-Kemper, T.C. (1993) 'Long-term infertile couples: a study of their well-being', *Journal of Psychosomatic Obstetrics and Gynaecology* 14, Special Edition: 53–60.

——— (1995) 'Involuntarily childless couples: their desire to have children and their motives', *Journal of Psychosomatic Obstetrics and Gynaecology* 16: 137–44.

Van Guens, S. and Morris, Z. (2001) 'Fertility doctor faces GMC inquiry', *Evening Standard*, 4 October 2001: 1–2.

Van Keep, P.A. and Schmidt-Elmendorff, H. (1975) 'Involuntary childlessness', *Journal of Biosocial Science* 7: 37–48.

Venn, A., Watson, L., Lumley, J., Giles, G., King, C. and Healy, D. (1995) 'Breast and ovarian cancer incidence after infertility and in-vitro fertilization', *Lancet* 346: 995–1000.

Venn, A., Watson, L., Bruinsma, F., Giles, G. and Healy, D. (1999) 'Risk of cancer after use of fertility drugs with in-vitro fertilisation', *Lancet* 354: 1573–4.

Wallace, L.M. (1985) 'Psychological adjustment to and recovery from laparoscopic sterilization and infertility investigation', *Journal of Psychosomatic Research* 29: 507–18.

Weiss, H.A., Troisi, R.A., Rossing, M.A., Brogen, D., Coates, R.J., Gammon, M.D., Potischman, N., Swanson, C.A. and Brinton, L.A. (1998) 'Fertility problems and breast cancer risk in young women: a case-control study', *Cancer Causes Control* 9: 331–9.

Whittemore, A.S. (1994) 'The risk of ovarian cancer after treatment for infertility', *New England Journal of Medicine* 331: 805–6.

Whittemore, A.S., Harris, R., Itnyre, J. and Halpern, J. (1992a) 'Collaborative Ovarian Cancer Group. Characteristics relating to ovarian cancer risk: collaborative analysis of 12 U.S. case-control studies. I. Methods', *American Journal of Epidemiology* 136: 1175–83.

Whittemore, A.S., Harris, R. and Itnyre, J. (1992b) 'Collaborative Ovarian Cancer Group. Characteristics relating to ovarian cancer risk: collaborative analysis of 12 U.S. case-control studies. II. Invasive epithelial ovarian cancers in white women', *American Journal of Epidemiology* 136: 1184–203.

Winston, R. (1996) *Infertility. A Sympathetic Approach to Understanding the Causes and Options For Treatment*, London: Vermilion.

—— (2000) *The IVF Revolution. The Definitive Guide to Assisted Reproductive Techniques*, London: Vermilion.

Wolff, A. (1956) *Structural Forms of the Feminine Psyche*, privately printed in Zurich.

Young, S. (1999) *Dreaming the Lotus*, Boston: Wisdom Publications.

Afterword

Chapter 16

Afterword

Germaine Greer

Germaine Greer is Professor of English and Comparative Studies at Warwick University.

'Conception', as Hamlet says, 'is a blessing', but not as many people conceive nowadays, amid so much struggle, heartache, physical violation and pain that we might doubt whether the motives driving them are quite rational, whether wanting 'a child' so badly makes sense. The reasons suggested in this book for desperately desiring a child, such as 'cheating death of its finality' (Raphael-Leff) are not reasons at all. If 'failure to produce a child . . . confronts us with the realisation that we are neither special nor immortal' (Pawson) then it ought to be encouraged, because we are neither special nor immortal and the sooner we realise it the better. Miller takes the contrary view that it is having children that convinces us that we are mortal. There can be little consensus on just why people want to have children because the evidence is both contradictory and impressionistic. Women have been heard to say on the one hand that childlessness causes them to lose their identity, and on the other that motherhood causes their identity to dwindle so that instead of being somebody they become merely somebody's mother. Our children are no less mortal than ourselves and indeed often are or appear more vulnerable, especially if they are sick or disabled, or drinking, driving too fast, having unprotected sex or using drugs. No one feels the finality of death more keenly than the parent who stands by the grave of her child. It is not parents but children who think that they are immortal and wilfully jeopardise the lives their parents struggled so to give them. To have a child is instantly to offer a hostage to fortune, and thereby exponentially to increase one's own capacity for suffering, sometimes lifelong.

ART (assisted reproductive technology) can offer no antidote to the unwelcome spectre of mortality, because it occasions a great deal more death than life, the number of jettisoned embryos and failed implantations being many times greater than the number of live births. Nowhere in this book is it suggested that acceptors who believe that ART will help them cheat the finality of death should be helped to emerge from their delusional state rather than subjected to the miseries of the infertility treatment cycle. From a tacit acceptance of the desire to overcome mortality as rational it is but a short step to accepting reproductive cloning as offering a genuine answer to the problem of mortality which, in global rather than egocentric terms, is no problem at all. Refusal to die is also a refusal to give birth, for the finite space of the planet is already desperately overcrowded, principally because of the failure of the death rate to keep pace with the birth rate. In the future our beleaguered planet may be run by an elite of cloned immortals who will be indifferent to the sufferings of the poor who will continue to be born and die in the old-fashioned way, *inter faecem et urinam*, in the pestilential slums that daily spread over more and more of Africa and South America.

Our world already manifests a dangerous degree of contrast between the infertile rich and the fecund poor. While most of the world's shorter-lived inhabitants still become parents in a largely uncontrolled and uncontrollable way, and are still losing beloved children to bacterial and parasitic infections that ought by now to have become extinct, the fertility of the longer-lived rich world, where virtually every child born can be guaranteed to survive, is declining steeply. Consumerism actively discourages childbirth because offspring are portrayed as demanding, rival consumers. People postpone childbearing, because they think that they cannot 'afford' children. At the same time that huge amounts of money, time and energy are expended on efforts to reverse the infertility that results from such delay, the majority of birthing women are so traumatised by the experience that more and more of them each year decide not to repeat it. Highly trumpeted concern for the involuntarily childless goes hand in hand with a cool unconcern for the women who are actually producing children. Though this might seem a paradox there is an internal logic in a system which promotes and glamorises conception and implantation in the laboratory and at the same time characterises the uterus as the place where everything goes wrong. Mothers who conceive before taking folic acid must blame themselves if their children are born with neural tube defects. Mothers who smoke or drink alcohol, who eat soft candy or chocolate or drink cola, cocoa or coffee, or take any kinds of drugs, medical or recreational, must hold themselves responsible for their infants' failure to thrive. Mothers who smoked during pregnancy have even been blamed for 'persistent criminal outcome' in their adult male offspring. Exposure to exogenous sex steroids in utero has been blamed for all kinds of phenomena including masculinisation of female foetuses, and feminisation of male ones, and homosexual orientation in both sexes. Every day the drive to criminalise the uterine environment produces small triumphs of ingenuity in yokings of undesirable outcomes with maternal behaviour. Many a parturient woman feels that it is she who is the obstacle in the path to the production of the perfect child, and her feelings of inadequacy are reinforced in her day-to-day negotiations with the health establishment which will take little heed of her insights into her child's problems and will insist on its own systems of assessment whether relevant or not. The latest development in the creeping criminalisation of the mother is the theory that it is mother's touch and voice and eye contact in early infancy that complete the wiring up of the infant brain so that it can learn and replicate social behaviour. A child whose mother does not supply this fourth-trimester brain stimulation is many times more likely to become a violent criminal than a child whose mother behaved correctly, or so the theory goes.

Both fatherhood and motherhood are undergoing radical refiguring. Traditional accounts of the development of patriarchy assume that women were placed under the control of men because it was the only way of ensuring paternity, women being the only means of production of children. Fifty years on from the discovery of DNA which made possible the establishment of paternity beyond doubt, what is striking is that few or no men have attempted to use the available technology so that they could claim any children who might be theirs. Instead it has been used principally in attempts to investigate whether the children of women men knew they had had sex with and whom they were supporting might not be carrying their genes and could therefore be denied. To suggest that men might be largely indifferent to whether they had children or not is to utter heresy; some of the essays in this book address men's deep psychic need to become fathers. No study has been made of men's need to preserve deniability of paternity, or of the common pattern among ART acceptors which finds a male partner going along with a female partner only because there will be no rest for either of them if her need is not addressed. No study of relationship breakdown after recourse to ART has ever been done, which is not surprising, for the publicity of ART centres on its successes, and there is no advantage to be gained by an assessment of the harm done by ART, not even in terms of obvious adverse outcomes such as abortion, prematurity and low birthweight, let alone the health problems both mental and physical faced by unsuccessful acceptors of ART.

Pro-ART rhetoric always identifies the child wanters as a couple: few studies have been done to ascertain whether it might not be the female in the partnership who is the prime driver of the process. She is certainly its prime victim; few male partners would feel justified in pressuring a reluctant woman to undergo what a determined woman will subject herself to repeatedly, even long after all hope is lost. One striking fact to emerge in this book is that a majority of ART acceptors want girl babies (Pawson), which could be taken as verification of the role played by narcissism. Narcissism will be better satisfied by what the promoters of reproductive cloning are promising, namely, that a woman will soon be able to clone herself so that she has an identical younger sister, who might as well be called her 'daughter'. If the cloning extremists have their way, sexual reproduction will be phased out along with death, as new bodies are cloned and personalities down loaded from the lived brain on to their *tabula rasa*. Like so many technologies ART contains within it the seeds of its own rapid obsolescence.

Mothers now come in three varieties, genetic mothers who supply oocytes, womb mothers who provide the uterine environment, and legal mothers who are recognised in law as the parents of ART babies. In unassisted reproduction one woman fulfils all these roles. While all womb mothers are seen by themselves and others as potentially delinquent, the genetic mother who is involved in ART may be actually dispossessed, with impunity. No systematic study of egg donors has ever been undertaken; the evidence from British women's magazines is that women feel much closer to their oocytes than men to their spermatozoa, and worry about what might become of them, saying fiercely that they would be appalled to think that a child of theirs had been implanted in the womb of an elderly woman or a lesbian, for example. If the donors have accepted a deal with the ART practitioner whereby they received a treatment cycle or sterilisation free of charge on condition that they undergo ovarian hyperstimulation and surrender the superfluous oocytes to the clinic, there is nothing whatsoever they can do to determine what becomes of them. Even if a woman puts herself through the ordeal to help a non-ovulating friend, the friend will not get her eggs but the eggs of a different anonymous donor. This practice is justified in various ways; what is obvious is that in Britain at least ART practitioners believe that women can never be trusted after giving up their genetic children to forget all about them. So far in Britain the rights of the legal mother annihilate any rights of either the genetic mother or the womb mother.

At least from the time of the inception of the Human Fertilisation and Embryology Authority women have been treated as merely instrumental to the practice of ART and never under any circumstances are they allowed to be in control. Hence the long struggle of Diane Blood to be impregnated with her dead husband's sperm. The philosopher Mary Warnock in her 1984 report on ART specifically excluded rights of access for any woman to a dead partner's sperm, positioning the technicians firmly in control of human genetic material, as if their decisions, being dispassionate, would always be right and the women's, being emotional, would always be wrong. At present the identities of egg donors and recipients are recorded in a central register which is kept by the HFEA. The information is described in blandishments to potential egg donors as 'never to be released'. What this large claim might mean in practice is unknown. In the United States the scandal of the unauthorised implantation of pre-embryos at the fertility clinic of the University of California at Irvine gave rise to litigation and a rather confused legal attempt to establish ownership of gametes, oocytes, blastocysts and embryos. As a consequence genetic mothers may assist when the womb mothers give birth. The anonymity that is insisted on in Britain is seen as neither possible nor desirable, especially as relinquishing mothers can find closure in such circumstances and will say that they no longer think of their genetic children as theirs. It would be interesting to study what differences this makes to the experience for all parties, and whether the gestalt of parenthood is changing as a consequence so that it becomes a genuinely collective posture and less an opportunity for ownership and control.

What is bizarre about the studious cultivation of unknowability of genetic parenthood within the ART spectrum is that with every day that passes we come to know more about the importance of genetic factors in predisposition to disease. The array of diseases and disabilities in which family history would be a valuable diagnostic tool is added to every day, and at the same time we are raising a growing number of children who cannot know their true family history. In some countries children conceived through ART are allowed information about their genetic parents; we have yet to see how the opportunity will be used and what outcomes might be expected. One outcome which can be confidently predicted is that donor sperm will become a much scarcer commodity if paternity in a Petri dish ceases to be deniable. Systems for identifying and keeping track of gametes have yet to be standardised and in any case are often not fully implemented, resulting in a series of rapidly hushed up scandals when samples of reproductive material have been accidentally destroyed, mixed up, lost and sold.

In traditional societies children are full members, and may be seen everywhere. In post-industrial society children are segregated inferiors. To opt to spend your life with them is to opt out of public life and even out of society. Children are not welcome in places of business or entertainment, on public transport or in shops and malls. New mothers are rapidly made to feel sidelined, oppressed and disadvantaged and the nurses and teachers who work with children are penalised for their choice of career. Contemplation of the plight of mothers in economies that refuse to support them, refuse to invest in daycare or children's activities, and cripple education by inappropriate interventions coupled with insufficient funding, should be sufficient to persuade distraught women that having a child may not be the answer to their feelings of frustration and incompleteness. The notional child can serve as a container for all kinds of fantasy goals, for reliving the past, especially the relationship with the mother, for reliving one's own youth, accomplishing one's defeated ambitions, and so forth. The infant who is expected to play some such constellation of roles for a parent will rapidly become a child in trouble.

In the rich world every child is supposed to be a wanted child and yet children are ostracised, deprived of intimacy and physical contact, shut up all day in schools and routinely abused by those with responsibility for their care. An English individual is more likely to be murdered between the ages of nought and one year than at any other time in his or her life. Most of us live our lives with no contact with children whatsoever (Higgins). The sight of a group of children advancing on us in a street at night fills us with terror. Given the marginalisation of children in our society, the achievement of the fertility merchants in having childlessness characterised as a disease condition in need of treatment is remarkable, to say the least. Infertility treatments are expensive and, with no more than *one treatment cycle in five* resulting in a take-home baby, inefficient. Infertility treatments are grudgingly made available for selected patients under the same national health schemes that fail to deal adequately with the commonest childhood ailments such as asthma and eczema. In 2002 for the first time the British government earmarked funds for research into the causes of disorders in the autism spectrum, which are thought to afflict at least one British child in a thousand and perhaps as many as six children per thousand. So desperately do British parents fear the misery of living with an autistic child that they would rather run the proven risk of losing the child to measles than accept the MMR vaccine which is thought by a tiny minority of researchers to be a possible contributing cause of the development of autism. At £2.5 million the sum for research into the causes of autism is derisory, amounting to less than half of what was spent on an unsuccessful campaign to restore public confidence in the MMR vaccine. The development of a child-friendly brain scanner would cost many times that sum. Using existing neuroimaging scanners to study brain activity in autistic children would cost several hundred pounds an hour, so clearly a mere £2.5 million will not go very far. This essential work will continue to be funded by charities, and donations from individuals who have personal knowledge of the sufferings of both autistic children and the people who have the duty of care towards them.

ART acceptors clearly want a child, but do they want any child? Will a sick or a disabled child do? If recourse to ART for a child of one's own is primarily driven by narcissism, the birth of a damaged child could have more than usually catastrophic consequences. Given the fact that all adverse outcomes – miscarriage, stillbirth, prematurity and low birth-weight – are more common in ART pregnancies, how long will it be before the proliferating suits which have already made the practice of obstetrics almost impossible begin to pursue the fertility specialists? We might wonder why ART acceptors have yet to blame relationship breakdown, debt and subsequent psychiatric and other disorders on ART practitioners, if the readiness of women to blame themselves for the failures of others were not so familiar a phenomenon.

In the post-industrial world at the beginning of the twenty-first century, children are no longer gifts from God, nor do they simply come along of their own accord. People who reject the notion that childbearing is a self-conscious project, and fail to plan for it, are feckless. A good deal is said in these pages about the stigma of childlessness; it is suggested more than once that inexplicable infertility may result from a failure of certain maturational processes (Christie and Morgan). Rather more obvious in our society is the stigmatisation of parents of large families; the possibility that parents might want to use ART to have a fifth or sixth child is never discussed, yet such parents would know better than the childless what having a child means in reality. The wishes and priorities of multi-generational families as distinct from that strange two-headed individual the 'couple' are not just not taken into account, they may be virtually criminalised. Families who are painfully aware of a pressing need for a son will be told that termination of pregnancy on grounds of the sex of the foetus is illegal. Any woman who seeks to destroy her female foetus simply because it is female will be characterised as criminal, regardless of whether she has already gone through repeated pregnancies that resulted in daughters, regardless of whether she will be under great pressure to embark on another pregnancy if she produces the wrong-sex child this time, regardless of whether she is exhausted by the combination of demands made on her by her other children, her pregnancy and her role in the family business. In Britain selective abortion on the grounds of sex has been declared illegal on grounds characterised as pro-feminist because it is assumed that the foetuses aborted would be mostly female. In a recent case a woman who had borne three daughters in quick succession, and who was in poor health, exhausted by the demands both of her growing family and of the contribution she had to make to the family business, died in the course of a desperate attempt to abort her fourth daughter after she had been denied surgical abortion. The coroner commenting upon the case deplored her actions and made no comment on the failure of the duty of care on the part of those to whom she had turned for help.

Though we are told continually that we live in a multicultural society, no attempt has been made to identify different patterns and priorities in family-building. Our myopic attention goes no further than the couple; in traditional Asian families, the birth of a child affects every member, and all, even the young uncles, will be involved in the rearing of the child. No good reasons for 'wanting a baby' are ever attributed to very young mothers, who are also those more likely to be giving birth within a multi-generational family with their own mother present and involved. People who do not postpone the arrival of children until they can provide every-thing a child might be thought to need – a room of its own in a house with a garden, not too far from a school – are thought likely to neglect and even abuse their children. People who produce children year on year are considered too stupid to regulate their reproductive affairs and held responsible for perpetuating the cycle of poverty, violence and crime. Teenage pregnancy is a blight on society, a source of shame and embarrassment to progressive governments who spend disproportionate amounts of time and money trying to prevent it rather than supporting lone mothers. Three-quarters of the children born in this rich society are living in poverty.

Elites are usually relatively infertile, and have always feared and hated the fecundity of their inferiors, whether they were to be found in the seething slums of European industrial cities or in villages in India. The infertile nations are now threatened by the fertile nations, whose surplus young population they are obliged to import if they are to find a workforce sufficient to provide essential menial services for their ageing populations. In the new commonwealth of nations built out of the old Soviet Union, Muslim groups are reproducing at a much faster rate than others; the new pressure on the old elites is exacerbating old tensions between contrasting lifestyles, of which the more dynamic, the Islamic, is unapologetically militant and evangelical. Islamic law holds that children are an unqualified blessing from God who will provide for any that he sends.

In a surprising number of the infertility narratives in this book, release from the illusion of planning and control is followed by conception. In some cases ART practitioners take over the role of the divine agency (Miller). Infertility technicians are well aware that they are not in control, that there is much that they cannot predict, but this awareness is not shared by their clients. Though the acceptor of infertility treatment may decide that the particular practitioners with whom she is dealing are incompetent, she does not doubt that they ought to be in control or that control is possible. It is not God who decides the outcome, nor is it any longer the child who decides to 'come along', damaged or perfect, angel or demon. Child-bearing though unmanageable must be managed; adverse outcomes are the results of failures of management, which should identify and extirpate any imperfect conception and use all kinds of assessments in procuring and protecting a perfect one. Ever since the family planning lobbies declared that 'fewer babies means better babies' the production of children has been subjected to quality control.

After I underwent laser surgery to reconstruct my one remaining fallopian tube, my gynaecologist told me that any pregnancy I began would be closely monitored and I would have to accept amniocentesis. When I reminded him that amniocentesis carried a significant risk of complications of pregnancy including abortion and that

I would accept a Down's syndrome baby if that was what I was carrying, he told me that he had not worked so hard to reconstruct my reproductive apparatus to have me produce a defective child. Not only was I to have amniocentesis, but the delivery would have to be a Caesarian. 'We will be taking no chances', he said. 'What if the child's a serial murderer?' I said.

Some of the chapters in this book touch on the distorted perceptions of fertility that characterise our culture and its patterns of somatisation. Young women are encouraged to believe, long before they are ovulating regularly, that they are highly fertile and should use effective chemical contraception rather than relying on condoms. Whether they are fertile or not, they are very susceptible to infection which can, and in far too many instances will, lead to sterilising pelvic disease. Failure to persuade young heterosexuals to use condoms is a tragic dereliction of duty on the part of the most powerful marketing organisations the world has ever seen. It is the bitterest of ironies that this failure leads directly to a marketing triumph, namely, the selling of ART as a workable way of building a family for older women whose fertility was compromised by unprotected sex when they were young.

As a sex, women of any age are relatively infertile; not all unassisted cycles are ovulatory and those that are result in the release of a single egg every twenty-eight days. Though as every schoolboy knows it takes only one sperm to fertilise an ovum, men manufacture spermatozoa unceasingly morning, noon and night. Men are astonishingly, unreasonably, inexplicably fertile. This striking contrast has inspired a good deal of modish sociobiology and anthropology, without impinging at all on cultural perception. All women are encouraged to identify themselves as potential mothers from childhood; no men see themselves primarily as potential fathers nor are they under pressure from the inception of sexual activity to take steps to prevent accidental fatherhood.

Though the movers and shakers in the fund-raising business have managed to establish childlessness as a disease state, no concerted attempt to protect the nation's fecundity has been undertaken. We are now told that as many as one in five British couples has difficulty in conceiving, which is tantamount to an epidemic of infertility, an epidemic which could have been prevented and was not. No prophylactic measures to reduce the incidence of involuntary infertility have even been suggested, let alone implemented. Attitudes to the decline in male fertility range from trumpeted disbelief in the phenomenon to the inculpation of every known industrial chemical, including some universal packaging agents. The decline in the Californian sperm count was even attributed to the ubiquity of chlorinated swimming pools. Concern for a small if inexorable decline in male fertility which is already unimaginably high is not matched by a concern for female fertility which is already low, though a statistical decline in overall female fertility is probably manifest as total infertility for a significant number of individual women. This unconcern combined with the astonishing depth of our ignorance on the causes of miscarriage and stillbirth, and incuriosity about them, suggests a posture in which we can discern the contours of classic misogyny.

Though fertility barons might present themselves as chivalrous individuals who were attracted to the demanding speciality of ART because they wished to help unhappy women, we are entitled, I think, to look beyond this benign avuncular mask in search of the sources of the drive to produce 'perfect' human babies out of any old thing, out of 60-year-old women who smoke, out of dead women, and perhaps even out of a pig or a man's chemically prepared pelvis, with a placenta grown on the bowel wall, and ask ourselves whether what is really driving the industry forward is fear and loathing of the mother. Rejection of the mother is an essential part of the process of masculinisation; in so far as bureaucratic society is the ultimate phallic life form, it seems consistent that the dark and messy processes of uterine gestation and natural parturition be rationalised. The first stage in such a proceeding would be the rendering of the womb transparent, so that gestation could be monitored, which was eventually accomplished by ultrasound. The need for ultrasound was not articulated by mothers, but once ultrasound was available mothers expected to meet their child for the first time on a television screen and it is now impossible to roll back the routine use of ultrasound more and more often even in normal pregnancy where no problems are anticipated.

Ultrasound is used to confirm pregnancy, to detect whether a pregnancy might be molar or ectopic, or a case of blighted ovum, or multiple, and to monitor the progress of the foetus, to diagnose congenital conditions such as intestinal atresia, hydrops foetalis, renal dysplasia, hydrocephalus, anencephaly, myelomeningocoele, achondroplasia, spina bifida, and exomphalos. Anti-abortion campaigners found another use for ultrasound imaging; by showing it to women contemplating abortion, they found that they could more easily persuade them to go full term and deliver their babies, even if only to give them up for adoption (cf. Christie and Morgan). The argument was that women could only tolerate termination of pregnancy because they could not see what was being destroyed. Ultrasound enabled them to 'see' their 'child' and therefore to understand the gravity of their proposed course of action. What is actually displayed on the ultrasound screen is a sonogram built up of the signals collected by repetitive arrays of very high frequency sound waves emitted by a transducer and bounced back to it off the structures in the pelvis. The image is arrived at by recomposing data that are gathered in two-dimensional slices; more sophisticated techniques now present these data as a three-dimensional image, as if the belly really did have a glass pane let into it like an oven door and the equivalent of an oven light shining on the developing foetus as if it were a rising cake. The video artefact is recognised by the mother as her child, as if the screen were being fed by a CCTV camera showing her a person in another place. In a less body-blind culture the foetus might be known to its mother by more intimate means than the same act of recognition that she uses for characters in TV soap operas. Anti-abortion campaigners tell us that when the reluctant mother sees her child on TV, as it were, she instantly bonds with it and becomes incapable of destroying it. What consequences this has for her coming to terms with a spontaneous abortion or with the discovery at the time of delivery of a congenital disability not detected by ultrasound screening is nowhere recorded.

Mothers-to-be did not invent ultrasound so that they could look into their own uteri. The technology was born in the desire to visualise underwater structures, and gathered momentum after the collision of the Titanic with a largely submerged iceberg; during the First World War the instrument was further developed to detect German U-boats. In peacetime, sonar was used to detect flaws in metal structures; it was not until the 1950s that refined versions of the original echo sonography were developed for scanning the brain and heart. All the developers of the technology were male; women's priorities were not considered then and are not paramount now. Often in the clinical situation the ultrasound screen is angled away from the patient so that she cannot see what the technician is looking at and is only privy to as much of the information as the technician wishes to share with her. Ultrasound is not an instrument of which a woman may avail herself in the service of her own priorities even though she may have life and death reasons of her own.

The driving force behind so much ultrasound imaging and monitoring of the pregnant woman is not a concern for her but for her foetus, but whether it is actually good for the foetus is debatable. Pregnant midwives noticed that when they were carrying out ultrasound scans the foetuses responded with violent and spasmodic movements. Concerns have been voiced about effects of high-frequency vibration on the developing brain, and suspected links with dyslexia and left-handedness. However serious these unintended consequences might turn out to be, more obvious is the fact that there are as yet no viable treatments for disorders detected in utero. The only available treatment is abortion, which is not a therapeutic procedure. Few statistics are available on the number of abortions carried out as a consequence of ultrasound diagnosis of foetal anomaly, or the extent of over-diagnosis and the frequency of abortion of healthy foetuses.

If birthing women are already hooked up to machines which do the thinking for them, the human cyborg is well on the way to becoming reality. ART takes eggs from a woman's body and effects conception outside it only to return pre-embryos to that same unsatisfactory body which then, two out of three times even in best practice, lets the technologists down again. As more and more women grow up convinced that childbearing will be beyond them, the end of motherhood comes into sight. As yet there is no movement to prevent the obsolescence of the womb. Simone de Beauvoir and Shulamith Firestone both thought that women would not be free until they were liberated from the onerous duties of conception, gestation and birth. More and more women are opting for technological interventions in the birthplace, for elective Caesarian section, for scheduled induction and epidural, for intensive foetal monitoring, for whatever is going to give them a 'perfect' baby with minimum trauma. Other women are begging for birth to be recognised as a social and familial event, as well as an individual life choice, for the female body to be seen not as essentially inefficient and unsatisfactory, but as powerful and self-regulating, and for the individual's genetic inheritance to be respected, unsatisfactory as it might appear to the quality controllers. It would be good to be able to say that battle is about to be joined; truth is that the technologists are winning by a walkover.

Appendix

Glossary of terms used in ART (assisted reproductive technology)

Abandoned cycle In IVF, where a treatment cycle is cancelled after commencing administration of drugs but before embryo transfer.

Adjusted live birth rate The live birth rate (number of births for every 100 treatment cycles) once it has been adjusted to take account of the different types of patients which the clinic treated during the year.

Assisted hatching The mechanical, chemical or laser breaching of the gelatinous coating of the eggs.

Autosomal Pertaining to any chromosome that occurs in the nucleus, except for the sex chromosomes.

Autosomal dominant disorders Disorders where inheritance of a mutation from one parent only (or arising anew during egg or sperm formation) can be sufficient for the person to be affected. Important dominant disorders in the UK include familial hypercholesterolaemia, Huntington's disease, adult polycystic kidney disease and familial adenomatous polyposis coli (colon cancer).

Autosomal recessive disorders Disorders where, for a person to be affected, a mutation has to be inherited from both parents. Such parents are usually unaffected carriers because they only have a single copy of the mutant gene. Recessive disorders commonly have onset in childhood and include cystic fibrosis, sickle cell disease and thalassaemia.

Cervical mucus The secretions surrounding the cervical canal. The amount and texture change during ovulation to allow sperm penetration.

Chromosomes Small bodies within the nucleus of every cell in the body. They contain the genes.

Clinical pregnancy Ultrasound evidence of a foetal heart.

Clinical pregnancy rate This is calculated as a proportion of pregnancies with beating heart for every 100 treatment cycles commenced.

Clones Organisms that are genetically identical (share the same nuclear gene set).

Cloning The production of genetically identical (sharing the same nuclear gene set) individuals.

Congenital malformations, deformities, diseases, etc. are those which are either present at birth, or, being transmitted direct from the parents, show themselves soon after birth.

Congenital abnormalities Deformities or diseases which are either present at birth or show themselves soon after birth.

Consent Acceptance of the procedures involved in donation. A donor must give consent before any of the procedures begin. Before she gives consent, a clinic must have given her adequate information and offered counselling. Consent is given by completing and signing a form supplied by the HFEA to the clinic. This consent to the use and storage of eggs and embryos made from those eggs is called 'informed consent'. Consent to a medical procedure, such as egg collection, is called 'valid consent'. Consent can be changed – it may be withdrawn or varied at any time unless the embryo concerned has already been used.

Counselling All licensed clinics are required to offer patients counselling. Such counselling aims to enable the patient to understand the implications of treatment, to give emotional support and to help the patient cope with the consequences of treatment.

Cryopreservation The freezing of oocytes, spermatozoa or embryos and their storage in liquid nitrogen.

Cystic fibrosis A disorder of the mucus-secreting glands of the lungs, the pancreas, the mouth, and the gastro-intestinal tract. The commonest serious genetic disease in Caucasian children.

Cytoplasm The material between the nucleus and the cell surface.

Directions The HFE Act allows the HFEA to impose additional conditions on licensed activities. These Directions cover areas where primary legislation would be inappropriate because of the need for flexibility. Directions can be applied to an individual clinic or generally.

Donor The woman who gives eggs to help another woman become pregnant or for use in research.

Donor insemination (DI) The insemination of donor sperm into the vagina, the cervix or the womb itself.

Drugs which may be used in IVF treatment:

Buserelin is a hormone suppressant which is given by nasal spray or a daily injection. Buserelin suppresses the activity of a small gland in the brain called the pituitary gland which normally stimulates the ovaries to produce eggs. The ovaries can then be stimulated artificially.

HCG – human chorionic gonadotrophin is given by injection about 34 to 36 hours before egg collection. It helps to ripen the eggs within the follicles.

HMG – human menopausal gonadotrophin (may be called Pergonal or Humegon) stimulates the development of egg follicles.

FSH – follicle stimulating hormone (may be called Metrodin) can be given also to stimulate egg follicles.

Egg collection Procedure by which eggs are collected from the woman's ovaries by using an ultrasound guided needle or by using a laparoscope (an instrument for looking into the abdomen) and a needle. Also known as egg retrieval.

Embryo A fertilised egg up to eight weeks of development. At two weeks it is approximately 1–1.5 mm in diameter.

Embryo biopsy Removal and examination of one or more cells from a developing embryo for diagnostic purposes.

Embryo freezing Embryos not required for treatment in a cycle can be frozen and stored for future use. Freezing is also known as cryopreservation.

Embryo storage The storage of one or more frozen embryos for future use.

Embryo transfer Transfer of one or more embryos to the uterus.

Embryologist A scientist who creates, cultures and studies embryos in a clinical or research laboratory.

Endometriosis A female condition in which endometrial cells, which normally line the uterus, implant around the outside of the uterus and/or ovaries, causing internal bleeding, pain and reduced fertility.

Epididymis Coiled tubing outside the testicles which store sperm.

Fallopian tube(s) The tubes between the ovaries and the uterus. After release of the egg from one of the ovaries, the tube transports the egg to the uterus.

Female factor This term covers any reason why a woman is infertile, such as ovulation failure or damage to the fallopian tubes.

Foetus The term used for an embryo after the eighth week of development until birth.

Follicle(s) A small sac in the ovary in which the egg develops.

Gamete The male sperm or the female egg.

Gamete intra fallopian transfer (GIFT) A procedure in which eggs are retrieved from the woman, mixed with sperm and immediately replaced in one or other of the woman's fallopian tubes so that they fertilise inside the body.

Genetic counselling A process by which information is imparted to those affected by, or at risk of, a genetic disorder. It includes information on the nature of the disorder, the size and extent of genetic risks, the options, including genetic testing, that may help clarify the risks, and the available preventative, supportive and therapeutic measures. In the context of genetic testing it may include responding to the concerns of individuals referred and their families, discussing the consequences of a test, and helping them to choose the optimal decision for themselves, but not determining a particular course of action.

Genetic testing Testing to detect the presence or absence of, or change in, a particular gene or chromosome.

Gonadotrophins Drugs used to stimulate the ovaries, similar in composition to natural follicle stimulating hormone (FSH) produced by the pituitary gland.

Hamster test (HEPT) A test of the fertilising ability of human sperm by observing their penetration into the hamster egg.

Hepatitis   Refers to infection with one of the hepatitis viruses which causes acute or chronic inflammation of the liver cells.

HFEA   Human Fertilisation and Embryology Authority.

Hormone   Hormones are natural chemical substances produced by the body some of which control the development and release of the egg from the ovary during each menstrual cycle. Natural and synthetic preparations of those hormones are used to increase the number of eggs produced in a cycle.

Intra cytoplasmic sperm injection (ICSI)   A micromanipulation technique. A variation of IVF treatment where a single sperm is injected into the inner cellular structure of the egg. This technique is used for couples where the male partner has severely impaired or few sperm.

Intra-uterine insemination   Insemination of sperm into the uterus of a woman.

In vitro fertilisation (IVF)   Eggs and sperm are collected and put together to achieve fertilisation outside the body. Up to three of the resulting embryos can be transferred into the woman's womb and a pregnancy may occur.

Laparoscopy   This is a surgical procedure for looking inside the pelvic cavity. Usually under a general anaesthetic, a small cut is made below the navel and a fine optical instrument is inserted. Laparoscopy is used in egg collection.

Late onset disorder   Disorders that normally become symptomatic in adult life.

Live birth   The delivery of one or more babies.

Live birth rate   The number of live births achieved from every 100 treatment cycles commenced.

Male factor   This term covers any reason why the male partner's sperm may be less effective or incapable of fertilisation, including the absence of viable sperm and a failed reversal of a vasectomy.

Menstrual cycle   A cycle of approximately one month in the female during which the egg is released from an ovary, the uterus is prepared to receive the fertilised egg, and blood and tissue are lost via the vagina if a pregnancy does not occur.

Micromanipulation   This term covers any technique used in IVF to bypass the zona pellucida (protein shell) which surrounds the egg, as this frequently prevents sperm which have poor motility or morphology from penetrating and fertilising the egg. ICSI is the most commonly used method of micromanipulation.

Microsurgical epididymal sperm aspiration (MESA)   Retrieving sperm directly from the epididymis.

Miscarriage   Spontaneous complete loss of a pregnancy before twenty-four weeks.

Monogenic disorders   Disorders arising from defects in a single gene.

Multiple birth   Birth of more than one baby from a pregnancy (these are counted as single live births irrespective of the number of babies born).

Multiple birth rate   This is the percentage of all births in which more than one baby was born.

Multiple pregnancy   A pregnancy in which two or more foetal hearts are present.

Multiple pregnancy rate   This rate is calculated as a proportion of all clinical pregnancies.

Muscular dystrophy   A hereditary condition where muscles slowly waste away.

Mutation   The change in a gene or chromosome that causes a disorder or the inherited susceptibility to a disorder.

Natural/unstimulated cycle   A cycle in which no drugs are given to stimulate egg production.

Neonatal death   The death of a baby within twenty-seven complete days of delivery.

Oocyte   Another name for an egg.

Ovarian hyperstimulation syndrome (OHSS)   A rare but serious consequence of taking the drugs used to stimulate the ovaries.

Ovary   One of a pair of female reproductive organs which produce eggs and hormones.

Partial zonal dissection (PZD)   A variation of IVF treatment in which a small hole is made in the outer membrane of the egg using a small glass needle, thereby easing the passage of sperm into the egg under their own motion.

Percutaneous epididymal sperm aspiration (PESA)   Retrieving sperm directly from the coiled tubing outside the testicles that store sperm (epididymis), using a needle.

Perinatal death   The death of a baby either in the uterus after twenty-four weeks of pregnancy (stillbirth) or within twenty-eight days after the birth.

Polygenic or multifactorial conditions   The interaction of several genes and the environment.

Pregnancy rate   The number of pregnancies achieved from every 100 treatment cycles commenced.

Preimplantation genetic diagnosis (PGD)   Use of genetic testing on a live embryo to determine the presence, absence or change in a particular gene or chromosome prior to implantation of the embryo in the uterus of a woman.

Prenatal diagnosis (PND):

Amniocentesis   This method involves examining foetal cells taken between 15 and 16 weeks of pregnancy from the amniotic fluid which surrounds the foetus. The foetal cells are cultured and the genetic make-up of the foetus determined. This allows testing for chromosomal abnormalities such as Down's syndrome and other birth defects.

Chorionic villus sampling (CVS)   This method involves the removal of a small sample of placental tissue between 9 and 11 weeks of pregnancy which is tested for genetic abnormalities.

Primitive streak   This develops in an embryo by day 14 when the cells which form the foetus separate from those which form the placenta and umbilical cord.

Recipient   The woman who receives eggs from another woman during treatment to help her to become pregnant.

Spermatid   An immature sperm cell.

Stillbirth   The birth of a dead infant.

Stimulated cycle   A treatment cycle in which stimulation drugs are used to produce more eggs than usual in the woman's monthly cycle.

Stimulation drugs   Drugs used to stimulate a woman's ovaries to produce more eggs than usual in a monthly cycle; also known as superovulatory drugs.

Sub zonal insemination (SUZI)   A variation of IVF treatment where a single sperm is deposited into the perivitelline space between the egg and its protein shell (the zona pellucida). This technique is aimed at patients who have sperm which fail to penetrate the zona.

Superovulation/stimulation   The stimulation of a woman's ovaries with drugs to produce more eggs than usual in a monthly cycle.

Superovulatory drugs   Hormones given to a woman so that she produces more eggs than usual in a monthly cycle. The drugs contain human menopausal gonadotrophin.

Testicular sperm extraction (TESE)   Retrieving sperm directly from the testis.

Testis   Testicle or male gonad.

Transport (or satellite) IVF   An arrangement whereby IVF is carried out at a primary centre (HFEA-licensed) but other parts of the treatment (e.g. ovulation induction or egg retrieval) are performed at a secondary centre (not necessarily HFEA-licensed). The embryology and embryo transfer take place at the primary centre.

Treatment cycle:
  (a) IVF with fresh embryos: a cycle begins with the administration of drugs for the purpose of superovulation or, if no drugs are used, with the attempt to collect eggs;
  (b) IVF with frozen-thawed embryos: a cycle begins with the removal of the stored embryo in order to be thawed and then transferred;
  (c) DI: a cycle begins when the first insemination with donor sperm takes place.

Triplet or trinucleatide repeat disorders   Disorders caused by the expansion of a triplet repeat of bases within a gene and usually associated with neurological disorders, e.g. fragile X, Huntington's disease, myotonic dystrophy. Each disease has a range of repeats associated with a spectrum from normal to affected individuals.

Ultrasound   Investigation using sound waves to make a picture of the womb and ovaries appear on a television screen. Ultrasound is used in monitoring egg development and in egg collection.

Unknown outcome   The outcome of a clinical pregnancy is unknown due to incomplete information being returned by a clinic to the HFEA.

Unstimulated   A cycle in which no drugs were given to stimulate egg production.

X-linked disorders   Disorders due to a mutation on the X chromosome. X-linked disorders usually only affect males, but the disorders can be transmitted through healthy female carriers.

Zona drilling (ZD)   Acid released to dissolve the gelatinous coating of the egg leaving a hole through which the sperm can enter.

Index